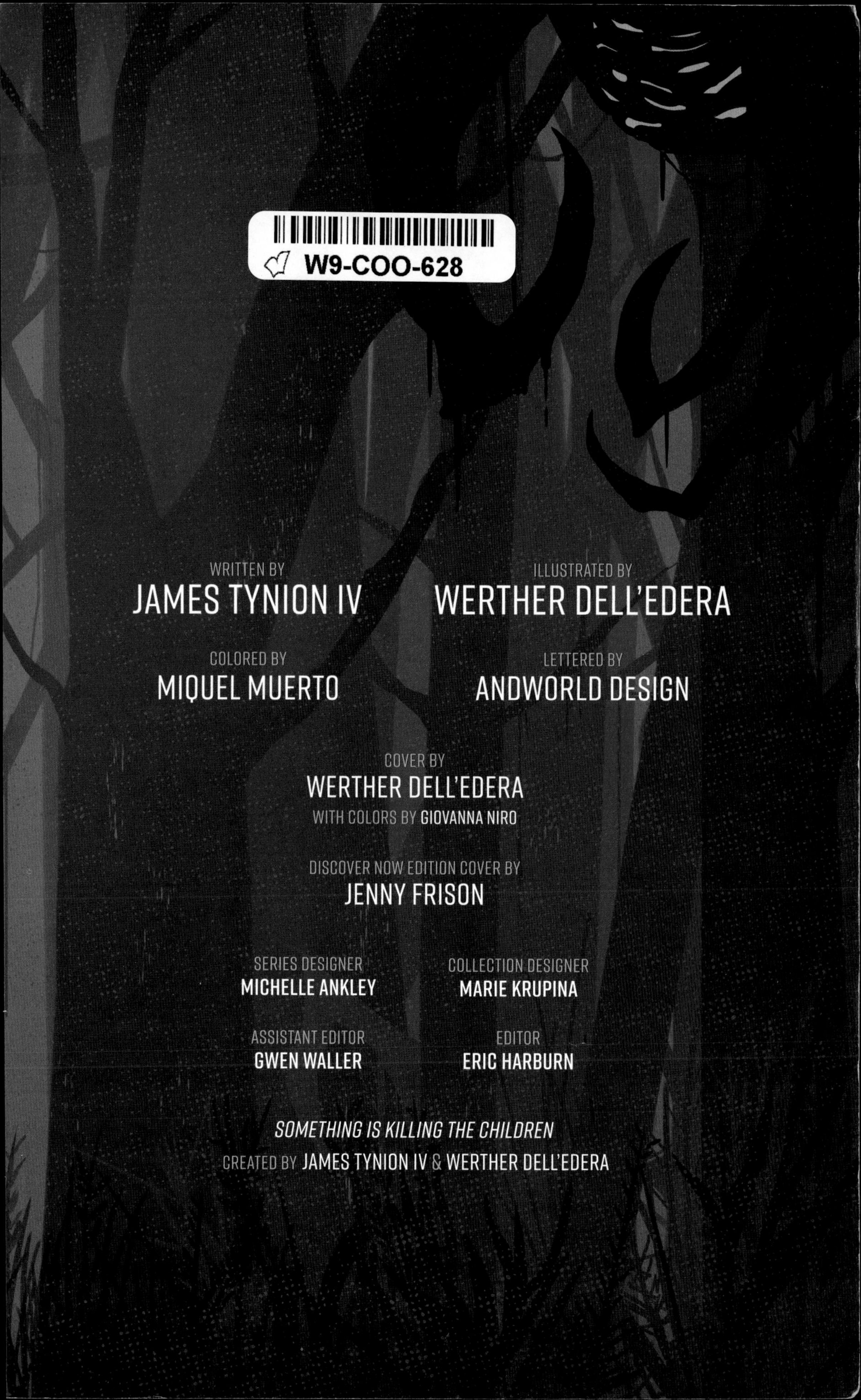

WRITTEN BY
JAMES TYNION IV

ILLUSTRATED BY
WERTHER DELL'EDERA

COLORED BY
MIQUEL MUERTO

LETTERED BY
ANDWORLD DESIGN

COVER BY
WERTHER DELL'EDERA
WITH COLORS BY GIOVANNA NIRO

DISCOVER NOW EDITION COVER BY
JENNY FRISON

SERIES DESIGNER
MICHELLE ANKLEY

COLLECTION DESIGNER
MARIE KRUPINA

ASSISTANT EDITOR
GWEN WALLER

EDITOR
ERIC HARBURN

SOMETHING IS KILLING THE CHILDREN
CREATED BY JAMES TYNION IV & WERTHER DELL'EDERA

CHAPTER
ONE

SOMETHING is KILLING the CHILDREN™

VOLUME ONE

BOOM!

SOMETHING IS KILLING THE CHILDREN Vol. 1, February 2020. Published by BOOM! Studios, a division of Boom Entertainment, Inc. Something is Killing the Children is ™ & © 2020 James Tynion IV. Originally published in single magazine form as SOMETHING IS KILLING THE CHILDREN No. 1-5. ™ & © 2019, 2020 James Tynion IV. All rights reserved. BOOM! Studios™ and the BOOM! Studios logo are trademarks of Boom Entertainment, Inc., registered in various countries and categories. All characters, events, and institutions depicted herein are fictional. Any similarity between any of the names, characters, persons, events, and/or institutions in this publication to actual names, characters, and persons, whether living or dead, events, and/or institutions is unintended and purely coincidental. BOOM! Studios does not read or accept unsolicited submissions of ideas, stories, or artwork.

For information regarding the CPSIA on this printed material, call: (203) 595-3636 and provide reference #RICH − 879551.

BOOM! Studios, 5670 Wilshire Boulevard, Suite 400, Los Angeles, CA, 90036-5679. Printed in USA. First Printing.

ISBN: 978-1-68415-558-3, eISBN: 978-1-64144-724-9

Discover Now Edition
ISBN: 978-1-68415-513-2

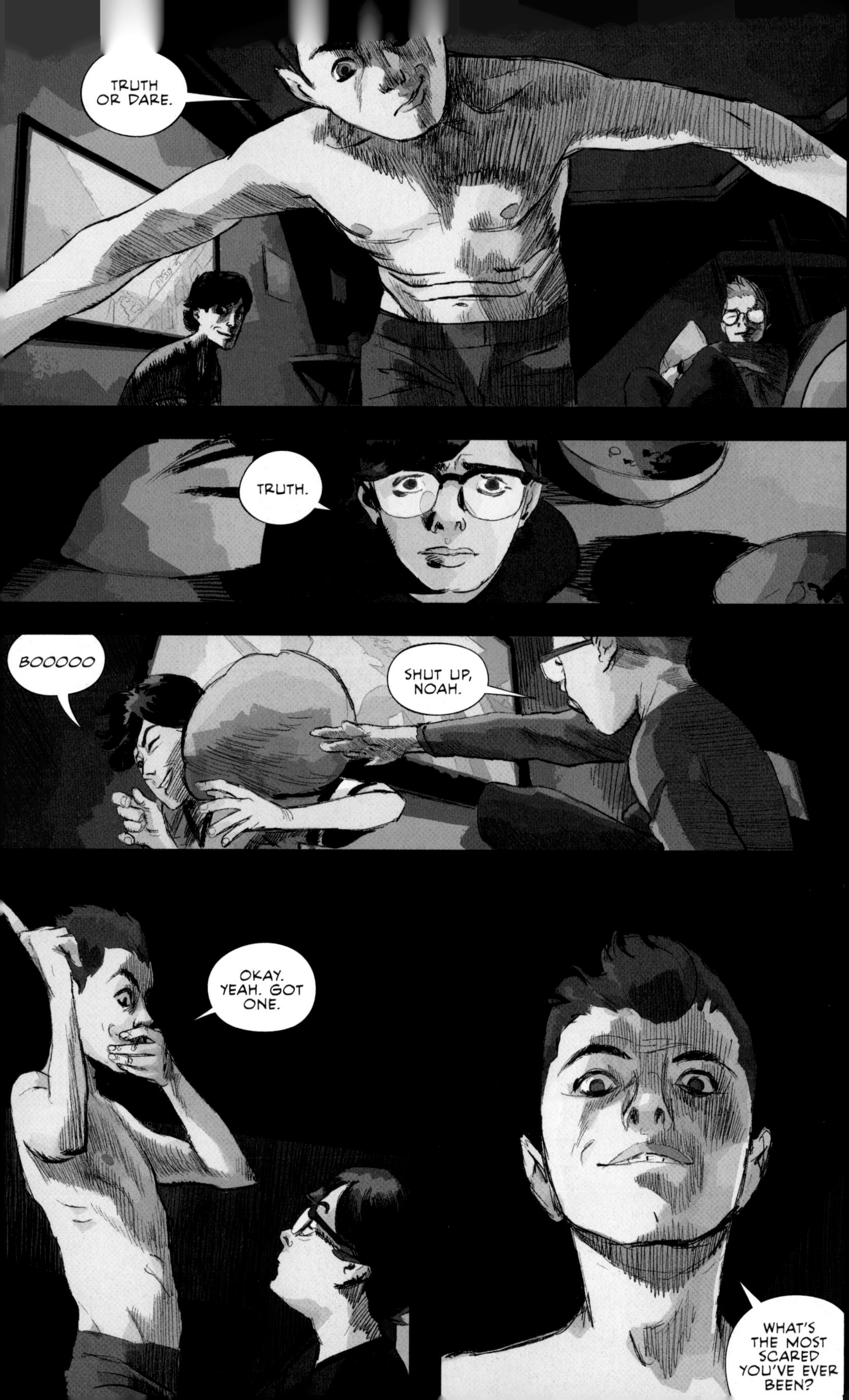
TRUTH OR DARE.
TRUTH.
BOOOOO
SHUT UP, NOAH.
OKAY. YEAH. GOT ONE.
WHAT'S THE MOST SCARED YOU'VE EVER BEEN?

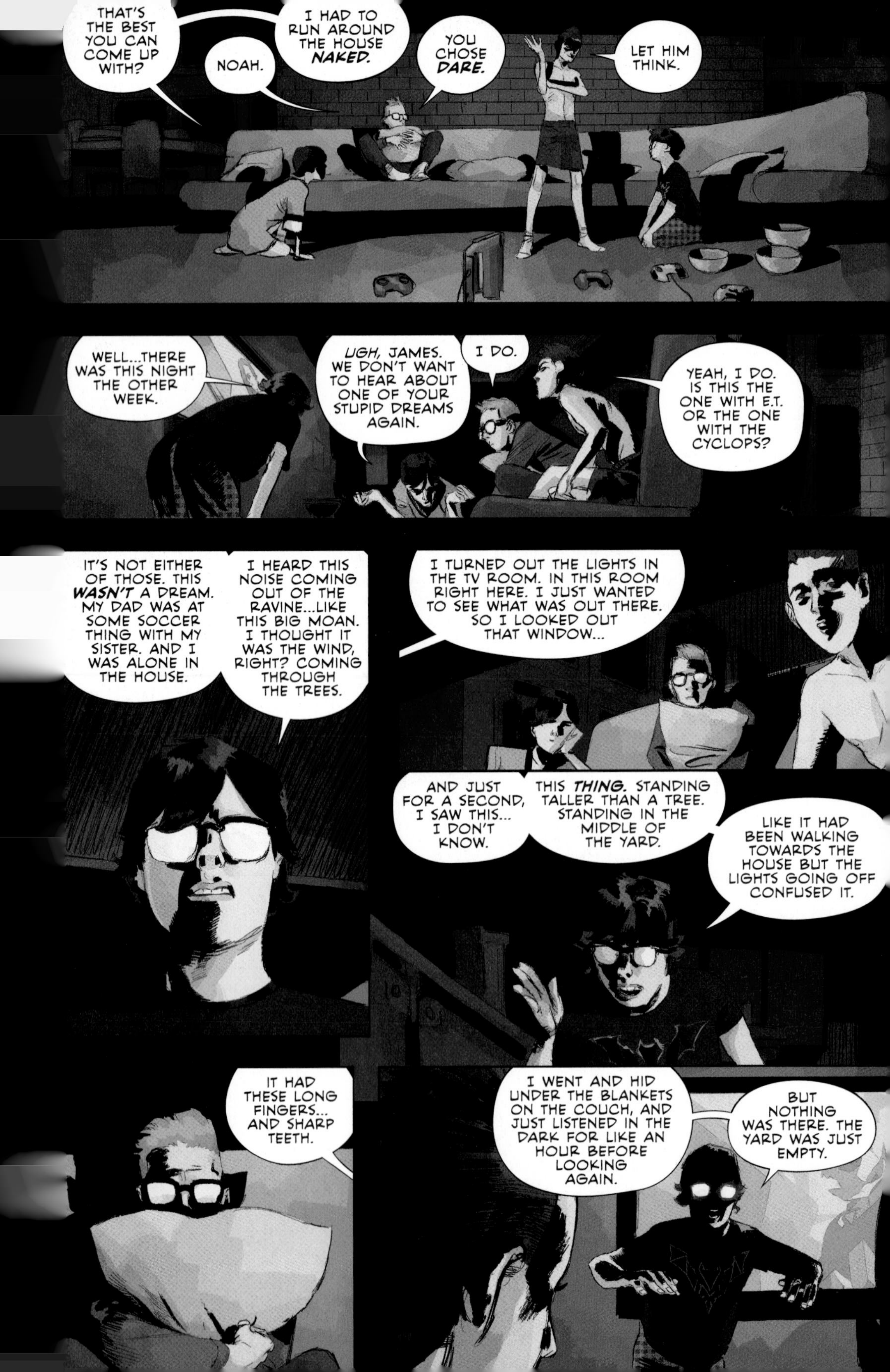
THAT'S THE BEST YOU CAN COME UP WITH?
I HAD TO RUN AROUND THE HOUSE *NAKED.*
NOAH.
YOU CHOSE *DARE.*
LET HIM THINK.
WELL...THERE WAS THIS NIGHT THE OTHER WEEK.
UGH, JAMES. WE DON'T WANT TO HEAR ABOUT ONE OF YOUR STUPID DREAMS AGAIN.
I DO.
YEAH, I DO. IS THIS THE ONE WITH E.T. OR THE ONE WITH THE CYCLOPS?
IT'S NOT EITHER OF THOSE. THIS *WASN'T* A DREAM. MY DAD WAS AT SOME SOCCER THING WITH MY SISTER. AND I WAS ALONE IN THE HOUSE.
I HEARD THIS NOISE COMING OUT OF THE RAVINE...LIKE THIS BIG MOAN. I THOUGHT IT WAS THE WIND, RIGHT? COMING THROUGH THE TREES.
I TURNED OUT THE LIGHTS IN THE TV ROOM. IN THIS ROOM RIGHT HERE. I JUST WANTED TO SEE WHAT WAS OUT THERE. SO I LOOKED OUT THAT WINDOW...
AND JUST FOR A SECOND, I SAW THIS... I DON'T KNOW.
THIS *THING.* STANDING TALLER THAN A TREE. STANDING IN THE MIDDLE OF THE YARD.
LIKE IT HAD BEEN WALKING TOWARDS THE HOUSE BUT THE LIGHTS GOING OFF CONFUSED IT.
IT HAD THESE LONG FINGERS... AND SHARP TEETH.
I WENT AND HID UNDER THE BLANKETS ON THE COUCH, AND JUST LISTENED IN THE DARK FOR LIKE AN HOUR BEFORE LOOKING AGAIN.
BUT NOTHING WAS THERE. THE YARD WAS JUST EMPTY.

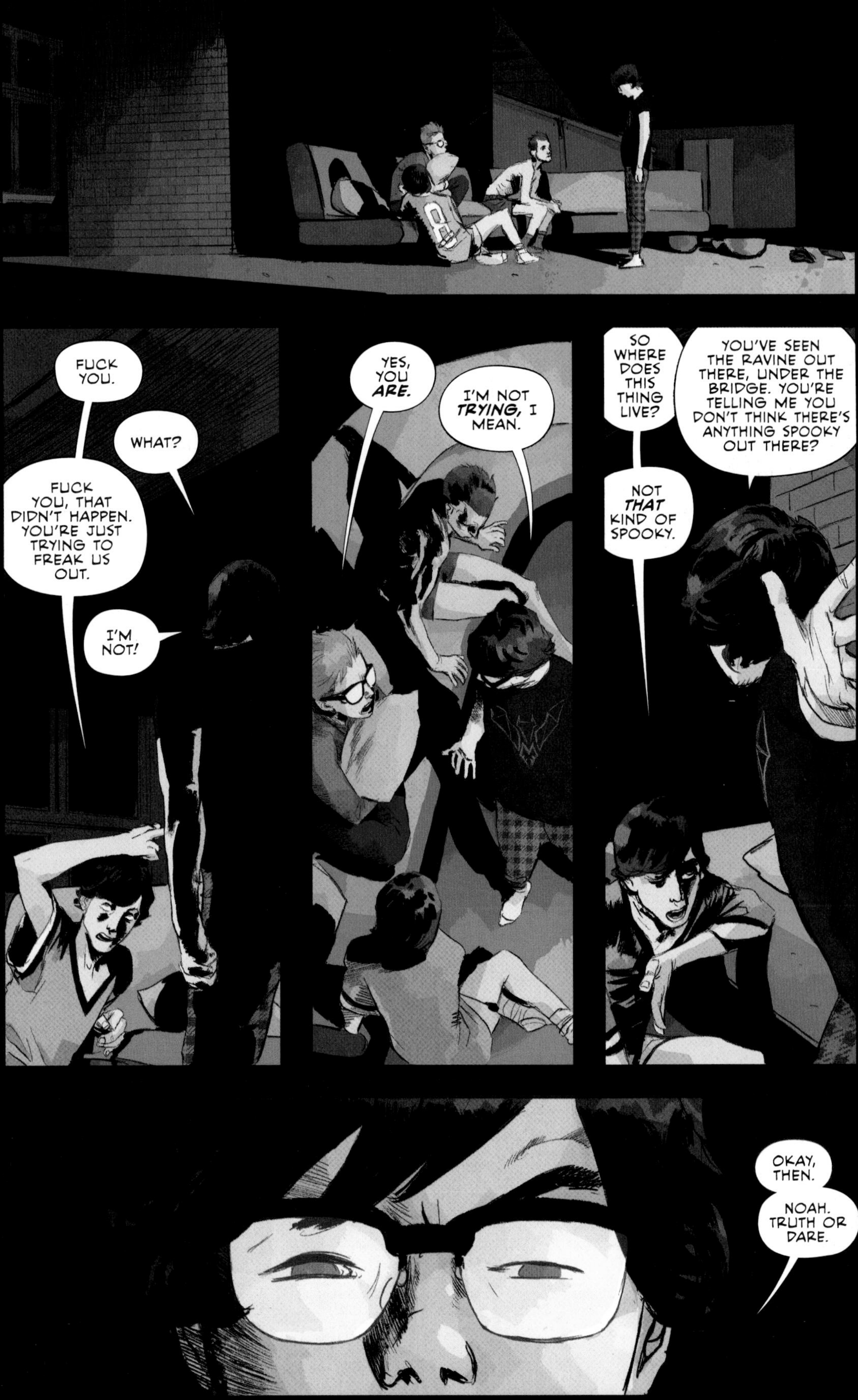
FUCK YOU.
WHAT?
FUCK YOU, THAT DIDN'T HAPPEN. YOU'RE JUST TRYING TO FREAK US OUT.
I'M NOT!
YES, YOU ARE.
I'M NOT TRYING, I MEAN.
SO WHERE DOES THIS THING LIVE?
YOU'VE SEEN THE RAVINE OUT THERE, UNDER THE BRIDGE. YOU'RE TELLING ME YOU DON'T THINK THERE'S ANYTHING SPOOKY OUT THERE?
NOT THAT KIND OF SPOOKY.
OKAY, THEN.
NOAH. TRUTH OR DARE.

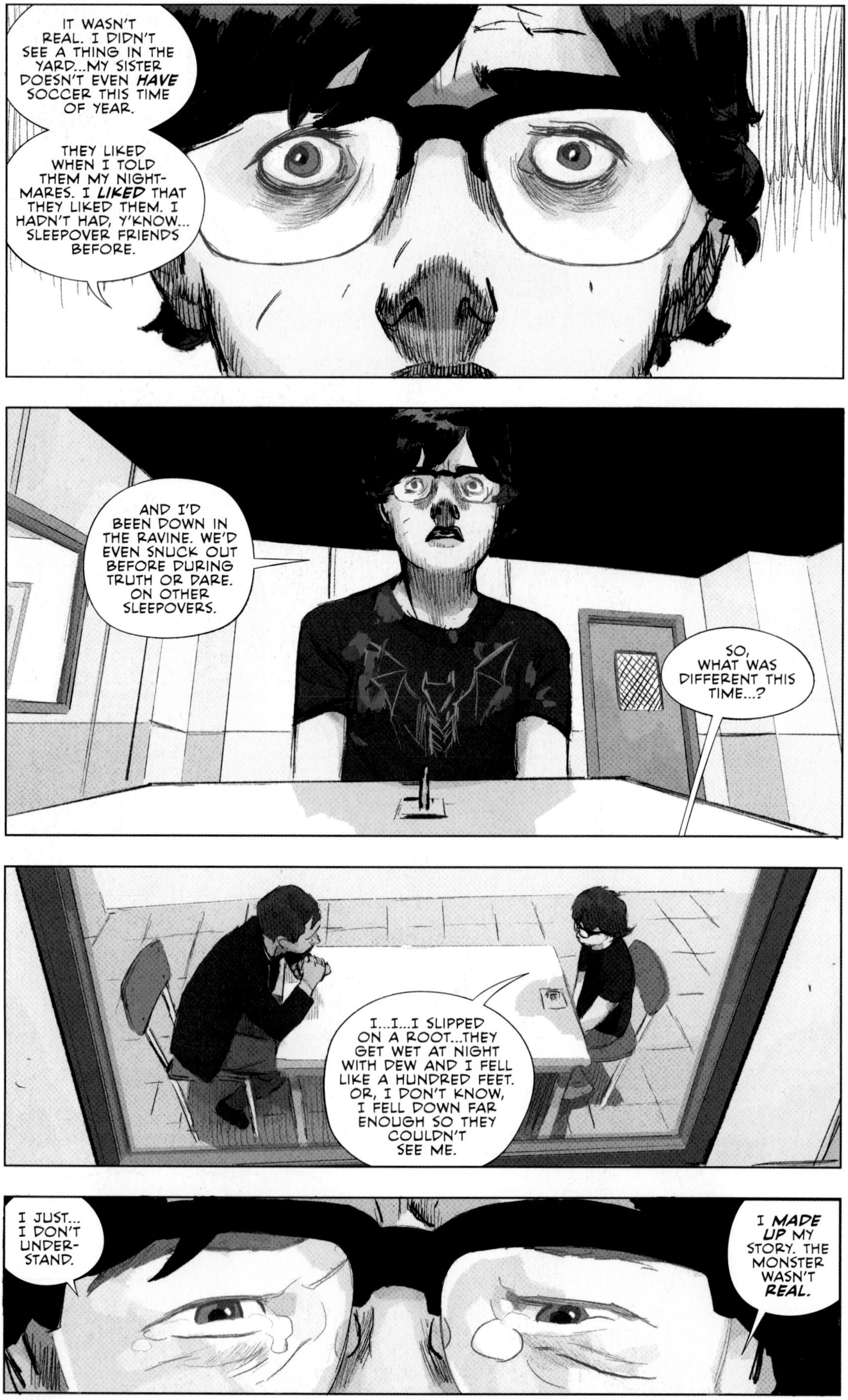
IT WASN'T REAL. I DIDN'T SEE A THING IN THE YARD...MY SISTER DOESN'T EVEN *HAVE* SOCCER THIS TIME OF YEAR.
THEY LIKED WHEN I TOLD THEM MY NIGHT-MARES. I *LIKED* THAT THEY LIKED THEM. I HADN'T HAD, Y'KNOW... SLEEPOVER FRIENDS BEFORE.
AND I'D BEEN DOWN IN THE RAVINE. WE'D EVEN SNUCK OUT BEFORE DURING TRUTH OR DARE. ON OTHER SLEEPOVERS.
SO, WHAT WAS DIFFERENT THIS TIME...?
I...I...I SLIPPED ON A ROOT...THEY GET WET AT NIGHT WITH DEW AND I FELL LIKE A HUNDRED FEET. OR, I DON'T KNOW, I FELL DOWN FAR ENOUGH SO THEY COULDN'T SEE ME.
I JUST... I DON'T UNDER-STAND.
I *MADE UP* MY STORY. THE MONSTER WASN'T *REAL.*

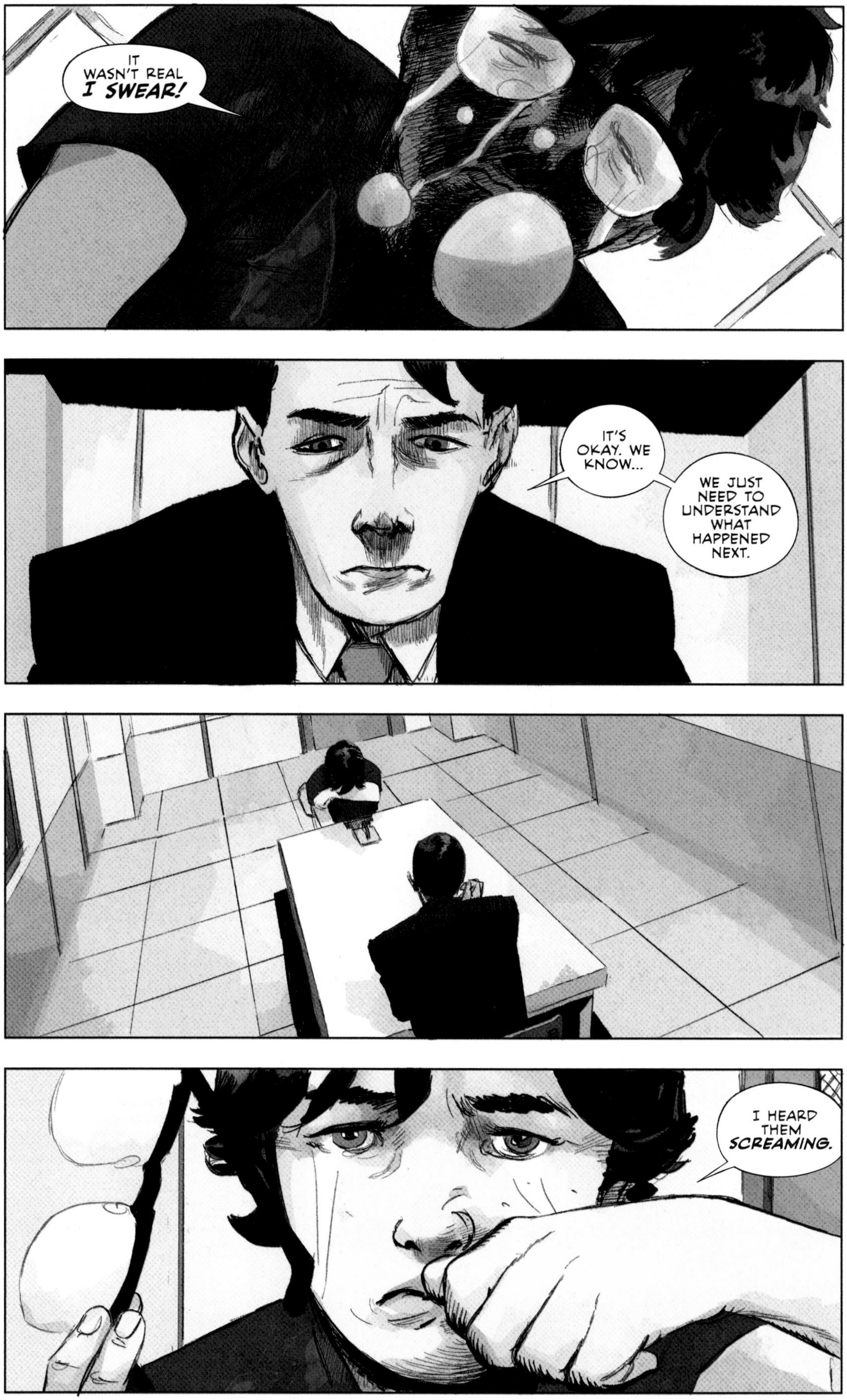
IT WASN'T REAL I SWEAR!
IT'S OKAY. WE KNOW...
WE JUST NEED TO UNDERSTAND WHAT HAPPENED NEXT.
I HEARD THEM SCREAMING.

SOME
is
KILL
CHILD

THING

LING

the

DREN

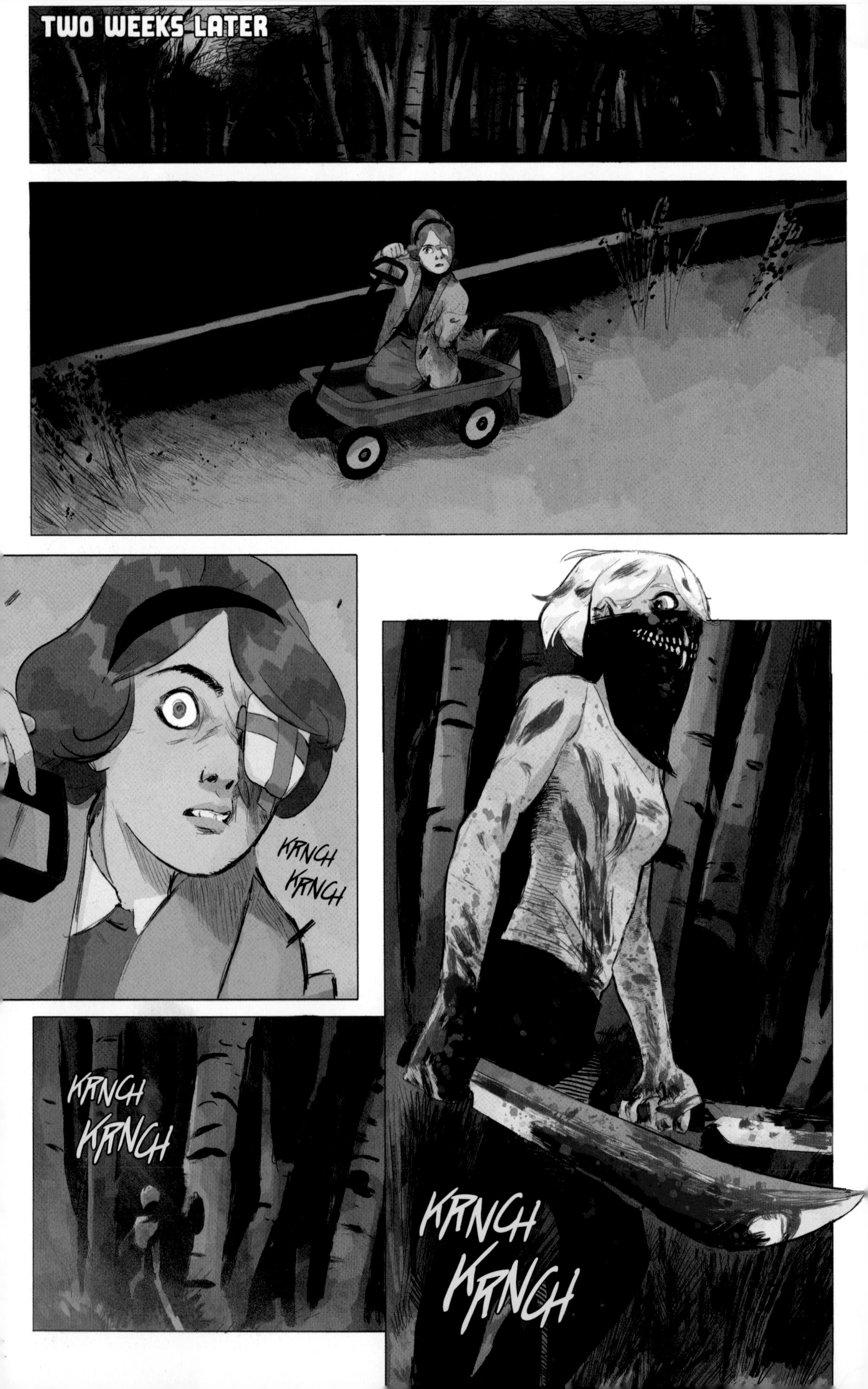
TWO WEEKS LATER
KRNCH
KRNCH
KRNCH
KRNCH
KRNCH
KRNCH

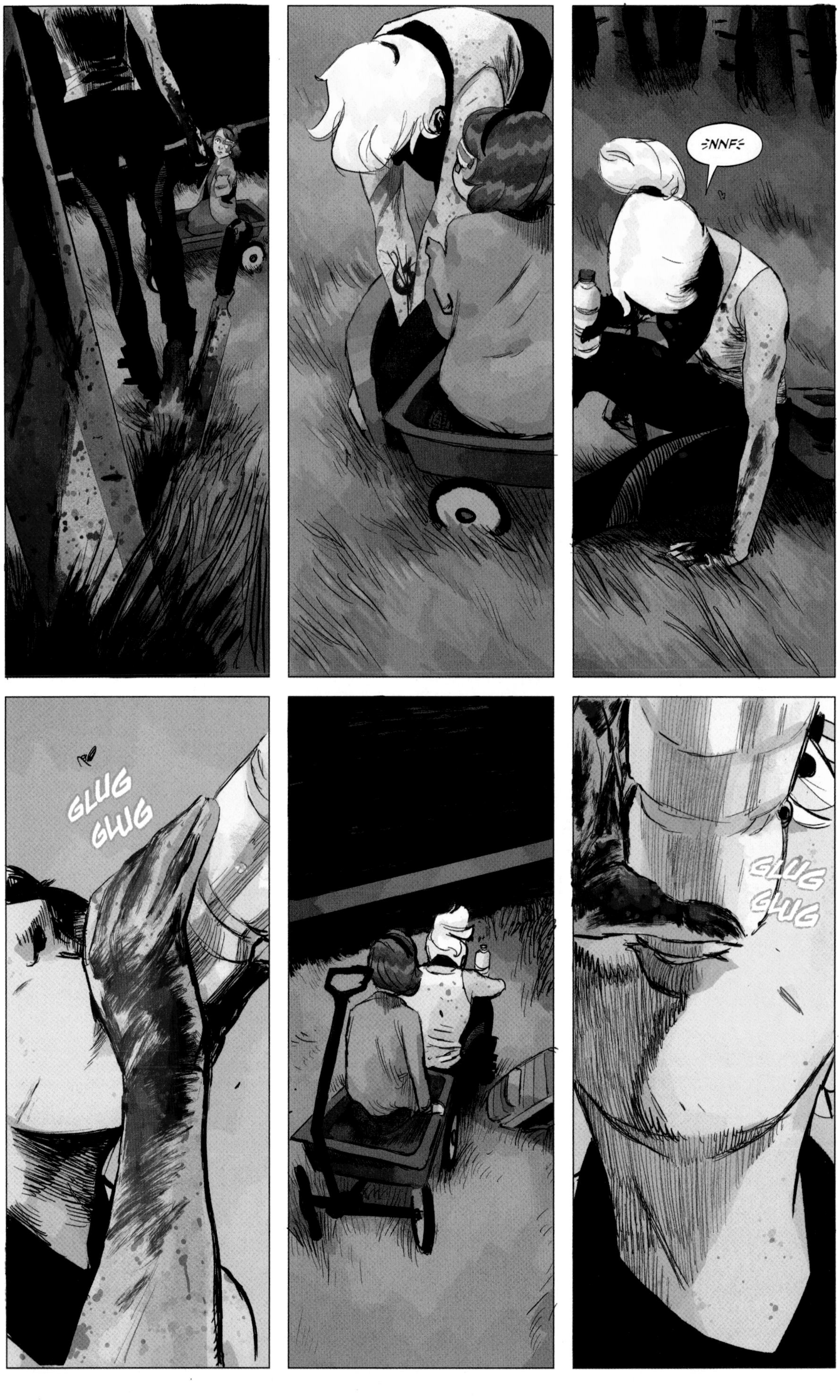
NNF
GLUG
GLUG
GLUG
GLUG

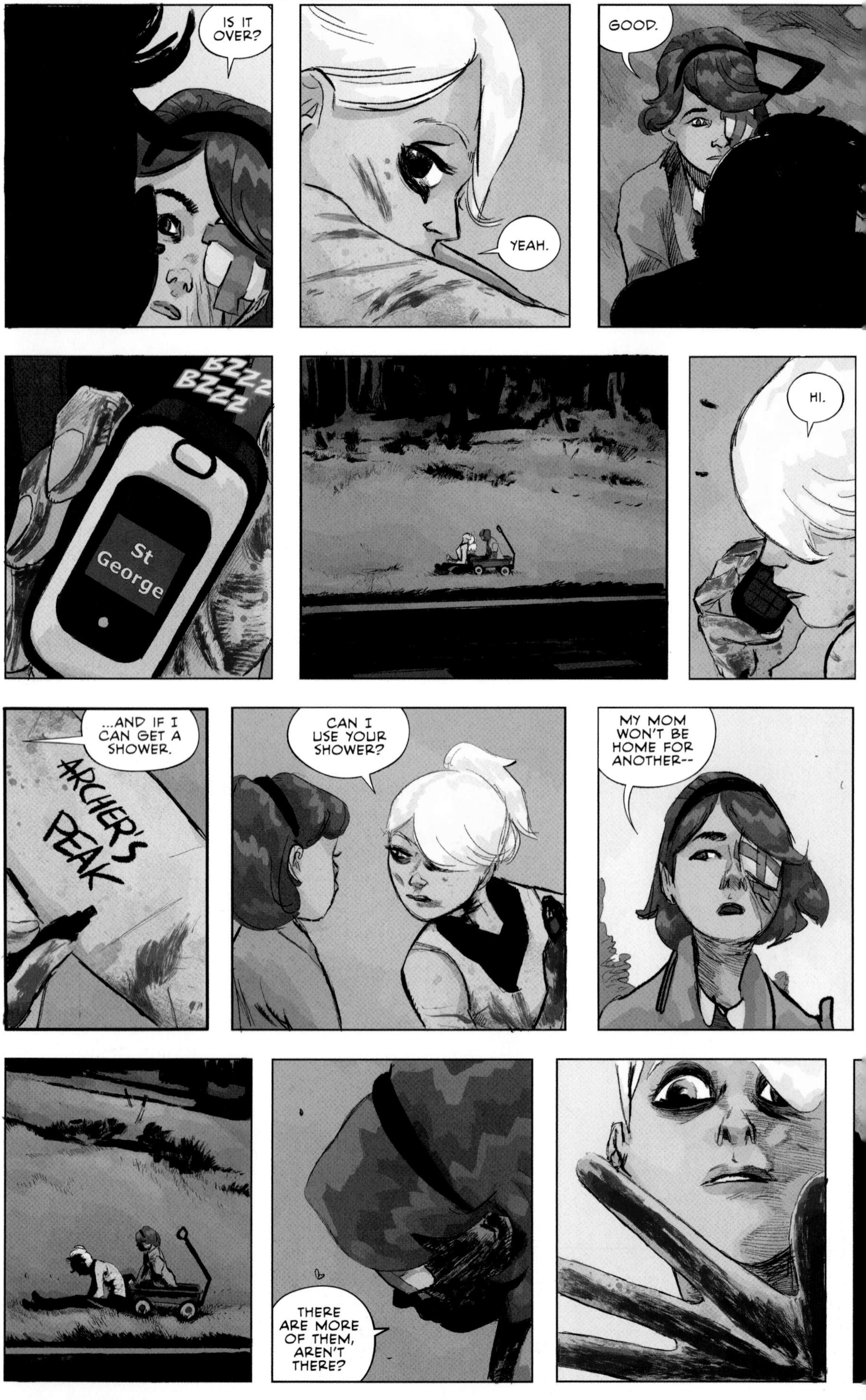
IS IT OVER?
YEAH.
GOOD.
BZZZ BZZZ
St George
HI.
...AND IF I CAN GET A SHOWER.
ARCHER'S PEAK
CAN I USE YOUR SHOWER?
MY MOM WON'T BE HOME FOR ANOTHER--
THERE ARE MORE OF THEM, AREN'T THERE?

GOOD.

BZZZ
BZZZ

SHIT.

THAT'S A BAD WORD.

I KNOW IT'S A FUCKING BAD WORD.

OKAY.

YEAH. YEAH, IT'S DONE.

SIXTEEN HOURS, I THINK? DEPENDING ON BUS SCHEDULES...

YEAH. SIXTEEN HOURS.

FINE.

CLACK

SHIT.

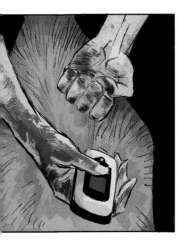

YEAH.

LET'S GET TO THAT SHOWER.

I STINK.

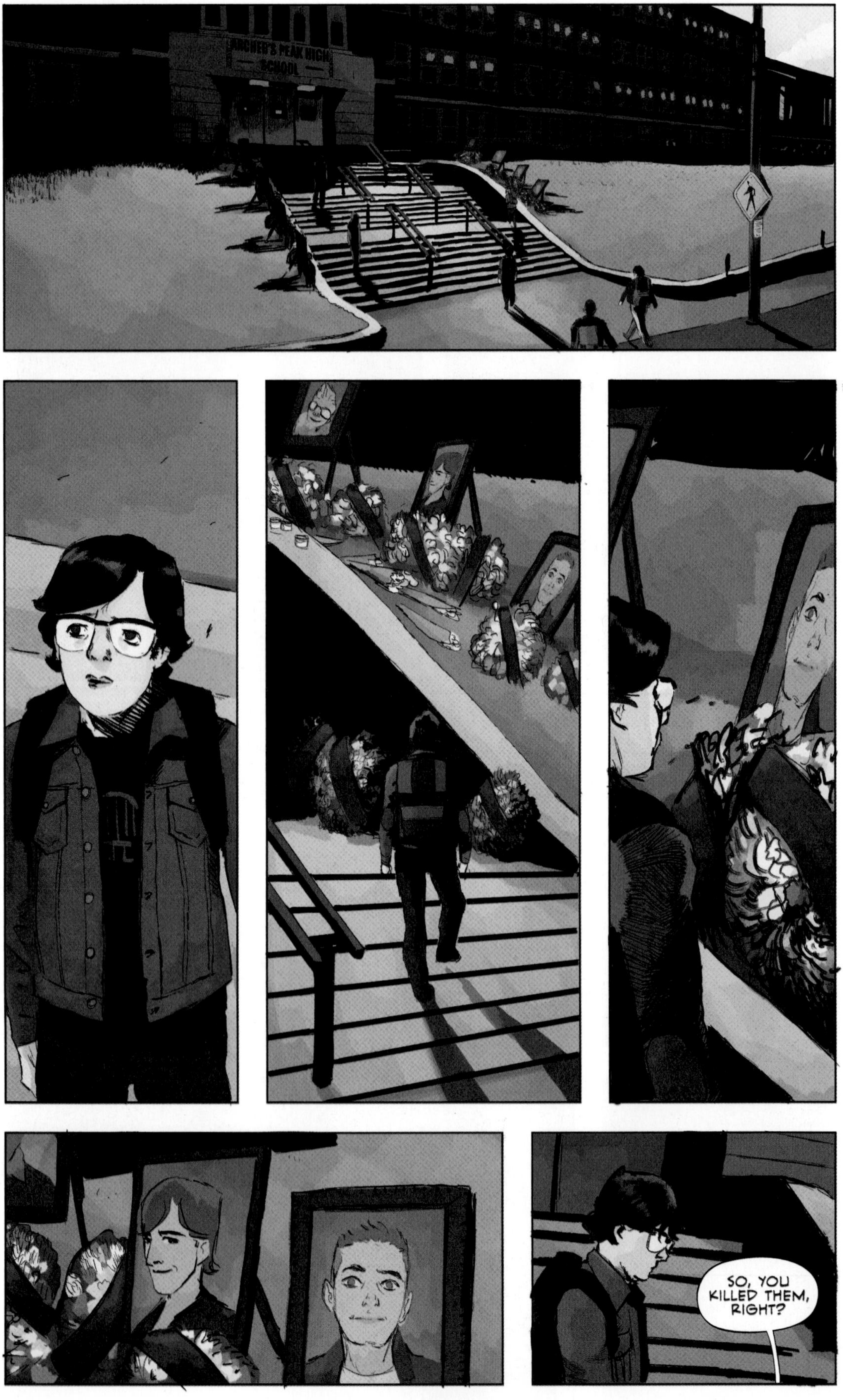
PEAK HIGH
SCHOOL
SO, YOU KILLED THEM, RIGHT?

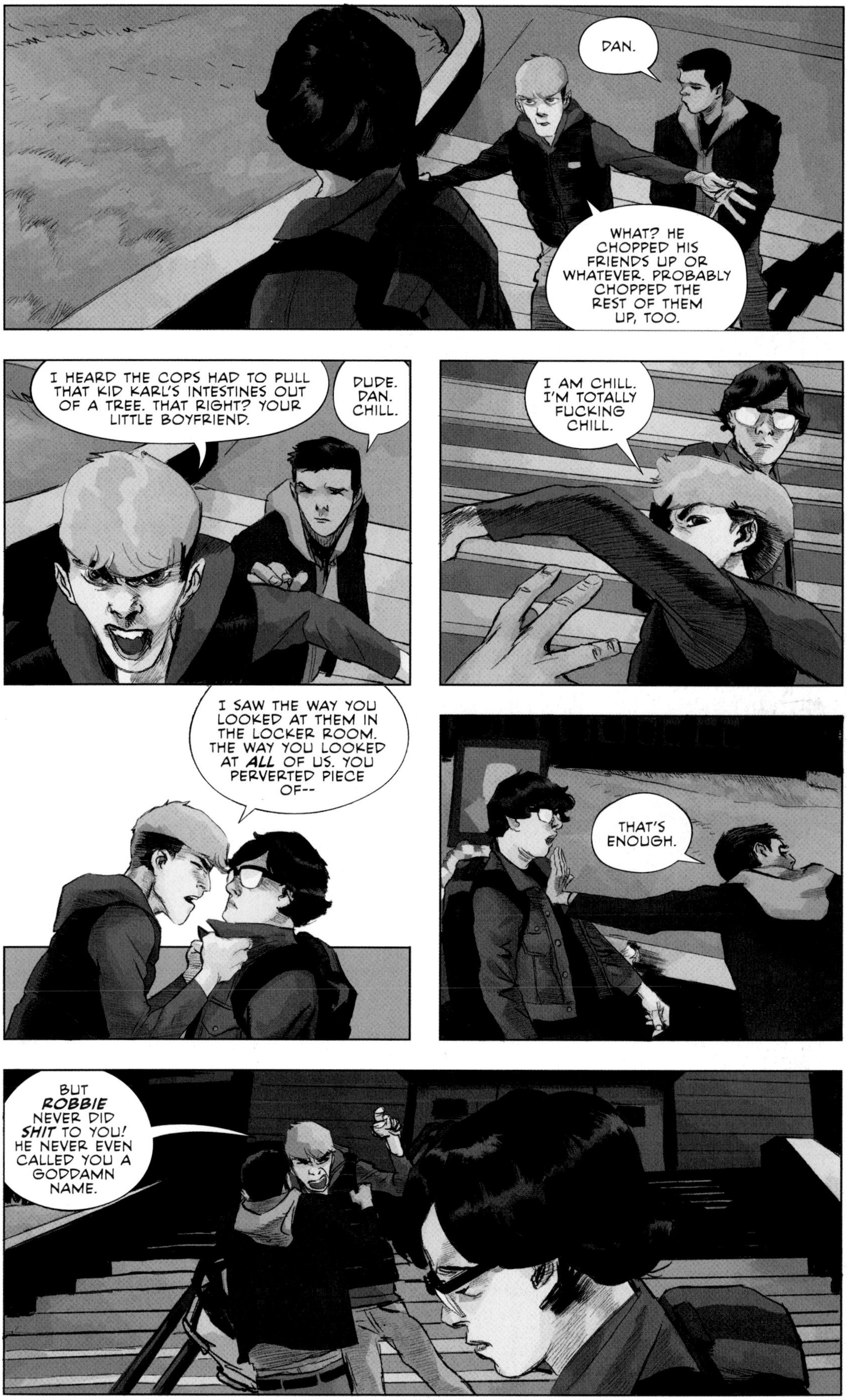
DAN.
WHAT? HE CHOPPED HIS FRIENDS UP OR WHATEVER. PROBABLY CHOPPED THE REST OF THEM UP, TOO.
I HEARD THE COPS HAD TO PULL THAT KID KARL'S INTESTINES OUT OF A TREE. THAT RIGHT? YOUR LITTLE BOYFRIEND.
DUDE. DAN. CHILL.
I AM CHILL. I'M TOTALLY FUCKING CHILL.
I SAW THE WAY YOU LOOKED AT THEM IN THE LOCKER ROOM. THE WAY YOU LOOKED AT ALL OF US. YOU PERVERTED PIECE OF--
THAT'S ENOUGH.
BUT ROBBIE NEVER DID SHIT TO YOU! HE NEVER EVEN CALLED YOU A GODDAMN NAME.

BUT HE WASN'T EVER GOING TO KISS YOU, SO YOU THOUGHT YOU'D JUST RIP HIS HEAD OFF. I DON'T EVEN WANT TO *THINK* ABOUT WHAT YOU--

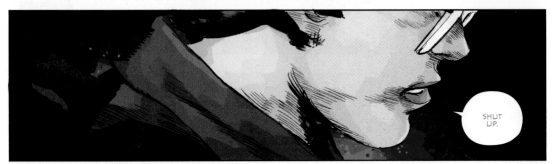

SHUT UP.

WHAT DID YOU SAY TO ME?

I SAID SHUT THE *FUCK* UP!

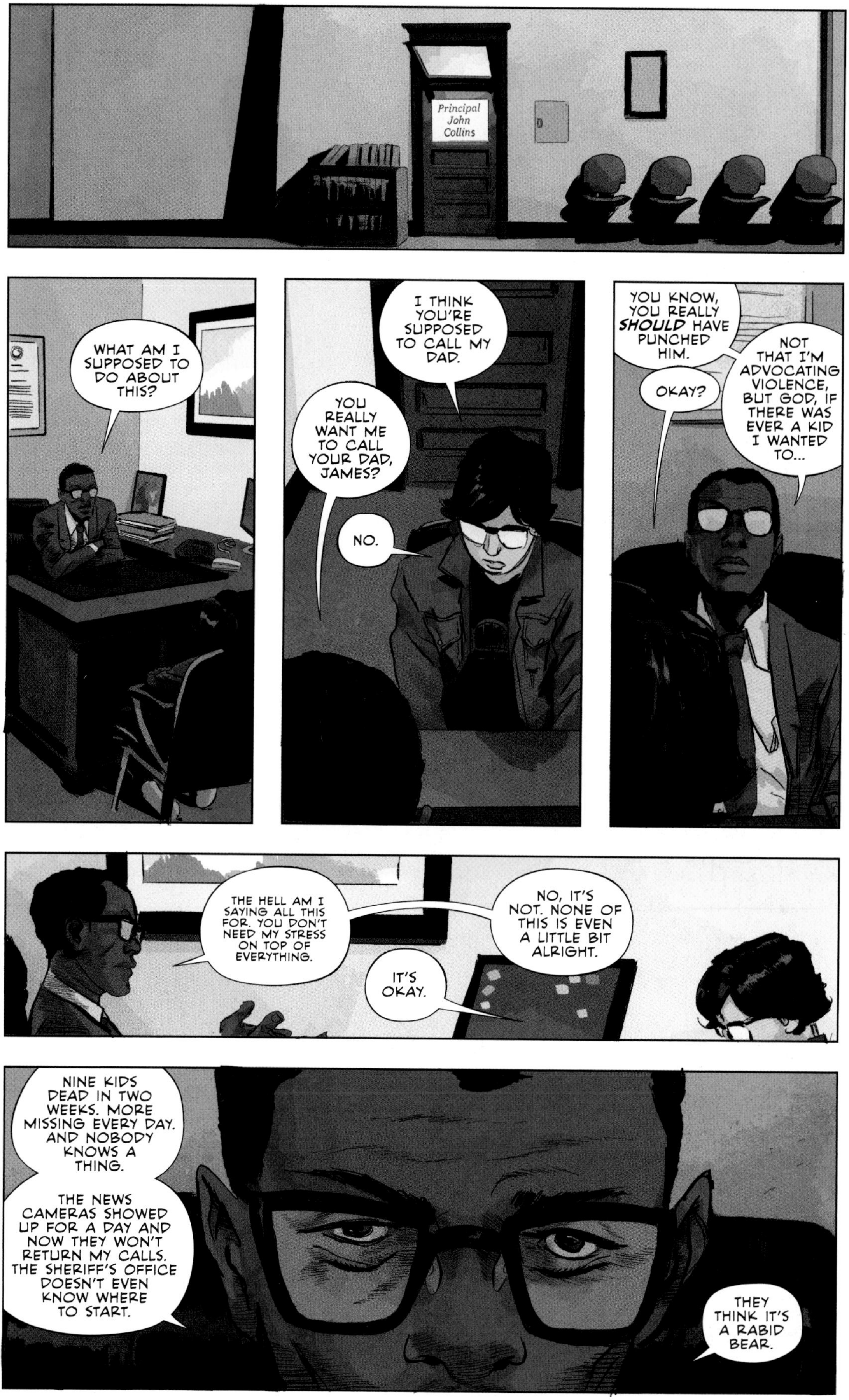
Principal John Collins
WHAT AM I SUPPOSED TO DO ABOUT THIS?
I THINK YOU'RE SUPPOSED TO CALL MY DAD.
YOU REALLY WANT ME TO CALL YOUR DAD, JAMES?
NO.
YOU KNOW, YOU REALLY SHOULD HAVE PUNCHED HIM.
OKAY?
NOT THAT I'M ADVOCATING VIOLENCE, BUT GOD, IF THERE WAS EVER A KID I WANTED TO...
THE HELL AM I SAYING ALL THIS FOR. YOU DON'T NEED MY STRESS ON TOP OF EVERYTHING.
IT'S OKAY.
NO, IT'S NOT. NONE OF THIS IS EVEN A LITTLE BIT ALRIGHT.
NINE KIDS DEAD IN TWO WEEKS. MORE MISSING EVERY DAY. AND NOBODY KNOWS A THING.
THE NEWS CAMERAS SHOWED UP FOR A DAY AND NOW THEY WON'T RETURN MY CALLS. THE SHERIFF'S OFFICE DOESN'T EVEN KNOW WHERE TO START.
THEY THINK IT'S A RABID BEAR.

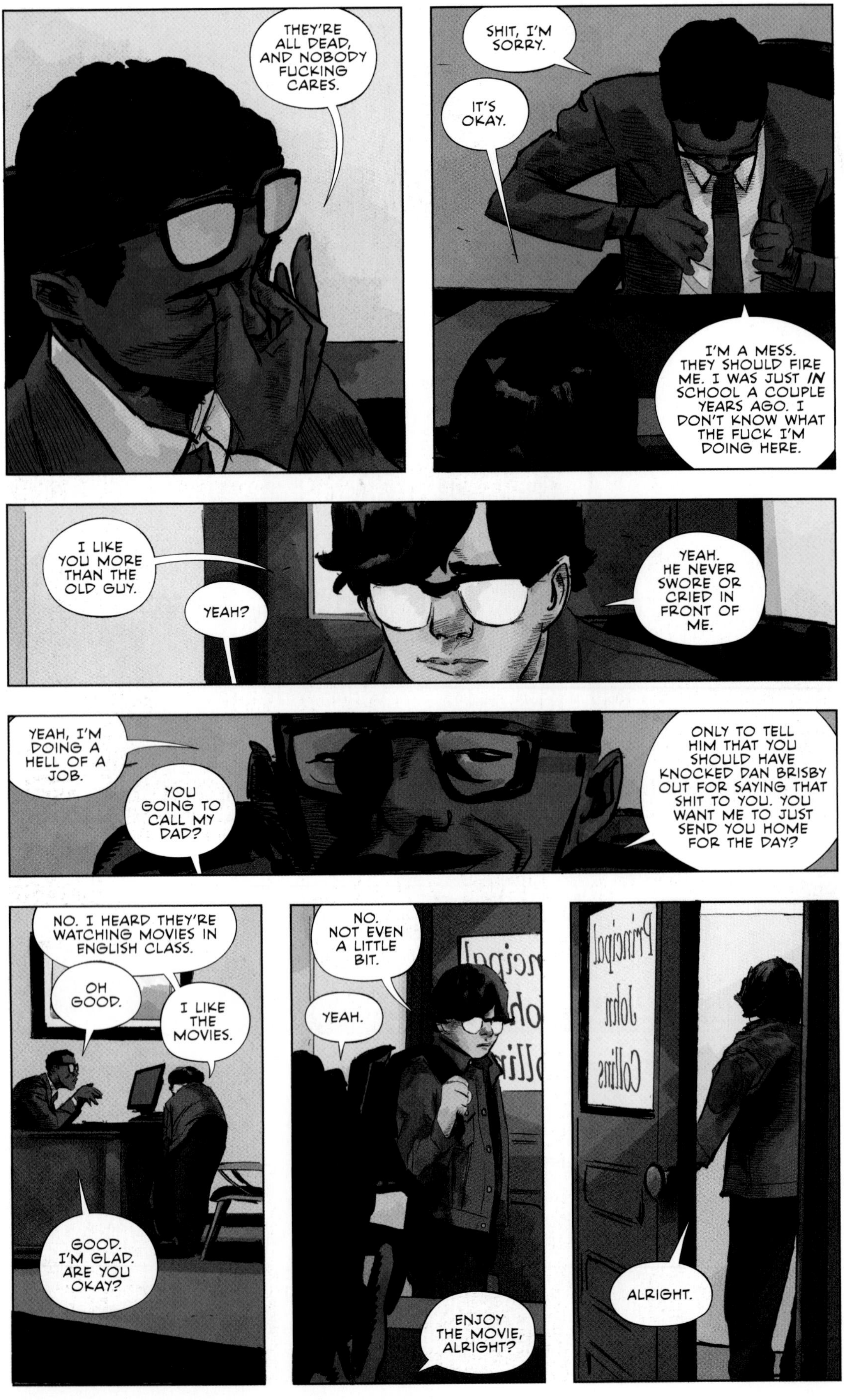
THEY'RE ALL DEAD, AND NOBODY FUCKING CARES.
SHIT, I'M SORRY.
IT'S OKAY.
I'M A MESS. THEY SHOULD FIRE ME. I WAS JUST IN SCHOOL A COUPLE YEARS AGO. I DON'T KNOW WHAT THE FUCK I'M DOING HERE.
I LIKE YOU MORE THAN THE OLD GUY.
YEAH?
YEAH. HE NEVER SWORE OR CRIED IN FRONT OF ME.
YEAH, I'M DOING A HELL OF A JOB.
YOU GOING TO CALL MY DAD?
ONLY TO TELL HIM THAT YOU SHOULD HAVE KNOCKED DAN BRISBY OUT FOR SAYING THAT SHIT TO YOU. YOU WANT ME TO JUST SEND YOU HOME FOR THE DAY?
NO. I HEARD THEY'RE WATCHING MOVIES IN ENGLISH CLASS.
OH GOOD.
I LIKE THE MOVIES.
GOOD. I'M GLAD. ARE YOU OKAY?
NO. NOT EVEN A LITTLE BIT.
YEAH.
ENJOY THE MOVIE, ALRIGHT?
Principal John Collins
ALRIGHT.

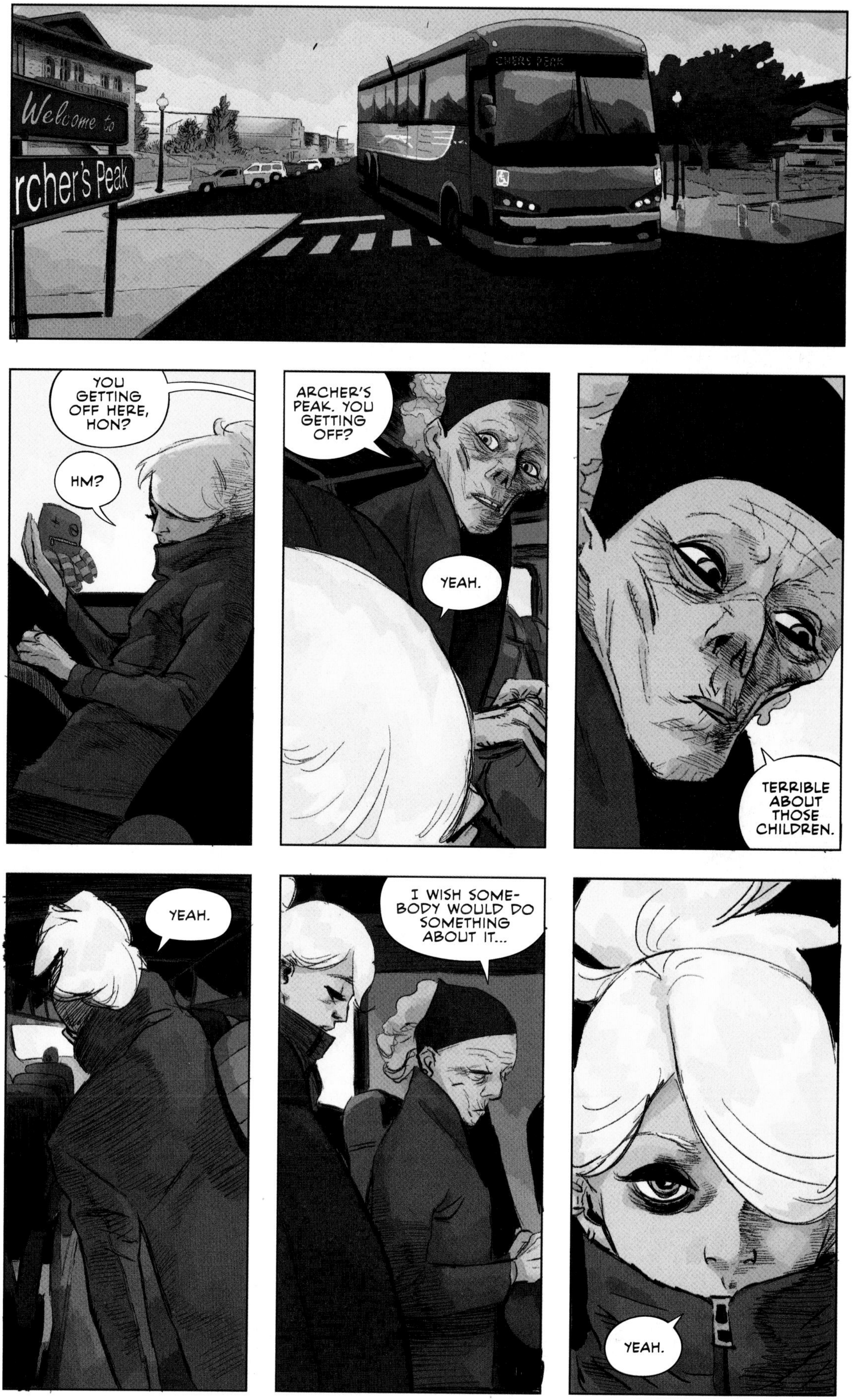
Welcome to
rcher's Peak
YOU GETTING OFF HERE, HON?
HM?
ARCHER'S PEAK. YOU GETTING OFF?
YEAH.
TERRIBLE ABOUT THOSE CHILDREN.
YEAH.
I WISH SOME-BODY WOULD DO SOMETHING ABOUT IT...
YEAH.

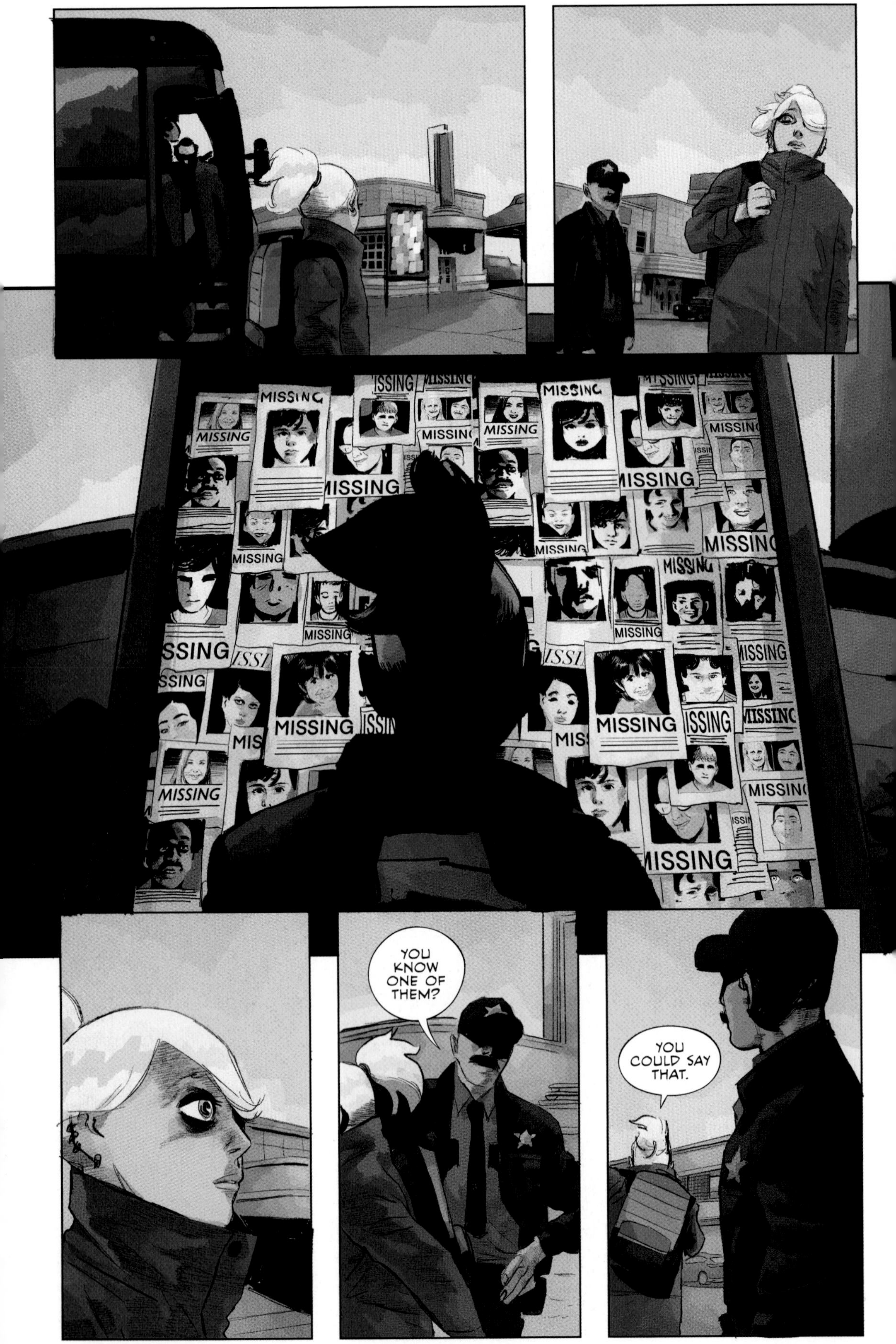
YOU KNOW ONE OF THEM?
YOU COULD SAY THAT.

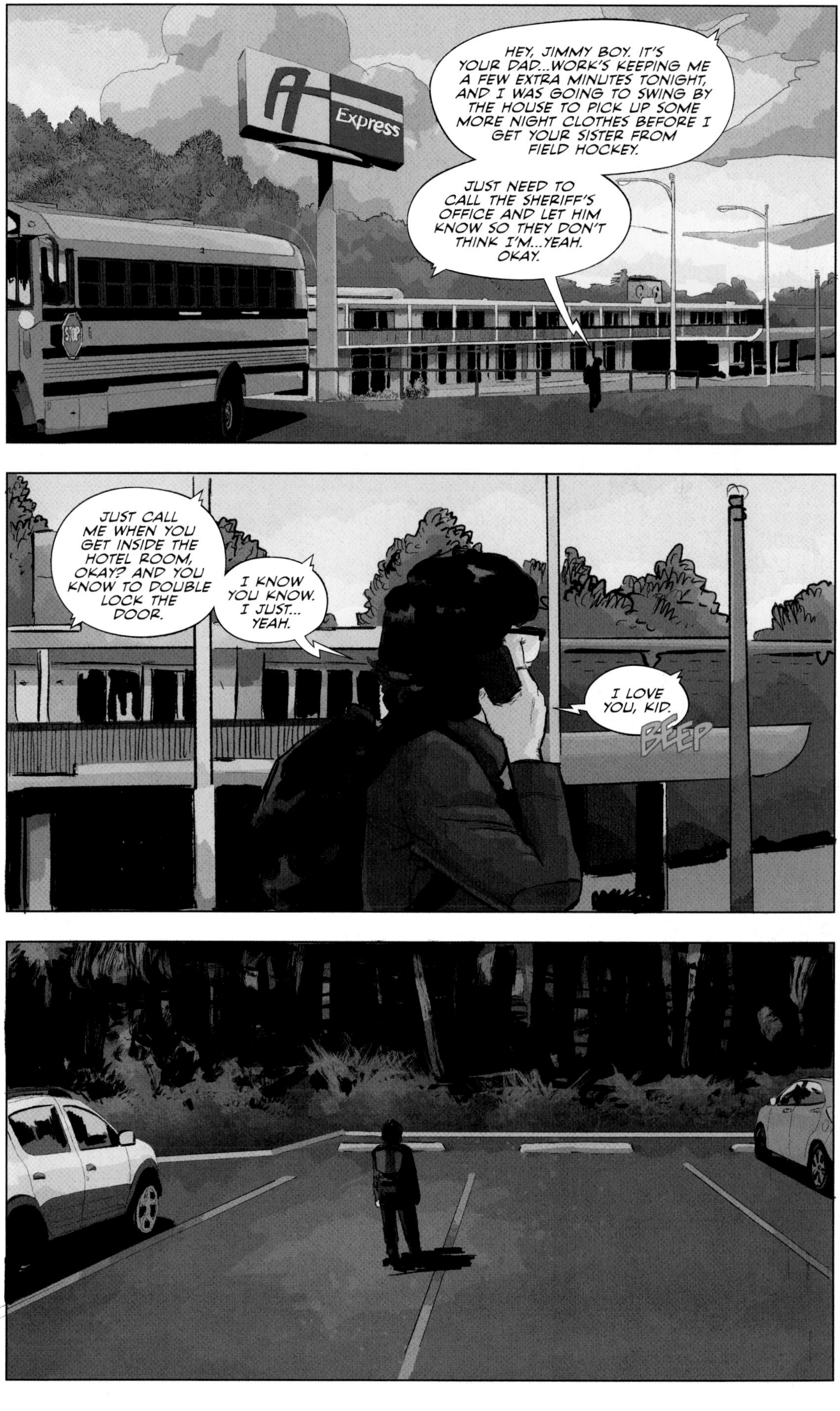

Express
HEY, JIMMY BOY. IT'S YOUR DAD...WORK'S KEEPING ME A FEW EXTRA MINUTES TONIGHT, AND I WAS GOING TO SWING BY THE HOUSE TO PICK UP SOME MORE NIGHT CLOTHES BEFORE I GET YOUR SISTER FROM FIELD HOCKEY.
JUST NEED TO CALL THE SHERIFF'S OFFICE AND LET HIM KNOW SO THEY DON'T THINK I'M...YEAH. OKAY.
JUST CALL ME WHEN YOU GET INSIDE THE HOTEL ROOM, OKAY? AND YOU KNOW TO DOUBLE LOCK THE DOOR.
I KNOW YOU KNOW. I JUST... YEAH.
I LOVE YOU, KID.
BEEP

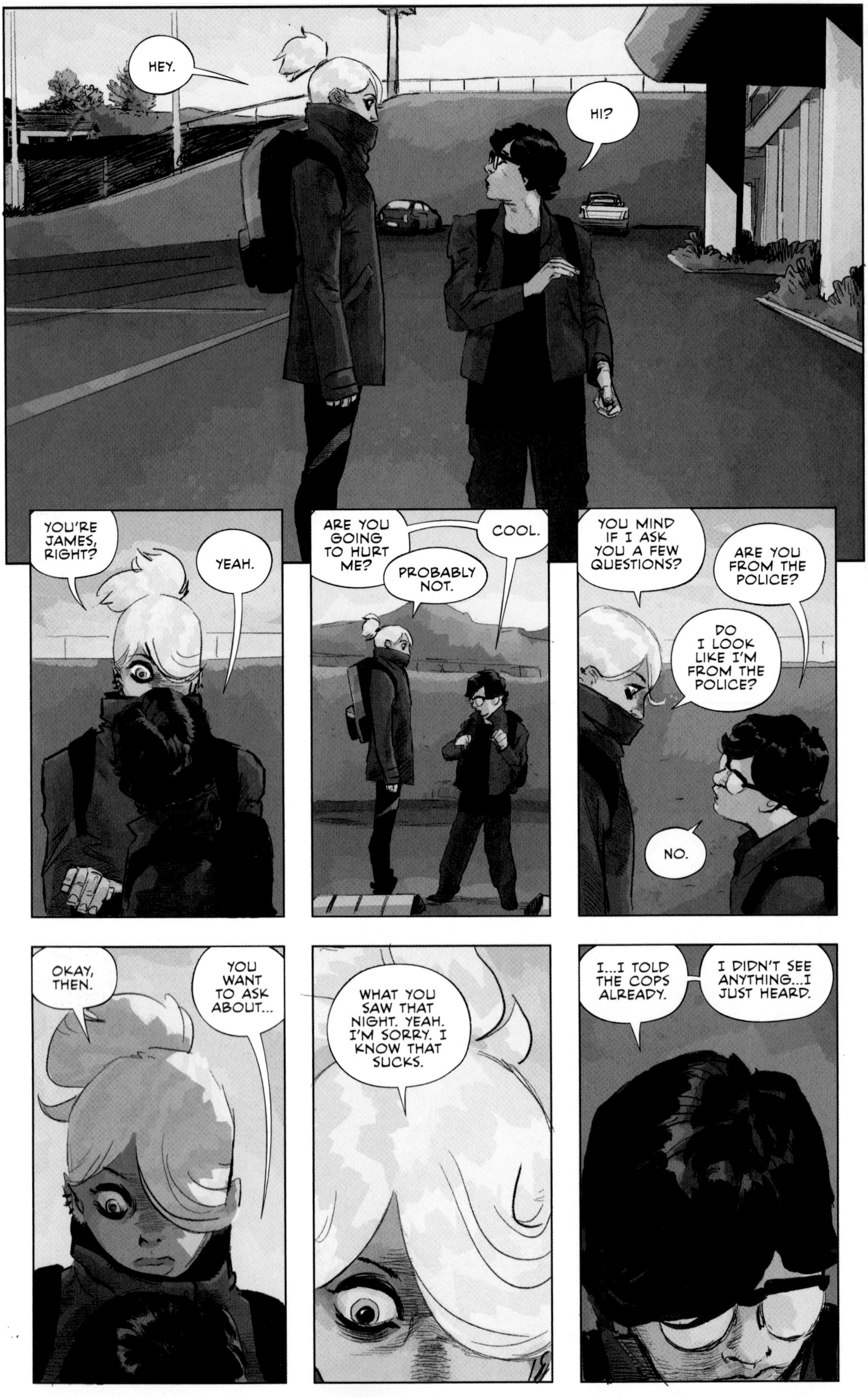
HEY.
HI?
YOU'RE JAMES, RIGHT?
YEAH.
ARE YOU GOING TO HURT ME?
PROBABLY NOT.
COOL.
YOU MIND IF I ASK YOU A FEW QUESTIONS?
ARE YOU FROM THE POLICE?
DO I LOOK LIKE I'M FROM THE POLICE?
NO.
OKAY, THEN.
YOU WANT TO ASK ABOUT...
WHAT YOU SAW THAT NIGHT. YEAH. I'M SORRY. I KNOW THAT SUCKS.
I...I TOLD THE COPS ALREADY.
I DIDN'T SEE ANYTHING...I JUST HEARD.

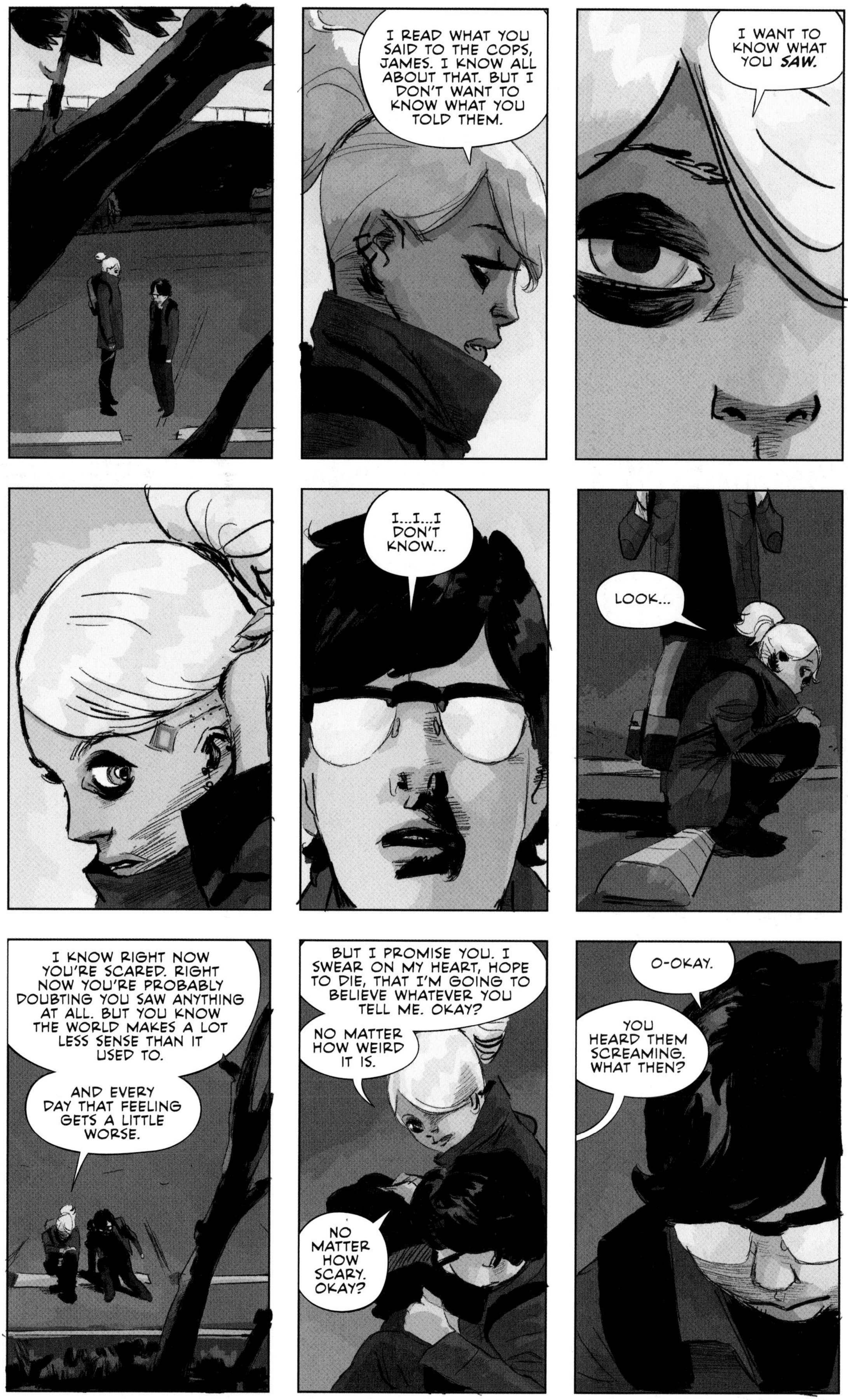
I READ WHAT YOU SAID TO THE COPS, JAMES. I KNOW ALL ABOUT THAT. BUT I DON'T WANT TO KNOW WHAT YOU TOLD THEM.
I WANT TO KNOW WHAT YOU SAW.
I...I...I DON'T KNOW...
LOOK...
I KNOW RIGHT NOW YOU'RE SCARED. RIGHT NOW YOU'RE PROBABLY DOUBTING YOU SAW ANYTHING AT ALL. BUT YOU KNOW THE WORLD MAKES A LOT LESS SENSE THAN IT USED TO.
AND EVERY DAY THAT FEELING GETS A LITTLE WORSE.
BUT I PROMISE YOU. I SWEAR ON MY HEART, HOPE TO DIE, THAT I'M GOING TO BELIEVE WHATEVER YOU TELL ME. OKAY?
NO MATTER HOW WEIRD IT IS.
NO MATTER HOW SCARY. OKAY?
O-OKAY.
YOU HEARD THEM SCREAMING. WHAT THEN?

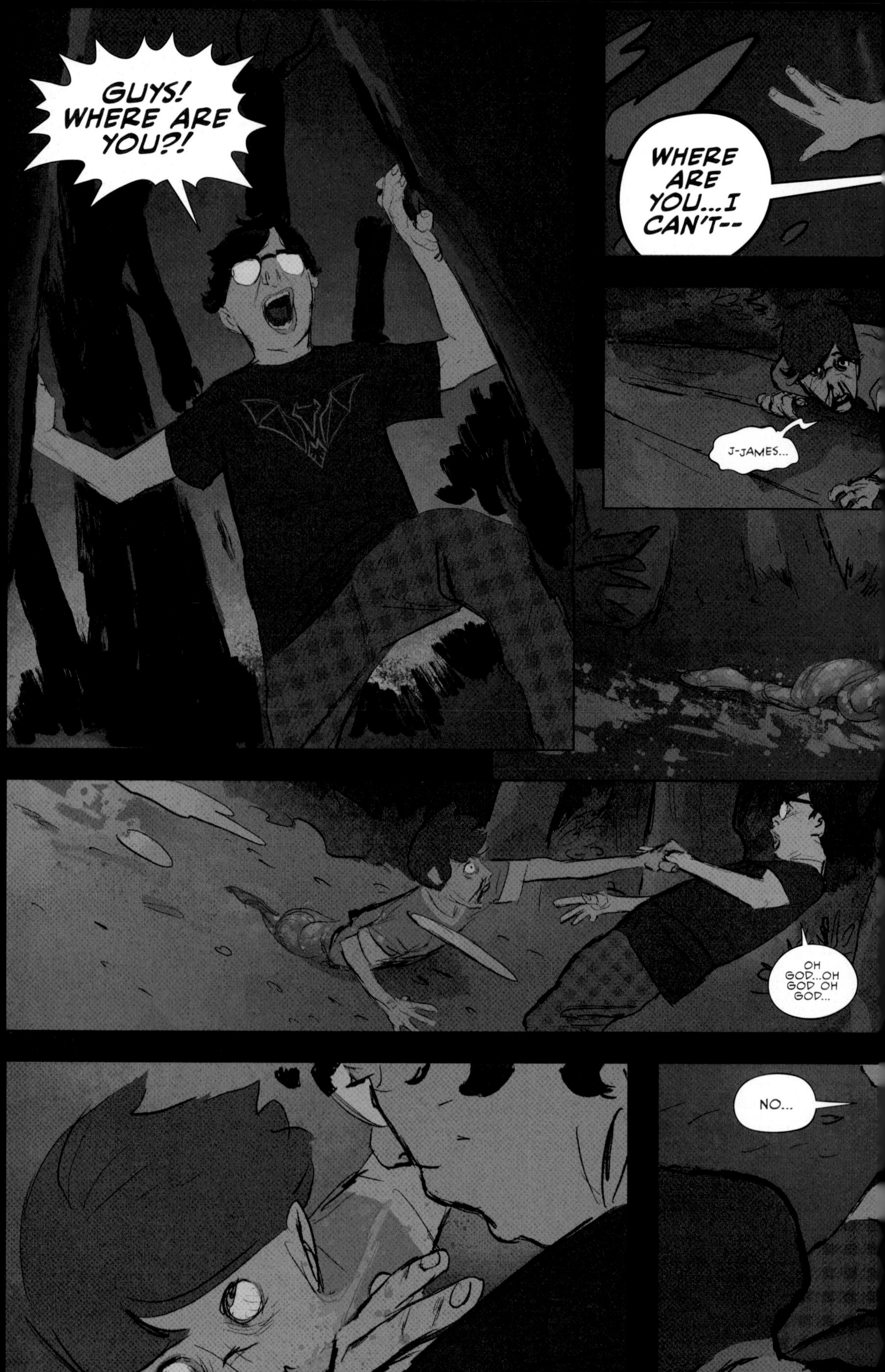
GUYS! WHERE ARE YOU?!
WHERE ARE YOU...I CAN'T--
J-JAMES...
OH GOD...OH GOD OH GOD...
NO...

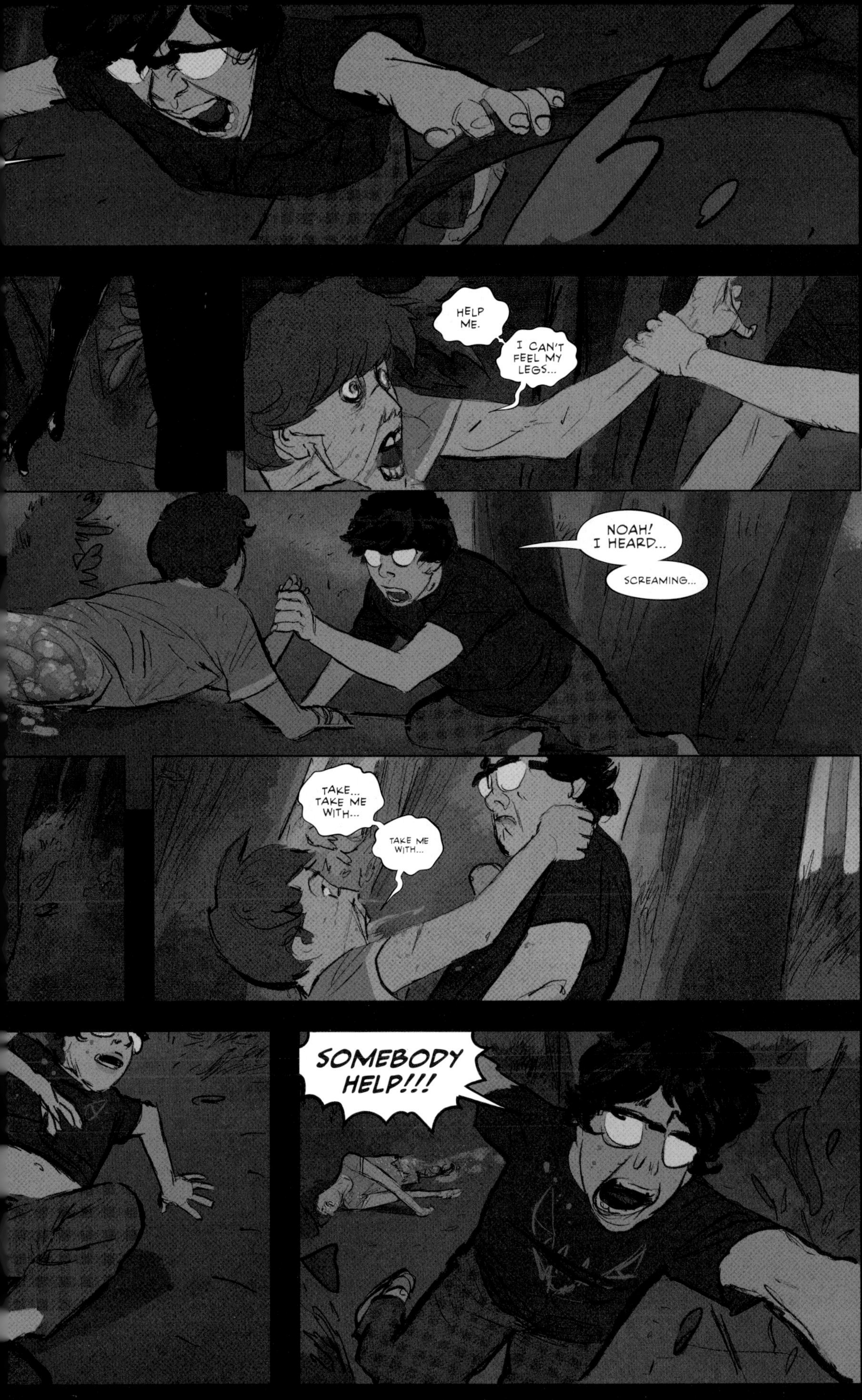
HELP ME.
I CAN'T FEEL MY LEGS...
NOAH! I HEARD...
SCREAMING...
TAKE... TAKE ME WITH...
TAKE ME WITH...
SOMEBODY HELP!!!

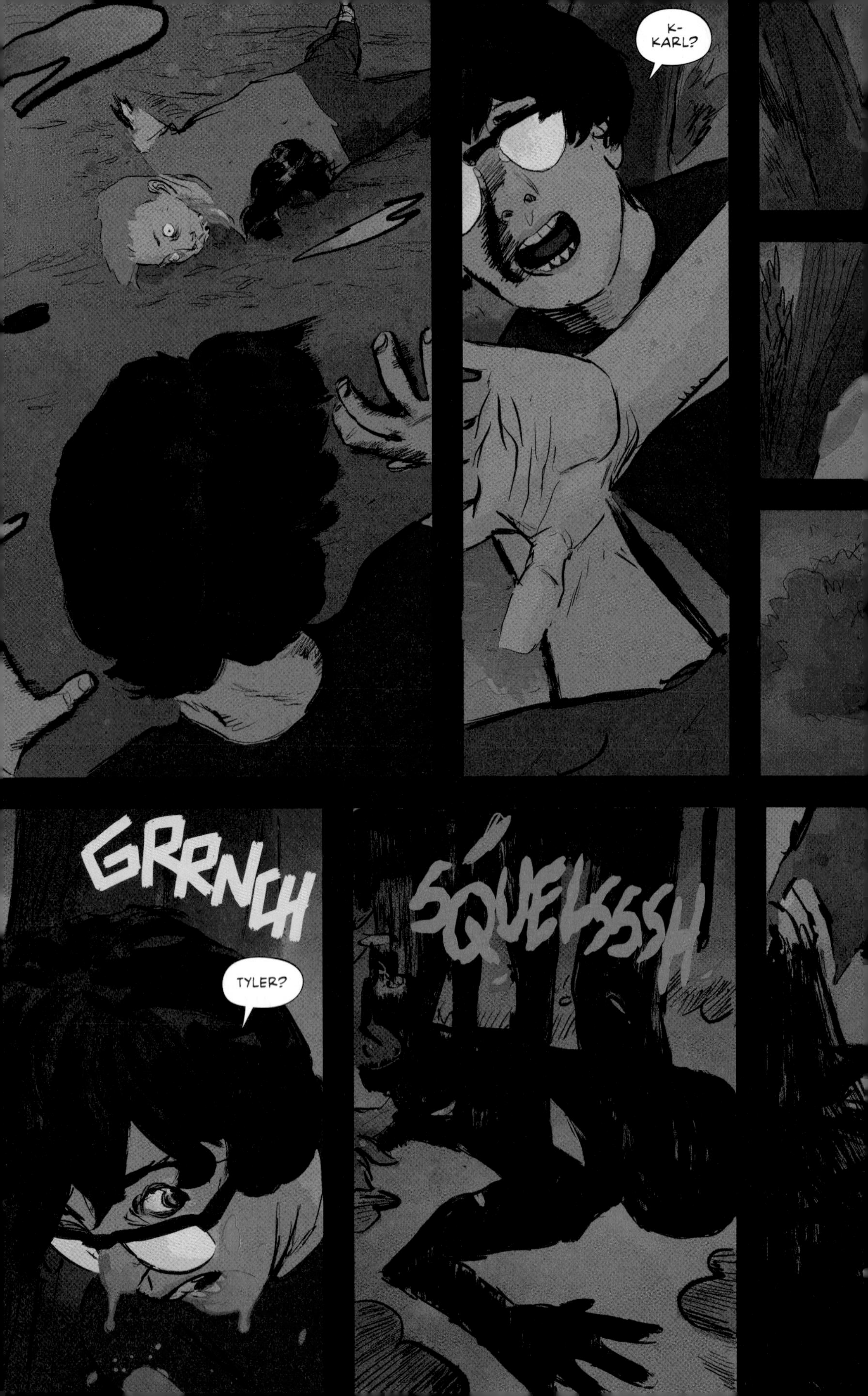
K-
KARL?
GRRNCH
TYLER?
SQUELSSSH

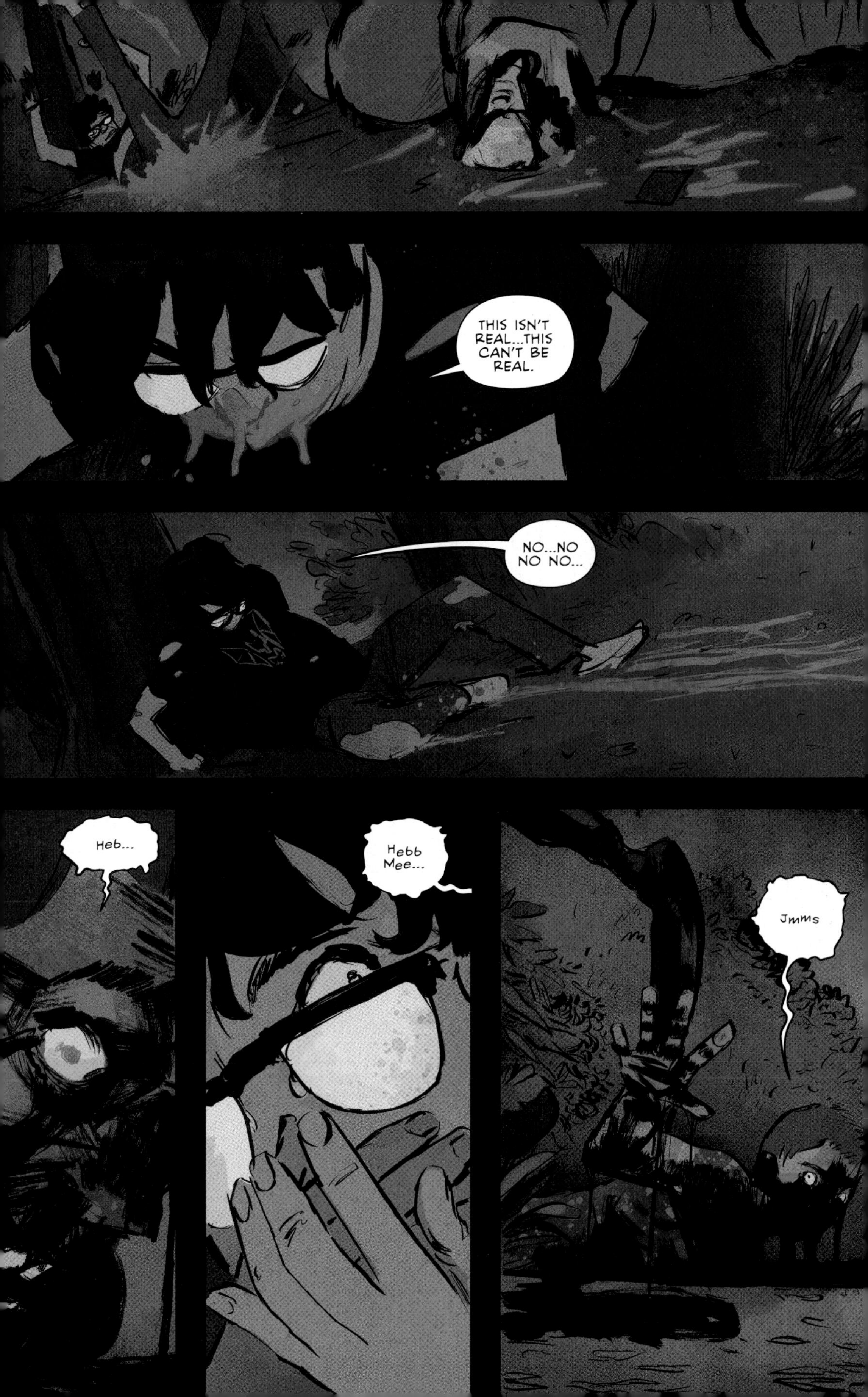
THIS ISN'T REAL...THIS CAN'T BE REAL.
NO...NO NO NO...
Heb...
Hebb Mee...
Jmms

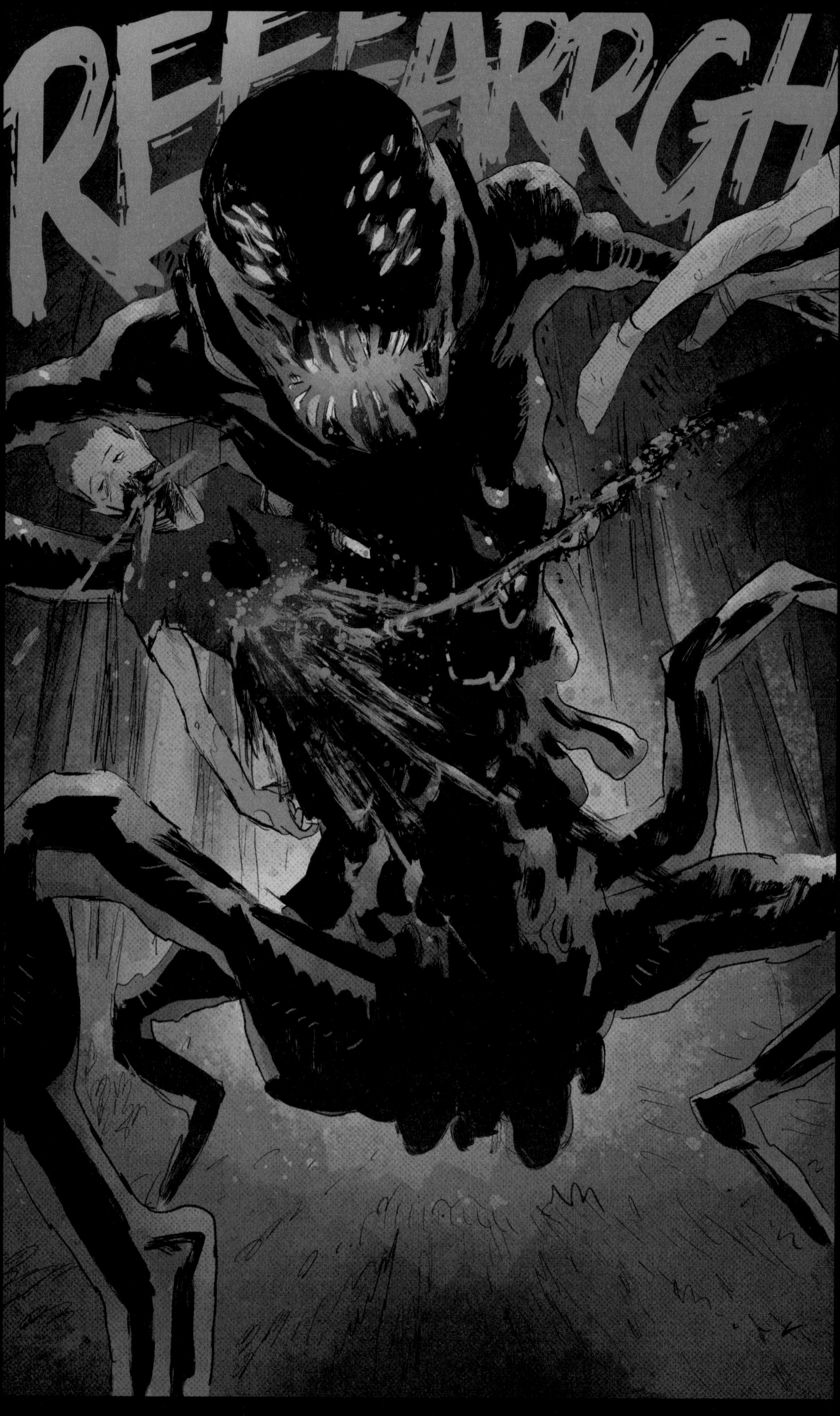
REEEARRGH

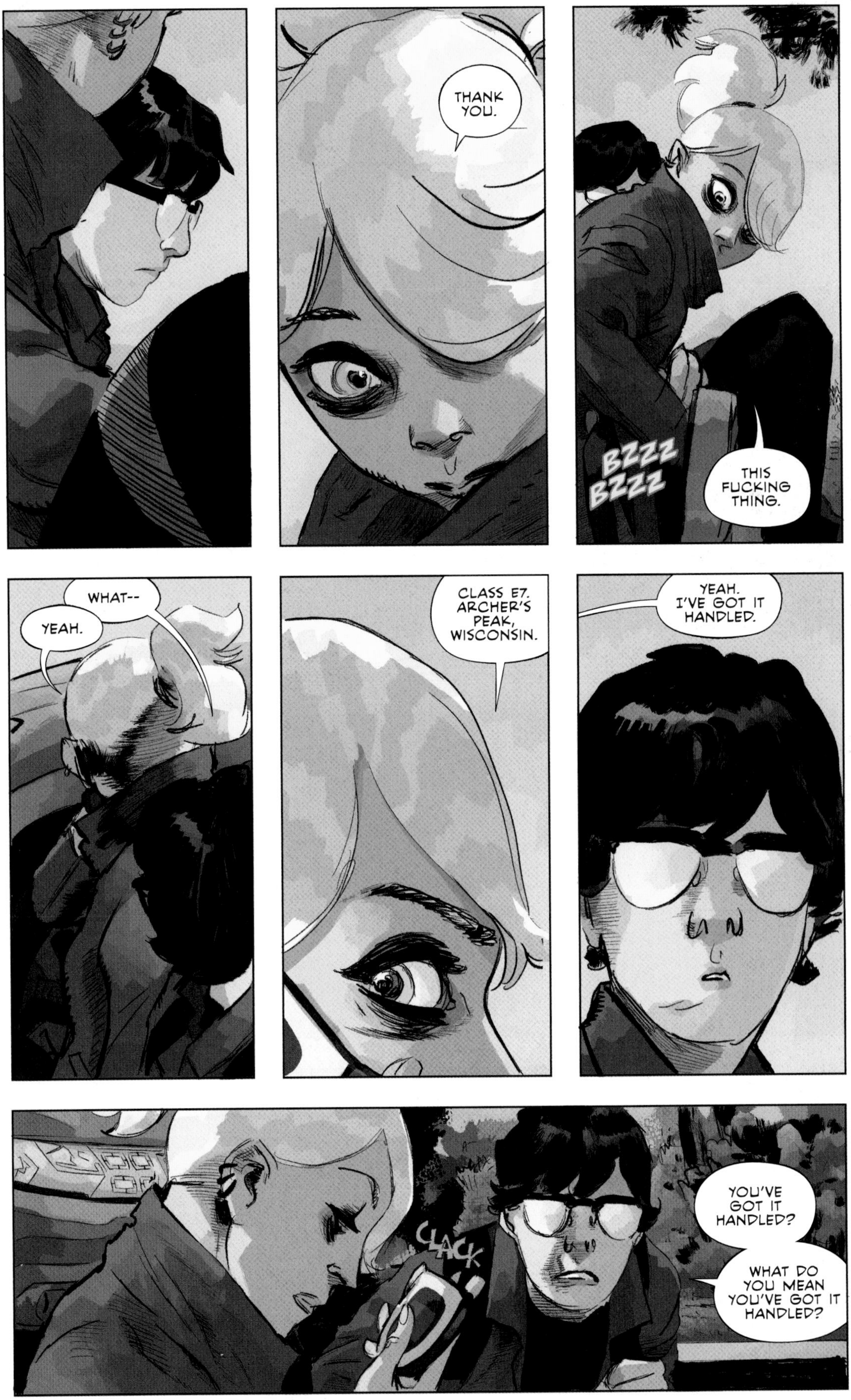

THANK YOU.
BZZZ BZZZ
THIS FUCKING THING.
WHAT--
YEAH.
CLASS E7. ARCHER'S PEAK, WISCONSIN.
YEAH. I'VE GOT IT HANDLED.
CLACK
YOU'VE GOT IT HANDLED?
WHAT DO YOU MEAN YOU'VE GOT IT HANDLED?

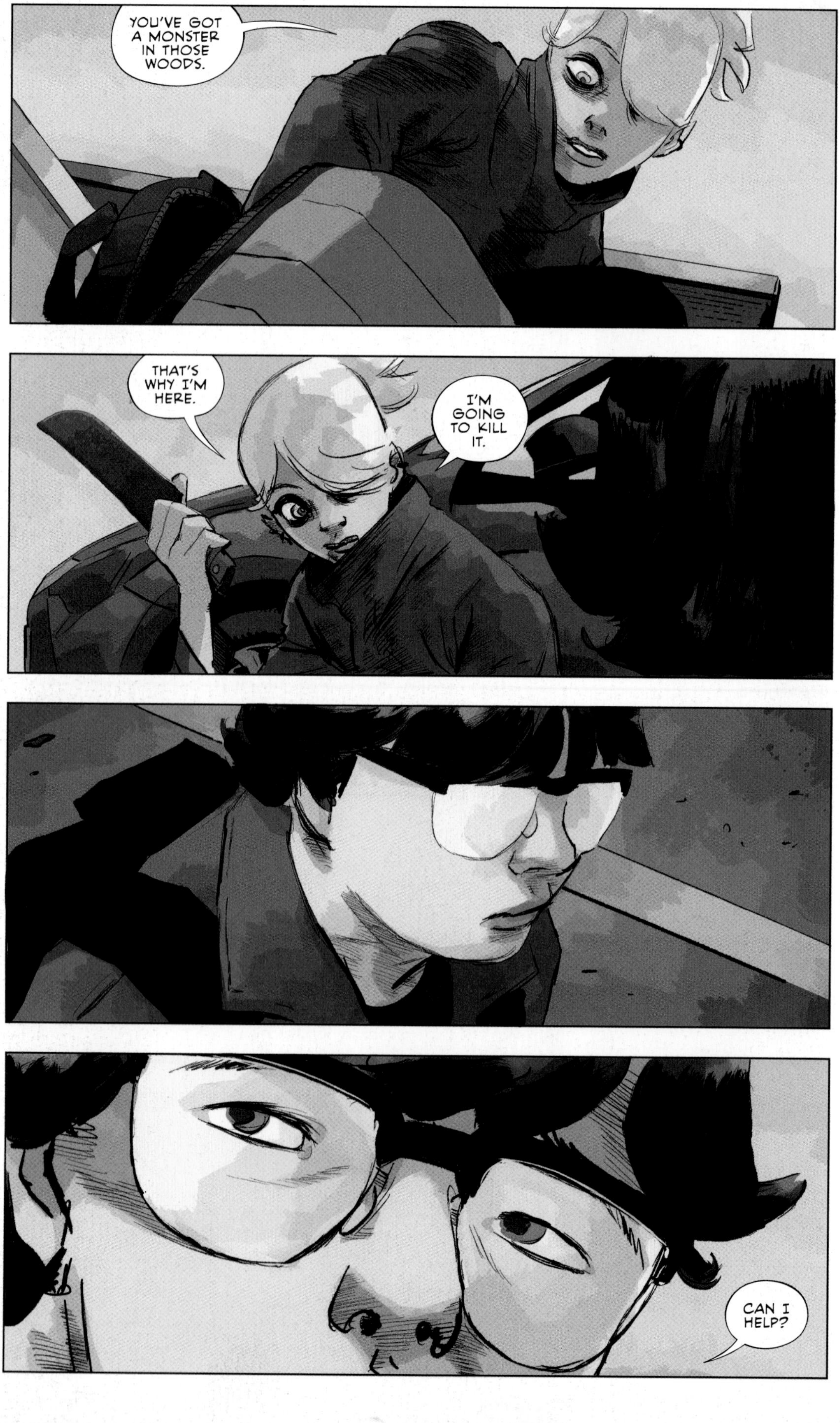
YOU'VE GOT A MONSTER IN THOSE WOODS.
THAT'S WHY I'M HERE.
I'M GOING TO KILL IT.
CAN I HELP?

CHAPTER
TWO

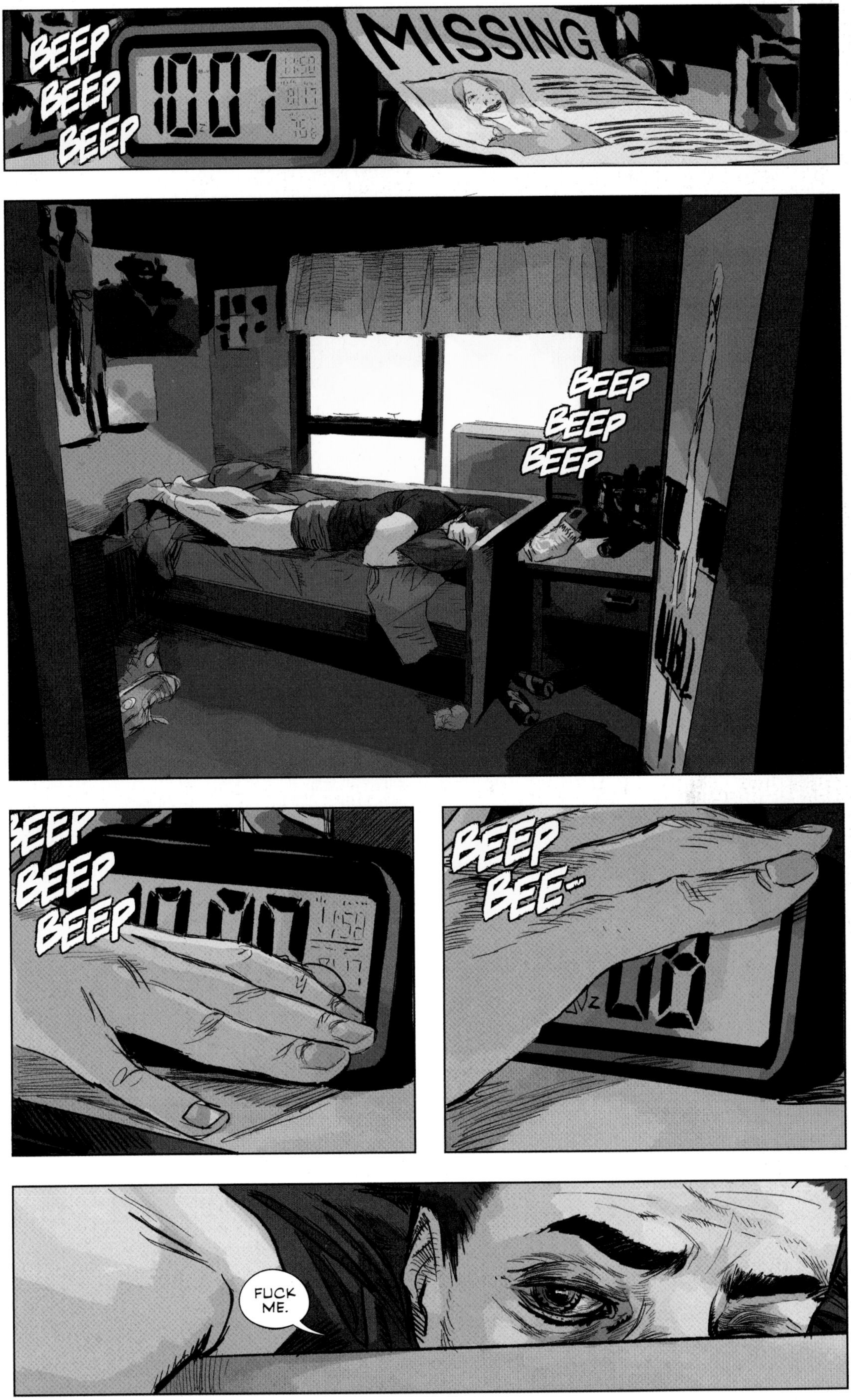
BEEP
BEEP
BEEP
MISSING
BEEP
BEEP
BEEP
BEEP
BEEP
BEEP
BEE--
FUCK ME.

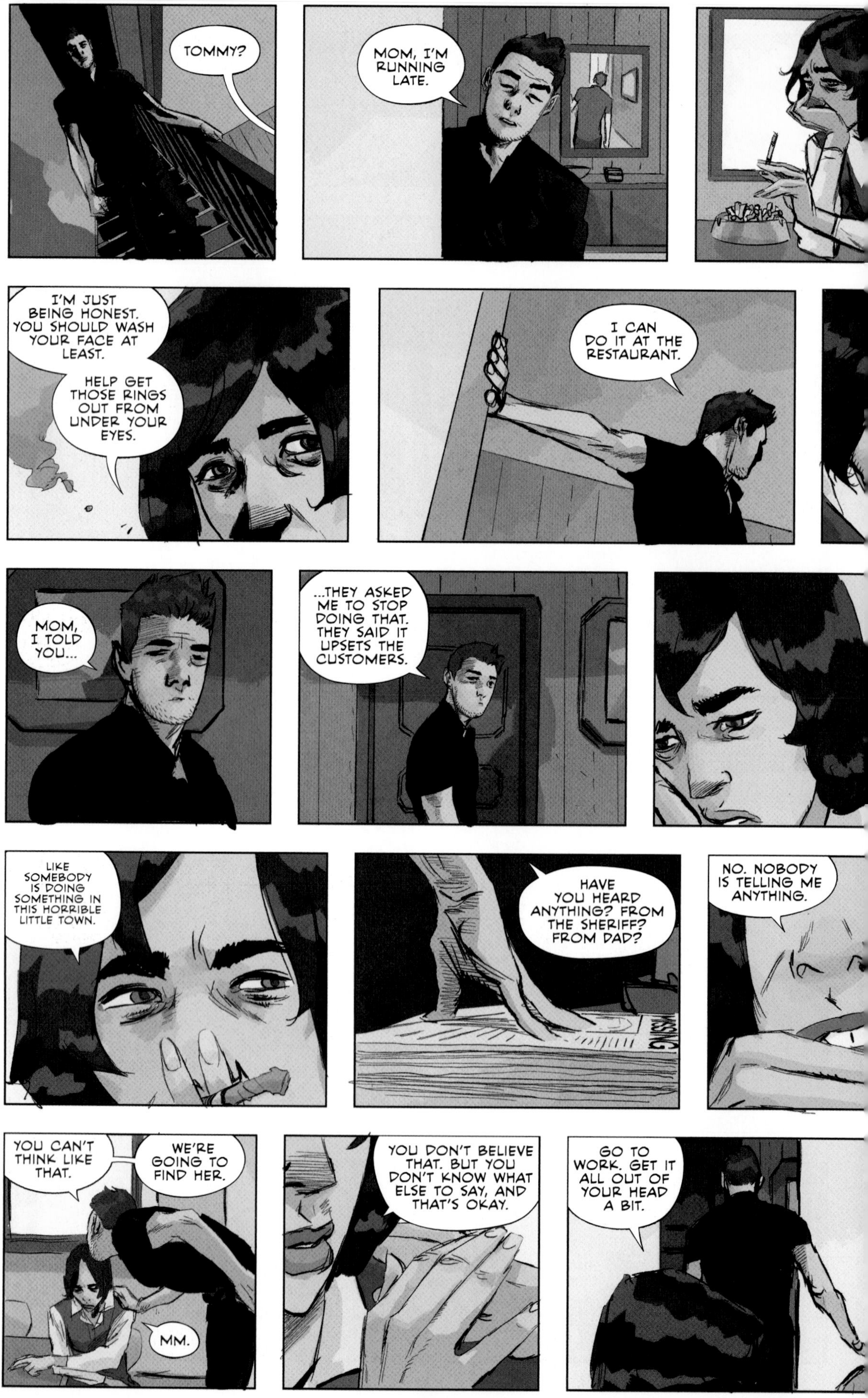
TOMMY?
MOM, I'M RUNNING LATE.
I'M JUST BEING HONEST. YOU SHOULD WASH YOUR FACE AT LEAST.
HELP GET THOSE RINGS OUT FROM UNDER YOUR EYES.
I CAN DO IT AT THE RESTAURANT.
MOM, I TOLD YOU...
...THEY ASKED ME TO STOP DOING THAT. THEY SAID IT UPSETS THE CUSTOMERS.
LIKE SOMEBODY IS DOING SOMETHING IN THIS HORRIBLE LITTLE TOWN.
HAVE YOU HEARD ANYTHING? FROM THE SHERIFF? FROM DAD?
NO. NOBODY IS TELLING ME ANYTHING.
YOU CAN'T THINK LIKE THAT.
WE'RE GOING TO FIND HER.
MM.
YOU DON'T BELIEVE THAT. BUT YOU DON'T KNOW WHAT ELSE TO SAY, AND THAT'S OKAY.
GO TO WORK. GET IT ALL OUT OF YOUR HEAD A BIT.

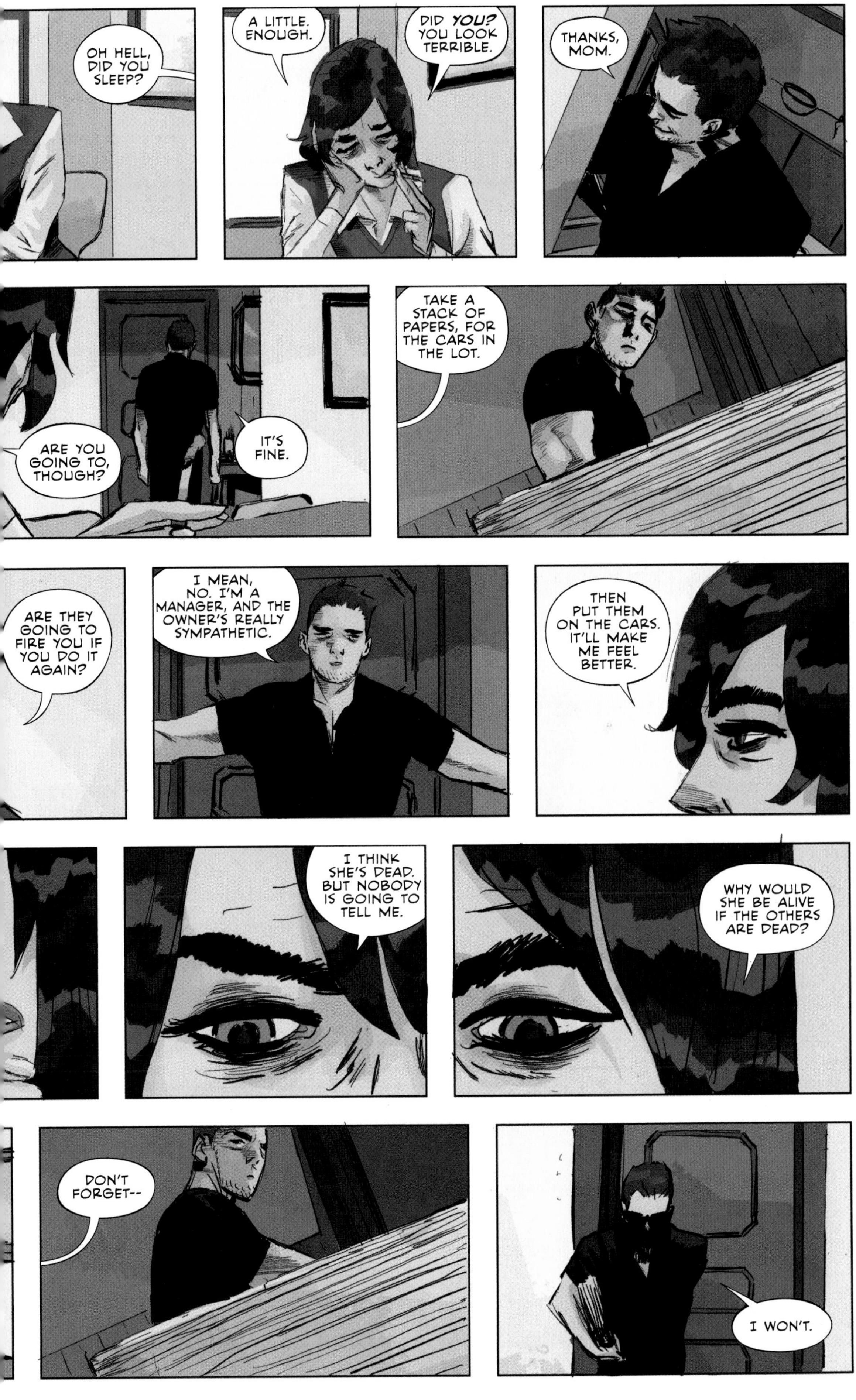
OH HELL, DID YOU SLEEP?
A LITTLE. ENOUGH.
DID YOU? YOU LOOK TERRIBLE.
THANKS, MOM.
ARE YOU GOING TO, THOUGH?
IT'S FINE.
TAKE A STACK OF PAPERS, FOR THE CARS IN THE LOT.
ARE THEY GOING TO FIRE YOU IF YOU DO IT AGAIN?
I MEAN, NO. I'M A MANAGER, AND THE OWNER'S REALLY SYMPATHETIC.
THEN PUT THEM ON THE CARS. IT'LL MAKE ME FEEL BETTER.
I THINK SHE'S DEAD. BUT NOBODY IS GOING TO TELL ME.
WHY WOULD SHE BE ALIVE IF THE OTHERS ARE DEAD?
DON'T FORGET--
I WON'T.

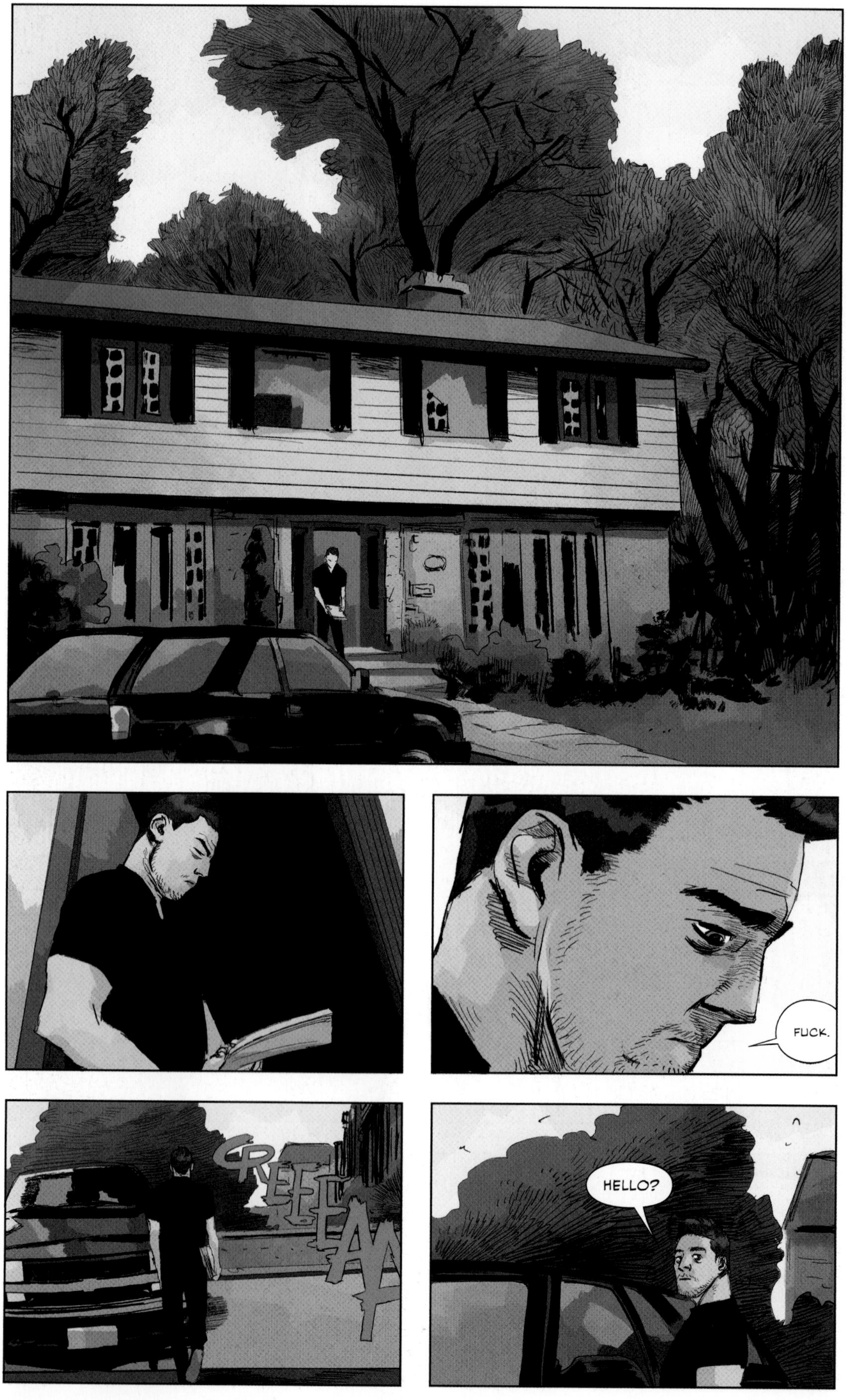
FUCK.
CREEEAA
HELLO?

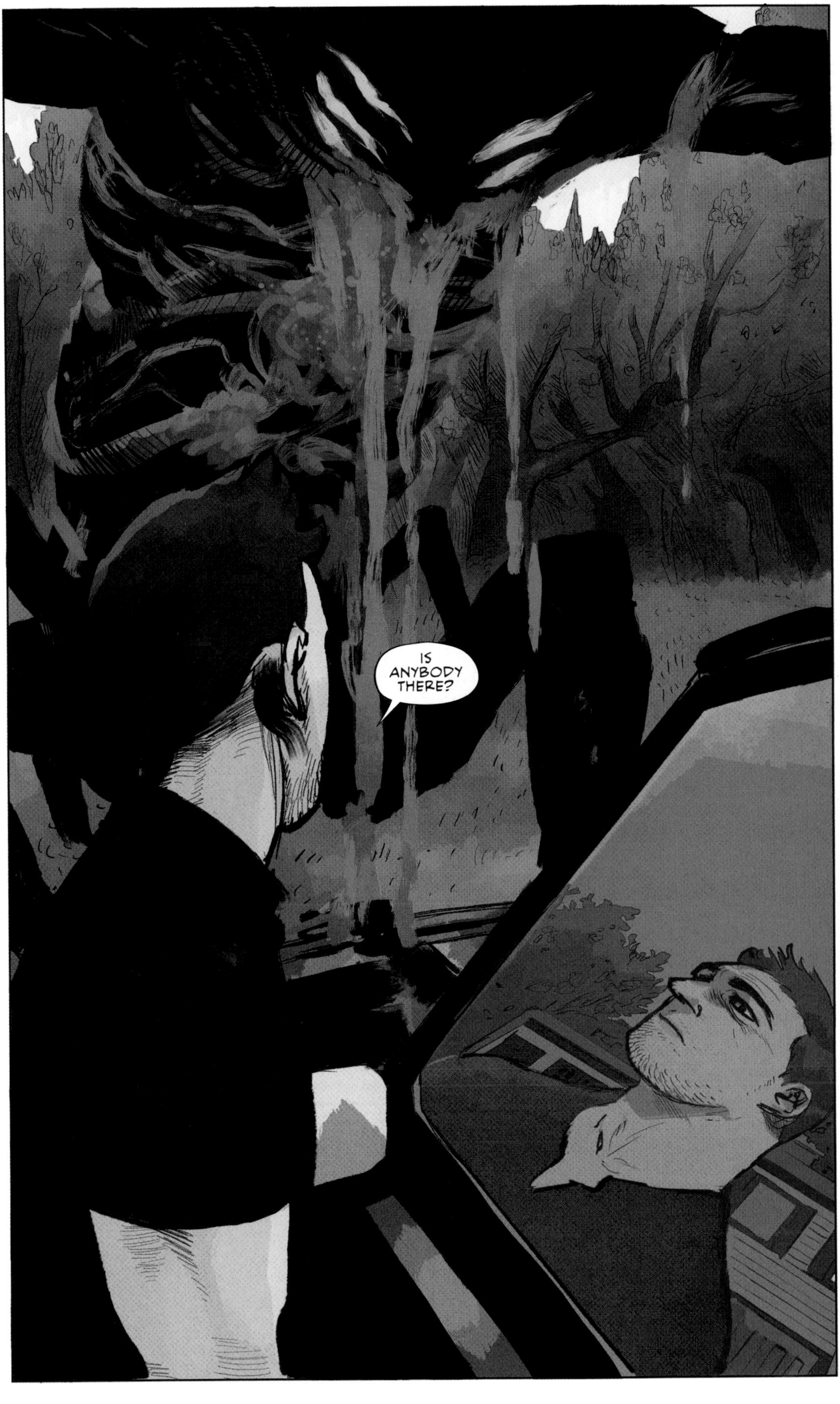
IS ANYBODY THERE?

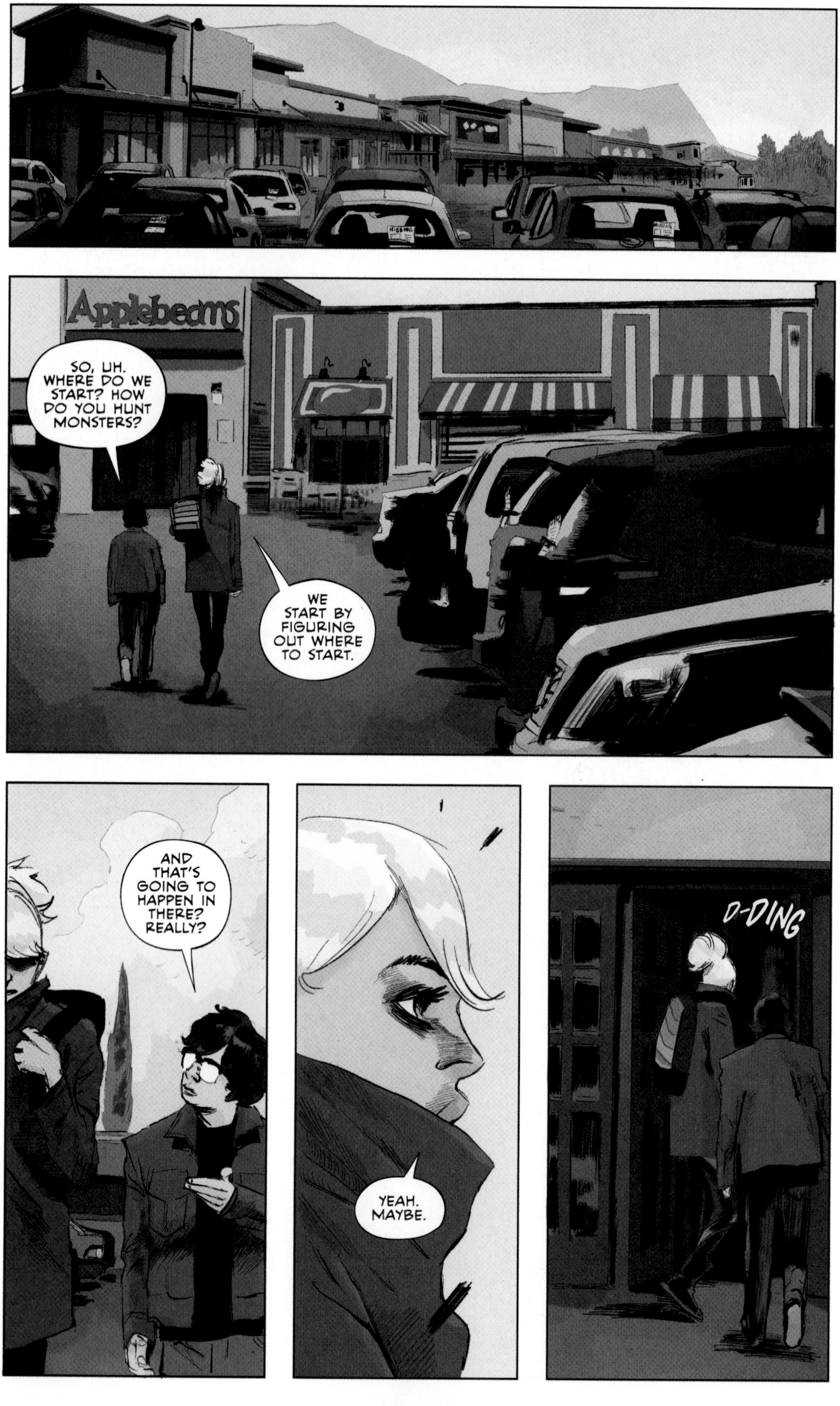
Applebeams
SO, UH. WHERE DO WE START? HOW DO YOU HUNT MONSTERS?
WE START BY FIGURING OUT WHERE TO START.
AND THAT'S GOING TO HAPPEN IN THERE? REALLY?
YEAH. MAYBE.
D-DING

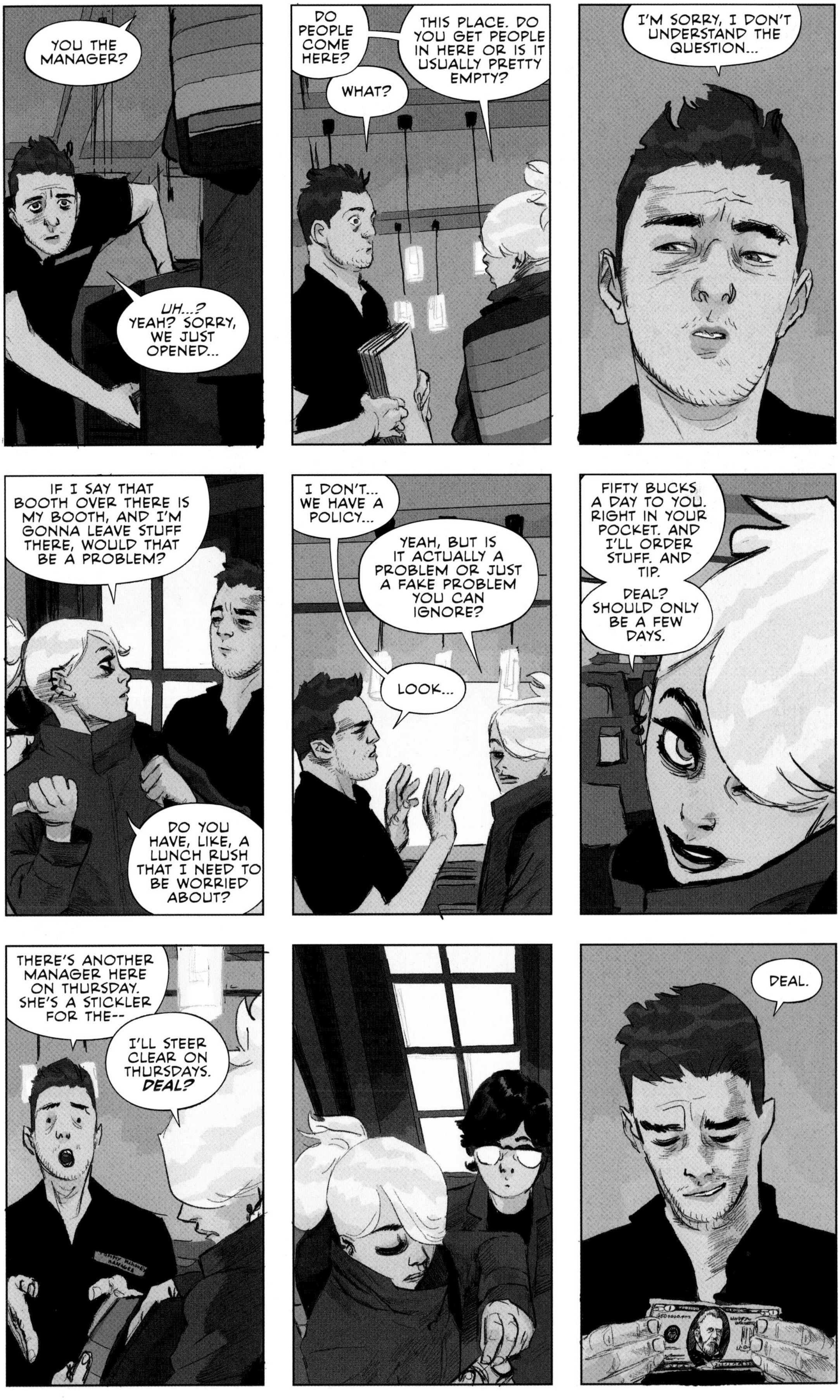
YOU THE MANAGER?
UH...? YEAH? SORRY, WE JUST OPENED...
DO PEOPLE COME HERE?
WHAT?
THIS PLACE. DO YOU GET PEOPLE IN HERE OR IS IT USUALLY PRETTY EMPTY?
I'M SORRY, I DON'T UNDERSTAND THE QUESTION...
IF I SAY THAT BOOTH OVER THERE IS MY BOOTH, AND I'M GONNA LEAVE STUFF THERE, WOULD THAT BE A PROBLEM?
DO YOU HAVE, LIKE, A LUNCH RUSH THAT I NEED TO BE WORRIED ABOUT?
I DON'T... WE HAVE A POLICY...
YEAH, BUT IS IT ACTUALLY A PROBLEM OR JUST A FAKE PROBLEM YOU CAN IGNORE?
LOOK...
FIFTY BUCKS A DAY TO YOU. RIGHT IN YOUR POCKET. AND I'LL ORDER STUFF. AND TIP.
DEAL? SHOULD ONLY BE A FEW DAYS.
THERE'S ANOTHER MANAGER HERE ON THURSDAY. SHE'S A STICKLER FOR THE--
I'LL STEER CLEAR ON THURSDAYS. ***DEAL?***
DEAL.

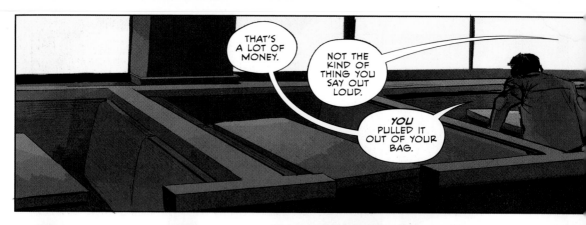

THAT'S A LOT OF MONEY.

NOT THE KIND OF THING YOU SAY OUT LOUD.

YOU PULLED IT OUT OF YOUR BAG.

YEAH, BUT YOU DON'T TALK ABOUT IT. YOU LET IT BE MYSTERIOUS.

YOU LIKE BEING MYSTERIOUS.

YEAH.

HE'S THE ONE... I KEEP WANTING TO FIND OUT THAT IT WAS A DREAM.

LIKE, I KNOW MY OTHER FRIENDS DIED, AND I MISS THEM, BUT I *KNOW* THEY'RE DEAD.

BUT KARL...

YOU REALLY LIKED HIM, HUH?

WERE YOU... MORE THAN FRIENDS?

HE DIDN'T THINK SO.

THAT'S OKAY.

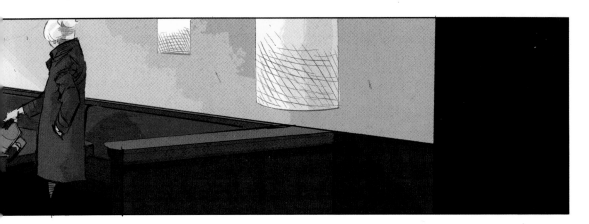

WHY THE OCTOPUS?

DON'T ASK ABOUT THE OCTOPUS.

WHAT *AM* I ALLOWED TO ASK ABOUT?

I DON'T KNOW. NOT A LOT.

THAT'S YOUR FRIEND, RIGHT?

YEAH. ONE OF THEM.

I'M SORRY.

WHERE'D YOU GET ALL OF THIS?

I PRINTED IT AT THE KINKO'S.

OH.

WHY ARE WE HERE? REALLY.

BECAUSE THESE KINDS OF PLACES ARE ALL GOING TO GO OUT OF BUSINESS IN A FEW YEARS, AND FOR THE MOST PART NOBODY GOES TO THEM ANYMORE.

AND THEY'VE GOT BIG TABLES.

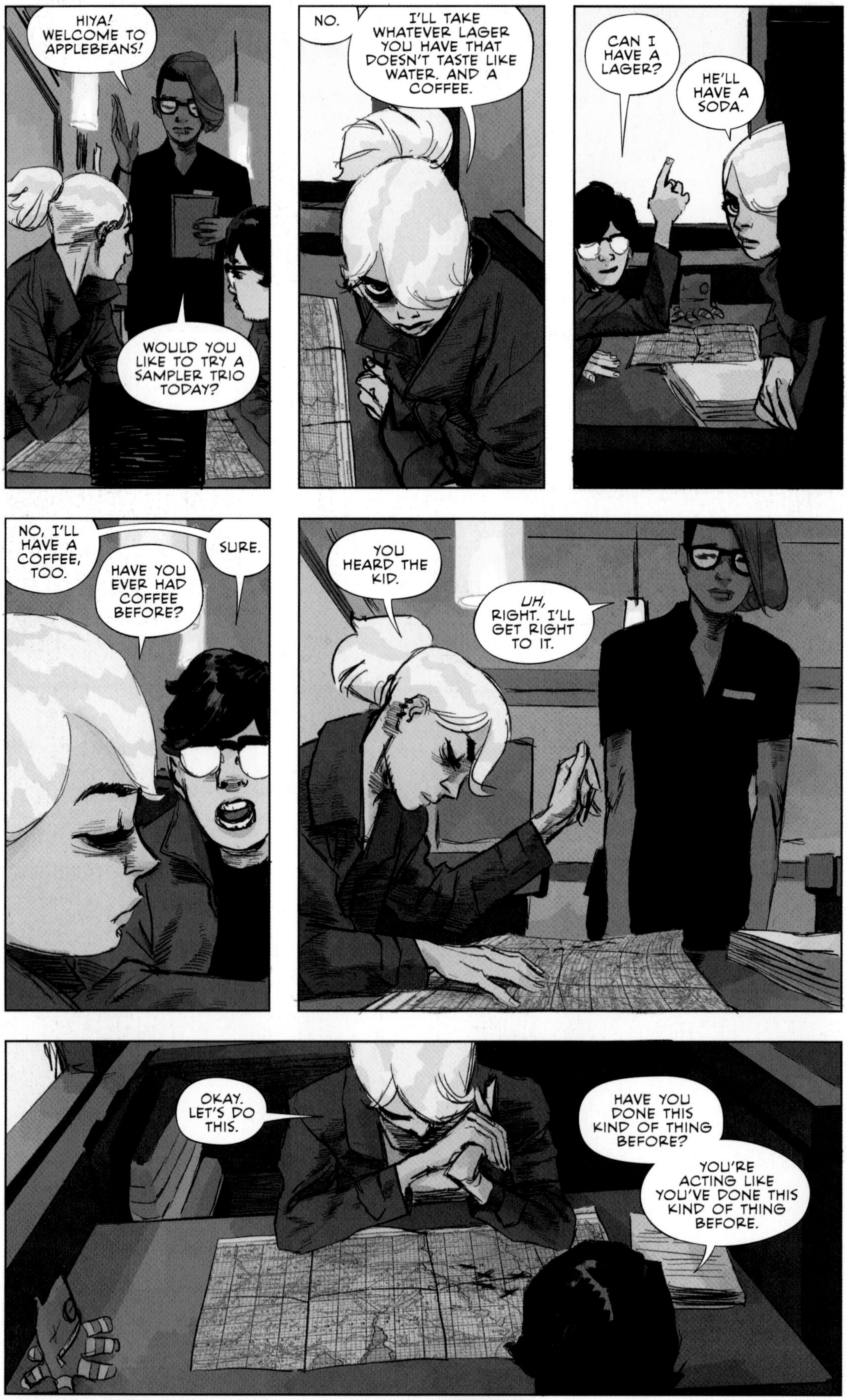
HIYA! WELCOME TO APPLEBEANS!
WOULD YOU LIKE TO TRY A SAMPLER TRIO TODAY?
NO.
I'LL TAKE WHATEVER LAGER YOU HAVE THAT DOESN'T TASTE LIKE WATER. AND A COFFEE.
CAN I HAVE A LAGER?
HE'LL HAVE A SODA.
NO, I'LL HAVE A COFFEE, TOO.
SURE.
HAVE YOU EVER HAD COFFEE BEFORE?
YOU HEARD THE KID.
UH, RIGHT. I'LL GET RIGHT TO IT.
OKAY. LET'S DO THIS.
HAVE YOU DONE THIS KIND OF THING BEFORE?
YOU'RE ACTING LIKE YOU'VE DONE THIS KIND OF THING BEFORE.

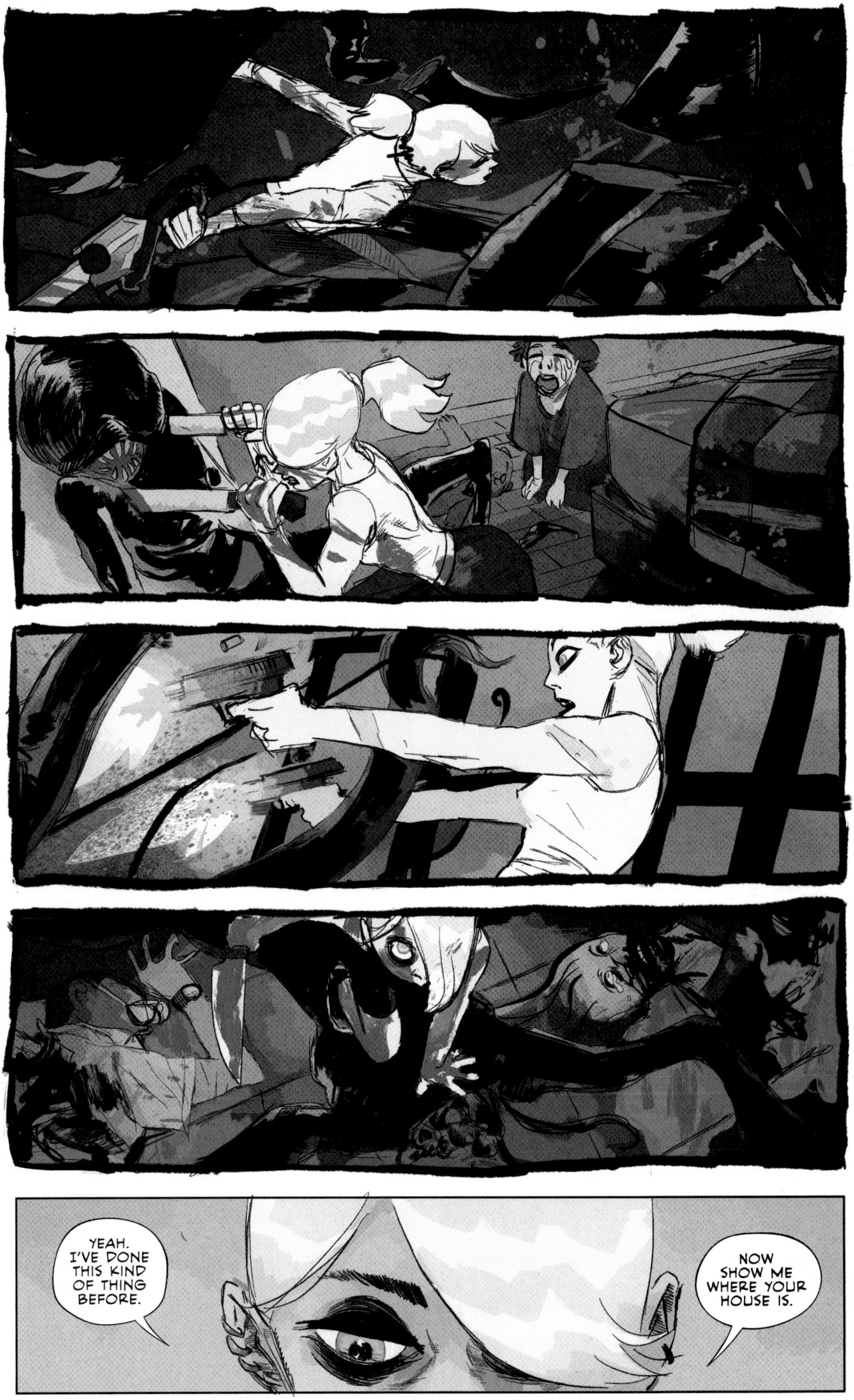
YEAH. I'VE DONE THIS KIND OF THING BEFORE.
NOW SHOW ME WHERE YOUR HOUSE IS.

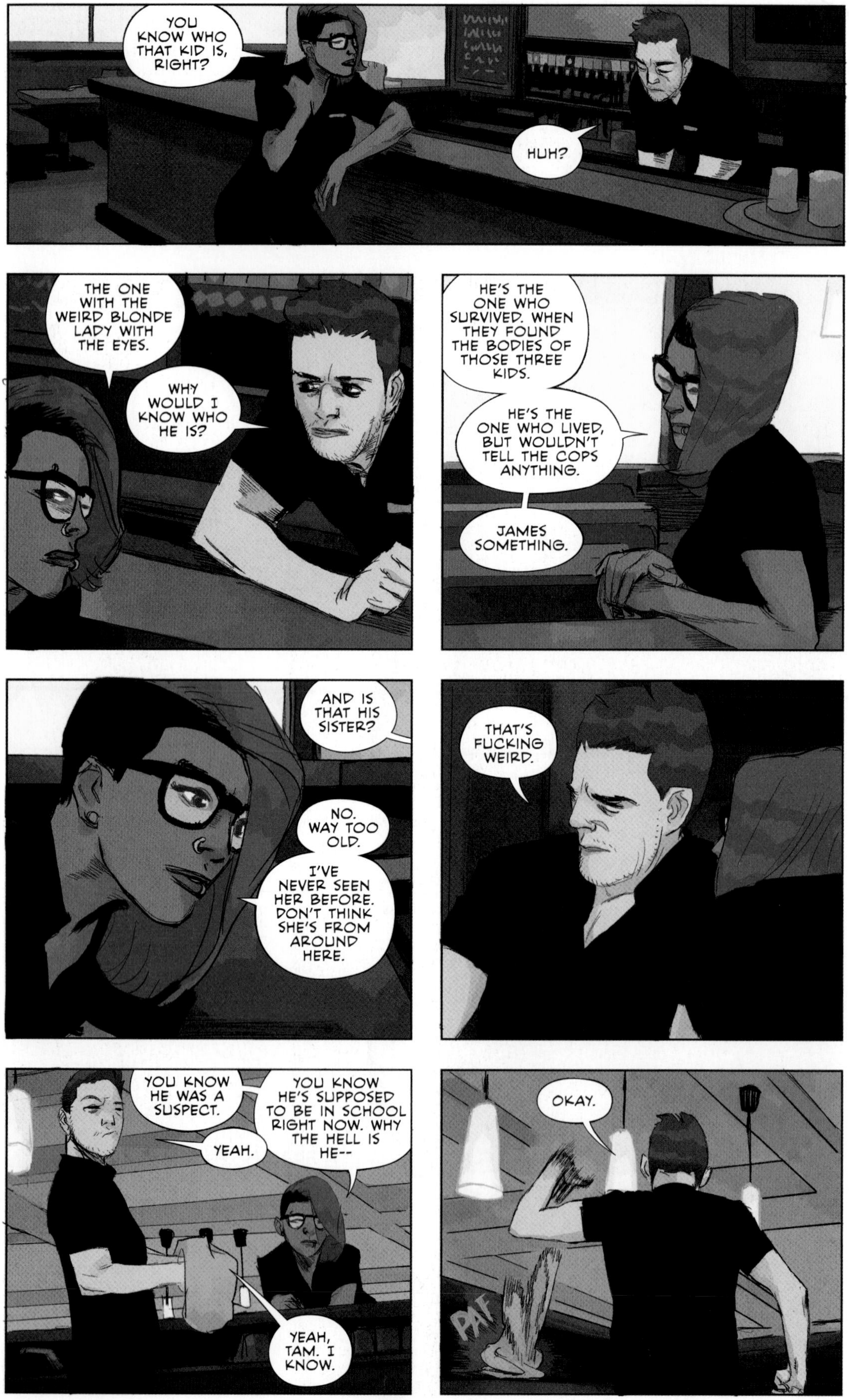
YOU KNOW WHO THAT KID IS, RIGHT?
HUH?
THE ONE WITH THE WEIRD BLONDE LADY WITH THE EYES.
WHY WOULD I KNOW WHO HE IS?
HE'S THE ONE WHO SURVIVED. WHEN THEY FOUND THE BODIES OF THOSE THREE KIDS.
HE'S THE ONE WHO LIVED, BUT WOULDN'T TELL THE COPS ANYTHING.
JAMES SOMETHING.
AND IS THAT HIS SISTER?
NO. WAY TOO OLD.
I'VE NEVER SEEN HER BEFORE. DON'T THINK SHE'S FROM AROUND HERE.
THAT'S FUCKING WEIRD.
YOU KNOW HE WAS A SUSPECT.
YEAH.
YOU KNOW HE'S SUPPOSED TO BE IN SCHOOL RIGHT NOW. WHY THE HELL IS HE--
YEAH, TAM. I KNOW.
OKAY.
PAF

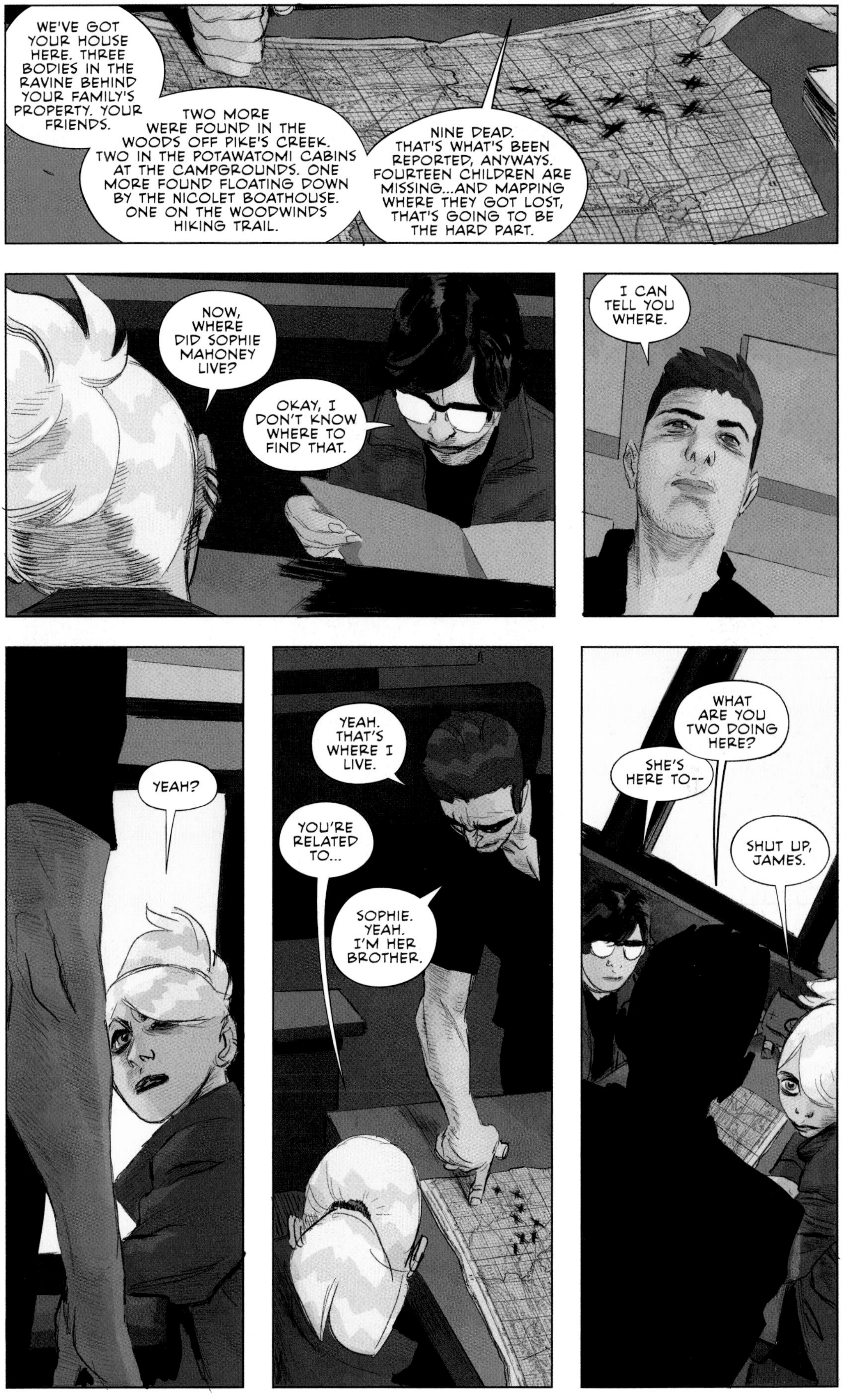
WE'VE GOT YOUR HOUSE HERE. THREE BODIES IN THE RAVINE BEHIND YOUR FAMILY'S PROPERTY. YOUR FRIENDS.
TWO MORE WERE FOUND IN THE WOODS OFF PIKE'S CREEK. TWO IN THE POTAWATOMI CABINS AT THE CAMPGROUNDS. ONE MORE FOUND FLOATING DOWN BY THE NICOLET BOATHOUSE. ONE ON THE WOODWINDS HIKING TRAIL.
NINE DEAD. THAT'S WHAT'S BEEN REPORTED, ANYWAYS. FOURTEEN CHILDREN ARE MISSING...AND MAPPING WHERE THEY GOT LOST, THAT'S GOING TO BE THE HARD PART.
NOW, WHERE DID SOPHIE MAHONEY LIVE?
OKAY, I DON'T KNOW WHERE TO FIND THAT.
I CAN TELL YOU WHERE.
YEAH?
YEAH. THAT'S WHERE I LIVE.
YOU'RE RELATED TO...
SOPHIE. YEAH. I'M HER BROTHER.
WHAT ARE YOU TWO DOING HERE?
SHE'S HERE TO--
SHUT UP, JAMES.

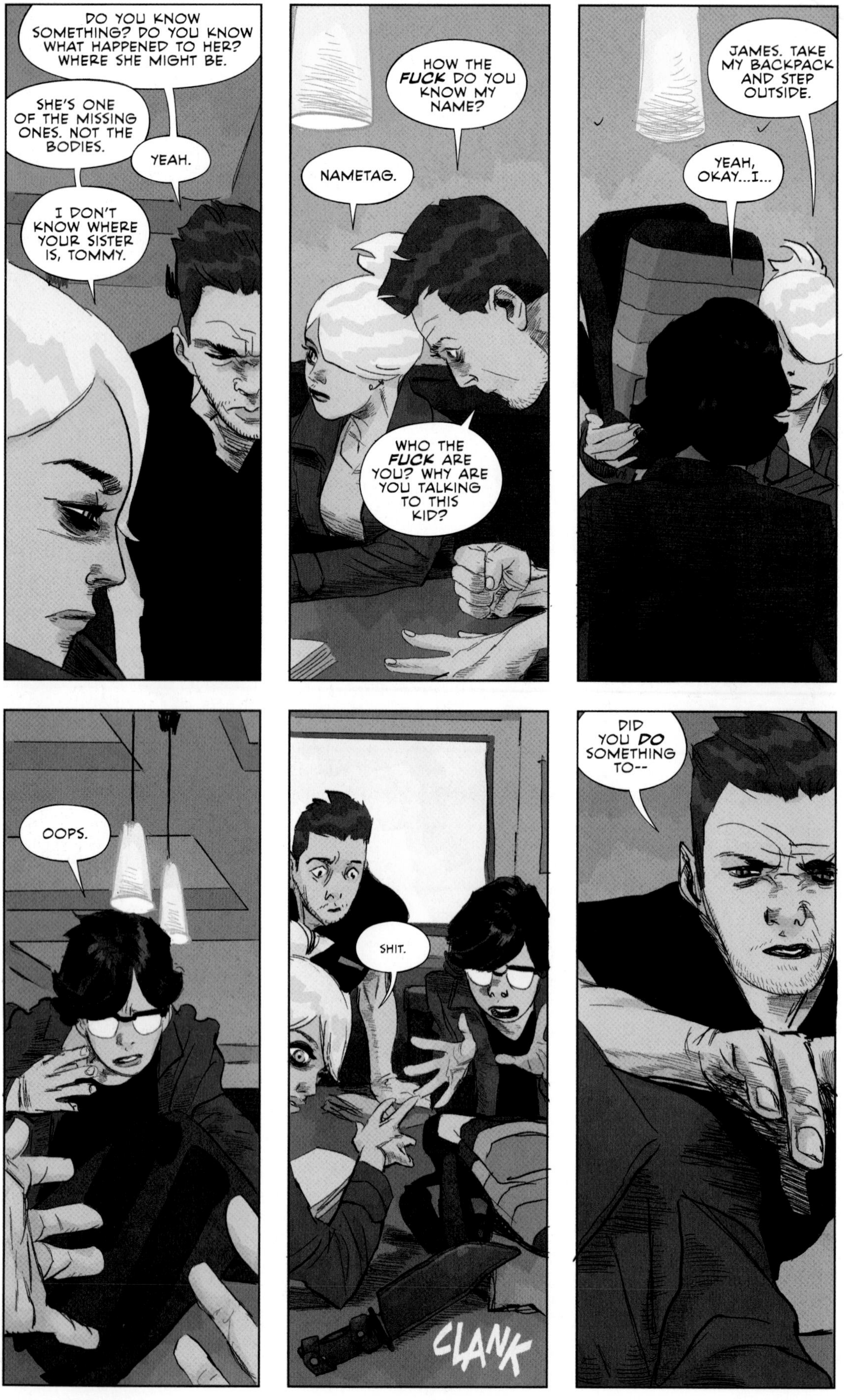

DO YOU KNOW SOMETHING? DO YOU KNOW WHAT HAPPENED TO HER? WHERE SHE MIGHT BE.
SHE'S ONE OF THE MISSING ONES. NOT THE BODIES.
YEAH.
I DON'T KNOW WHERE YOUR SISTER IS, TOMMY.
HOW THE FUCK DO YOU KNOW MY NAME?
NAMETAG.
WHO THE FUCK ARE YOU? WHY ARE YOU TALKING TO THIS KID?
JAMES. TAKE MY BACKPACK AND STEP OUTSIDE.
YEAH, OKAY...I...
OOPS.
SHIT.
CLANK
DID YOU DO SOMETHING TO--

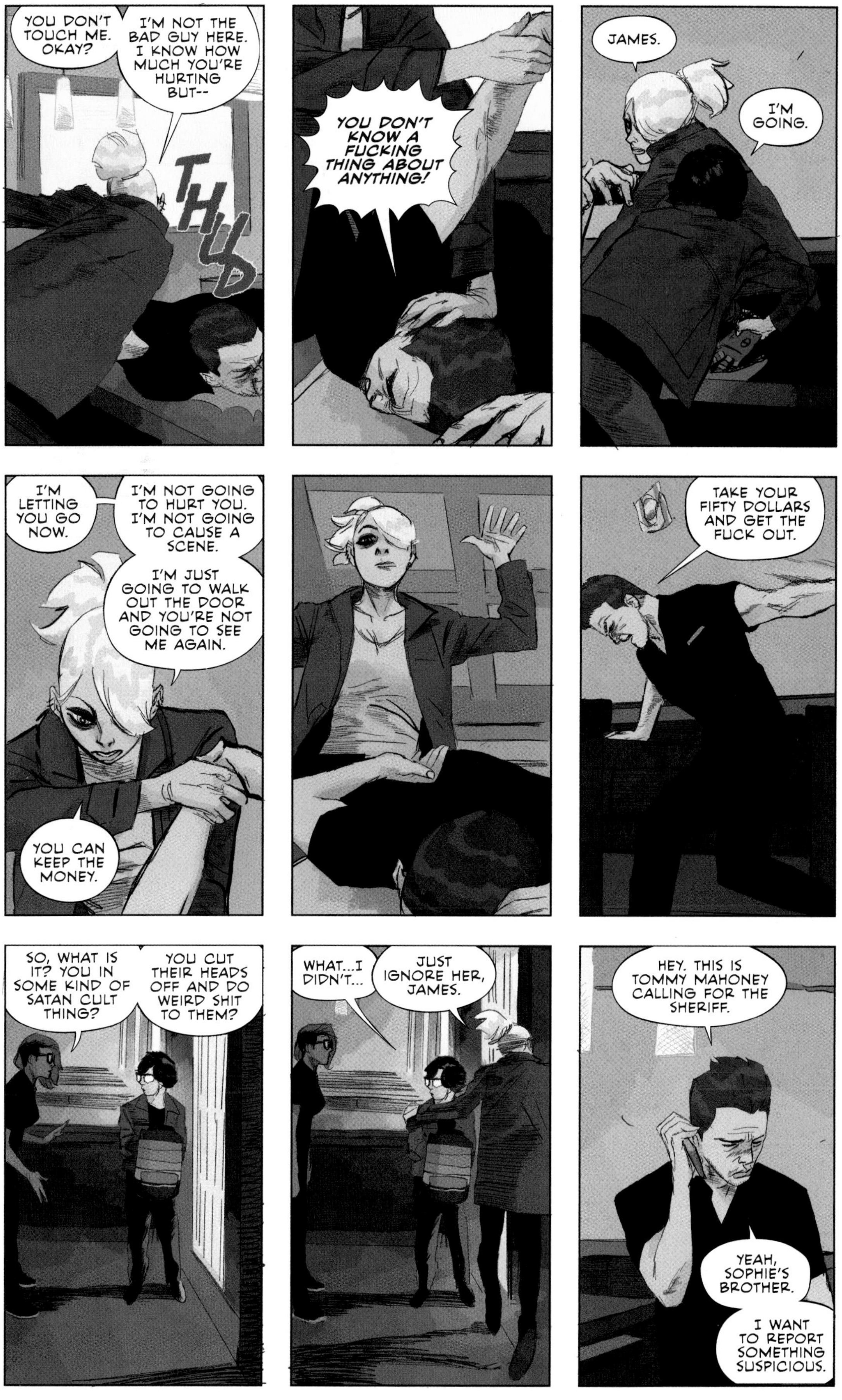
YOU DON'T TOUCH ME. OKAY?
I'M NOT THE BAD GUY HERE. I KNOW HOW MUCH YOU'RE HURTING BUT--
THUD
YOU DON'T KNOW A FUCKING THING ABOUT ANYTHING!
JAMES.
I'M GOING.
I'M LETTING YOU GO NOW.
I'M NOT GOING TO HURT YOU. I'M NOT GOING TO CAUSE A SCENE.
I'M JUST GOING TO WALK OUT THE DOOR AND YOU'RE NOT GOING TO SEE ME AGAIN.
YOU CAN KEEP THE MONEY.
TAKE YOUR FIFTY DOLLARS AND GET THE FUCK OUT.
SO, WHAT IS IT? YOU IN SOME KIND OF SATAN CULT THING?
YOU CUT THEIR HEADS OFF AND DO WEIRD SHIT TO THEM?
WHAT...I DIDN'T...
JUST IGNORE HER, JAMES.
HEY. THIS IS TOMMY MAHONEY CALLING FOR THE SHERIFF.
YEAH, SOPHIE'S BROTHER.
I WANT TO REPORT SOMETHING SUSPICIOUS.

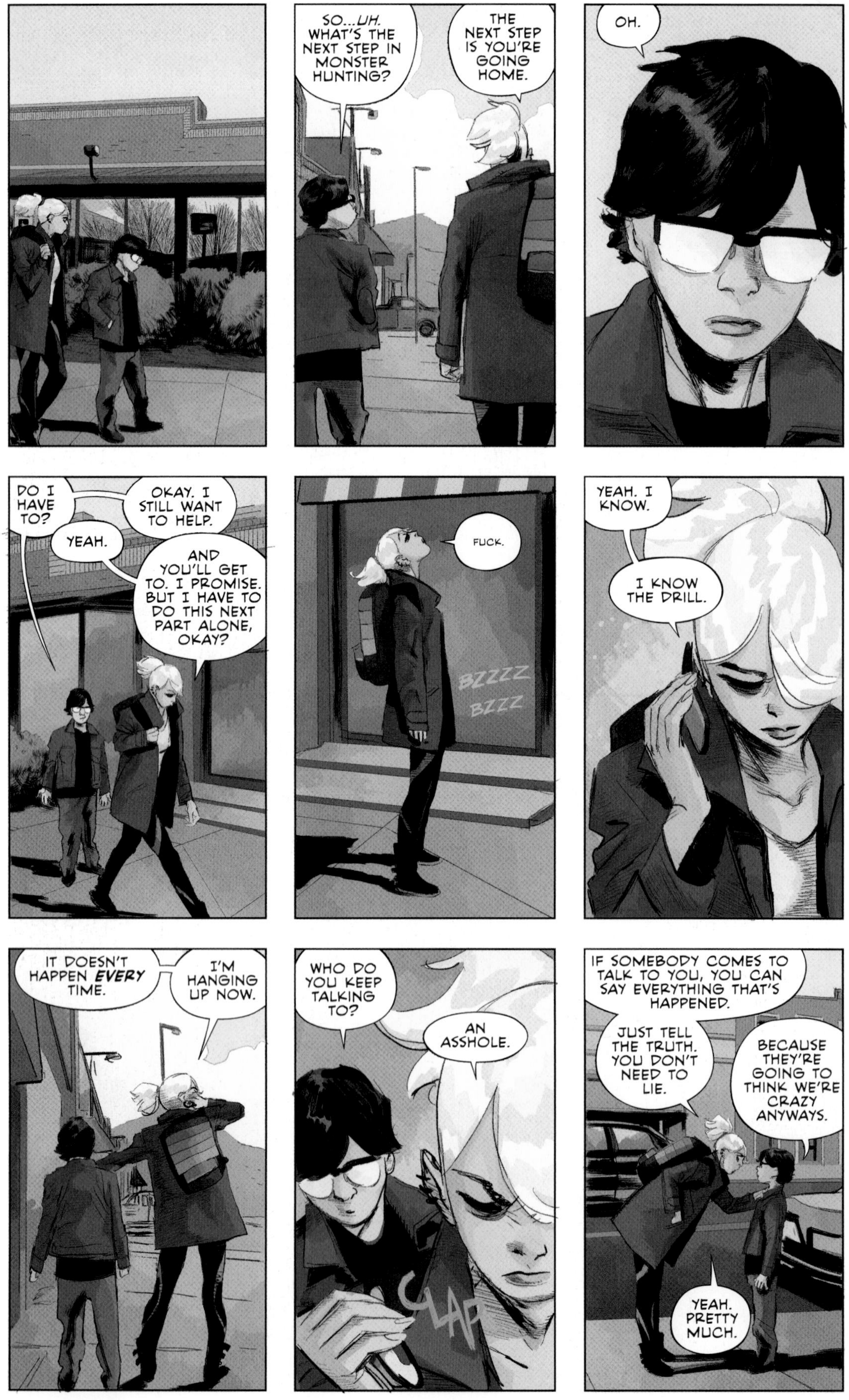
SO...UH. WHAT'S THE NEXT STEP IN MONSTER HUNTING?
THE NEXT STEP IS YOU'RE GOING HOME.
OH.
DO I HAVE TO?
YEAH.
OKAY. I STILL WANT TO HELP.
AND YOU'LL GET TO. I PROMISE. BUT I HAVE TO DO THIS NEXT PART ALONE, OKAY?
FUCK.
BZZZZ BZZZ
YEAH. I KNOW.
I KNOW THE DRILL.
IT DOESN'T HAPPEN EVERY TIME.
I'M HANGING UP NOW.
WHO DO YOU KEEP TALKING TO?
AN ASSHOLE.
CLAP
IF SOMEBODY COMES TO TALK TO YOU, YOU CAN SAY EVERYTHING THAT'S HAPPENED.
JUST TELL THE TRUTH. YOU DON'T NEED TO LIE.
BECAUSE THEY'RE GOING TO THINK WE'RE CRAZY ANYWAYS.
YEAH. PRETTY MUCH.

YOU HAD A CALL.

YEAH?

YEAH.

TOO BAD THEY MISSED ME.

HEY, I DON'T WANT TROUBLE.

ME NEITHER.

YOU SAW THE MAP. IT'S A CLASS E7. THERE ARE STILL KIDS MISSING, SO IT'S STASHING ITS FOOD SOMEWHERE. THERE ARE PROBABLY CAVES OFF THE LAKE.

I NEED TO KNOW WHAT KIND OF THING IT'S GOING TO BE BEFORE I GO LOOKING FOR IT. AND IT'S PROBABLY GOING TO BE A FEW DAYS BEFORE I CAN DO THAT.

SO I NEED YOU THINKING ON IT IN THE MEANWHILE, DO YOU UNDERSTAND?

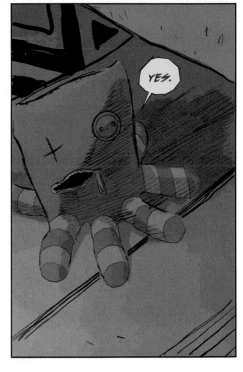

YES.

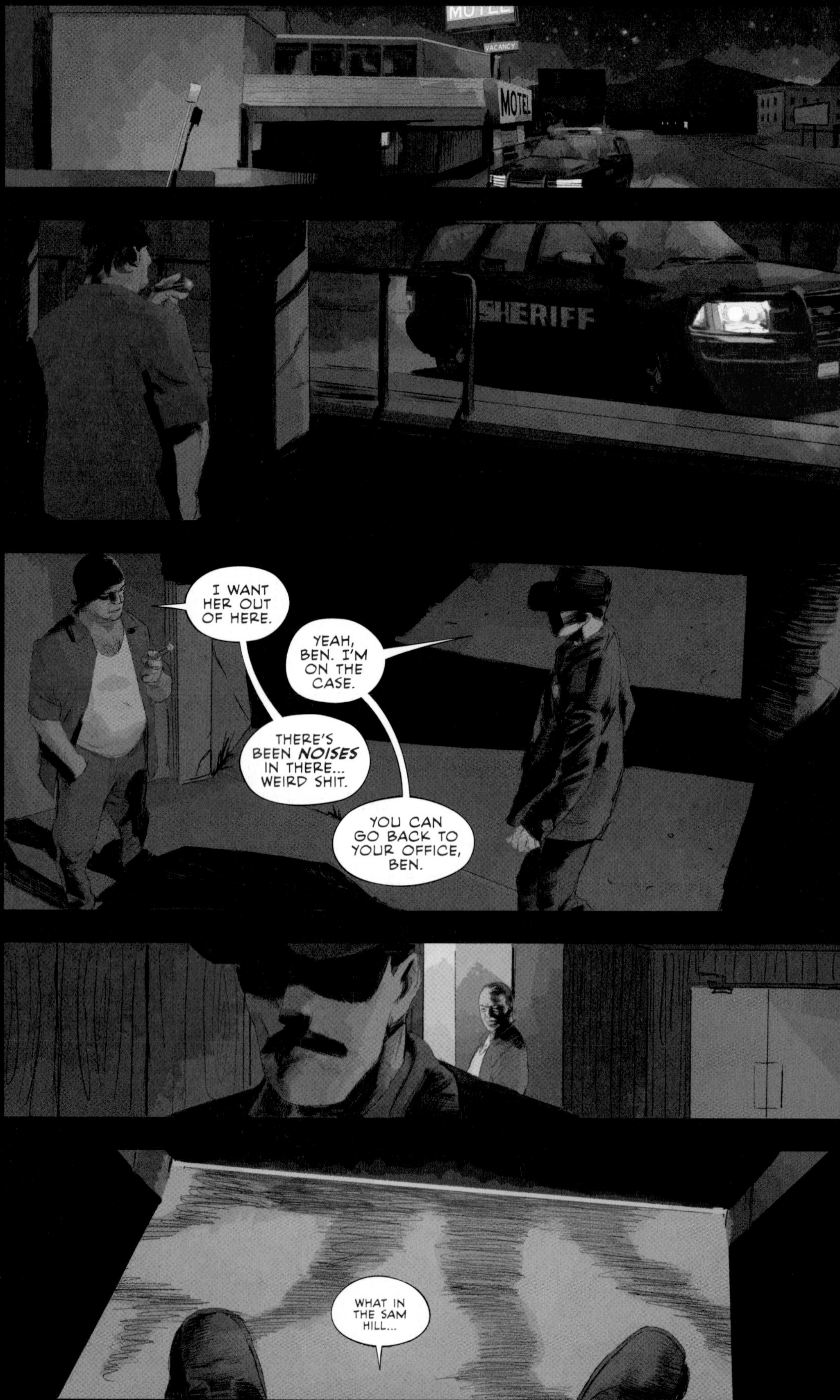
MOTEL
VACANCY
MOTEL
SHERIFF
I WANT HER OUT OF HERE.
YEAH, BEN. I'M ON THE CASE.
THERE'S BEEN *NOISES* IN THERE... WEIRD SHIT.
YOU CAN GO BACK TO YOUR OFFICE, BEN.
WHAT IN THE SAM HILL...

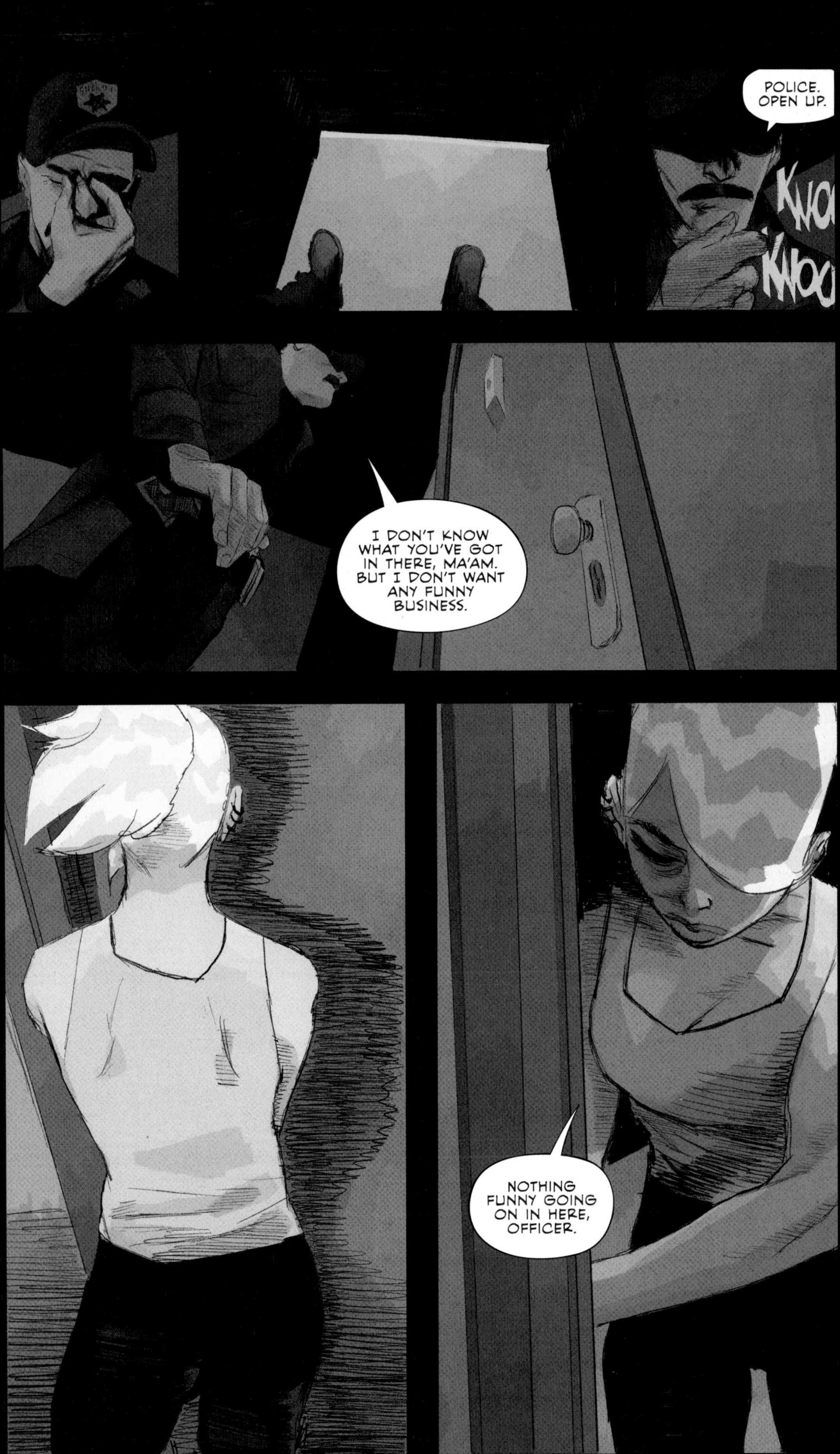
POLICE. OPEN UP.
KNOCK KNOCK
I DON'T KNOW WHAT YOU'VE GOT IN THERE, MA'AM. BUT I DON'T WANT ANY FUNNY BUSINESS.
NOTHING FUNNY GOING ON IN HERE, OFFICER.

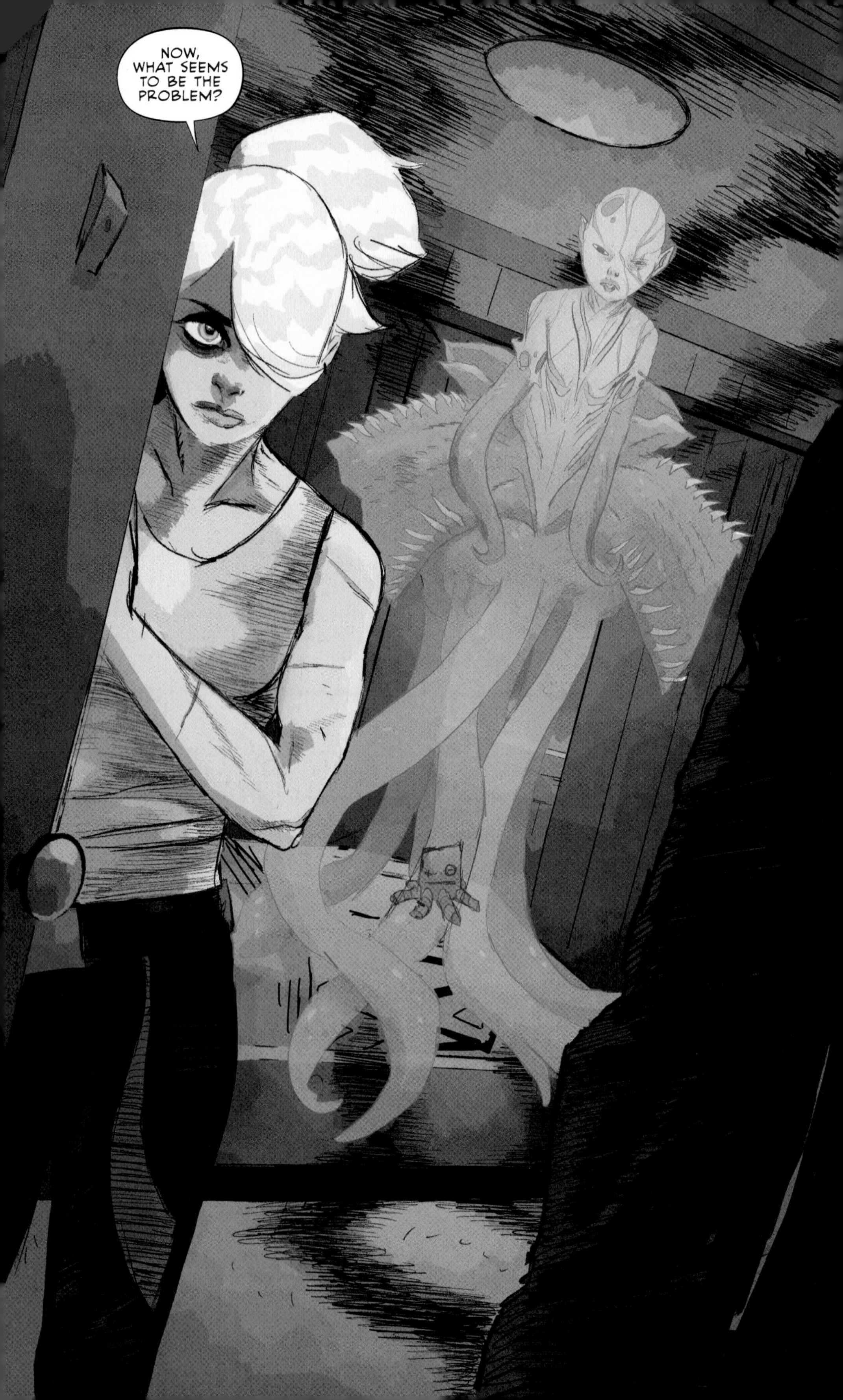
NOW, WHAT SEEMS TO BE THE PROBLEM?

CHAPTER
THREE

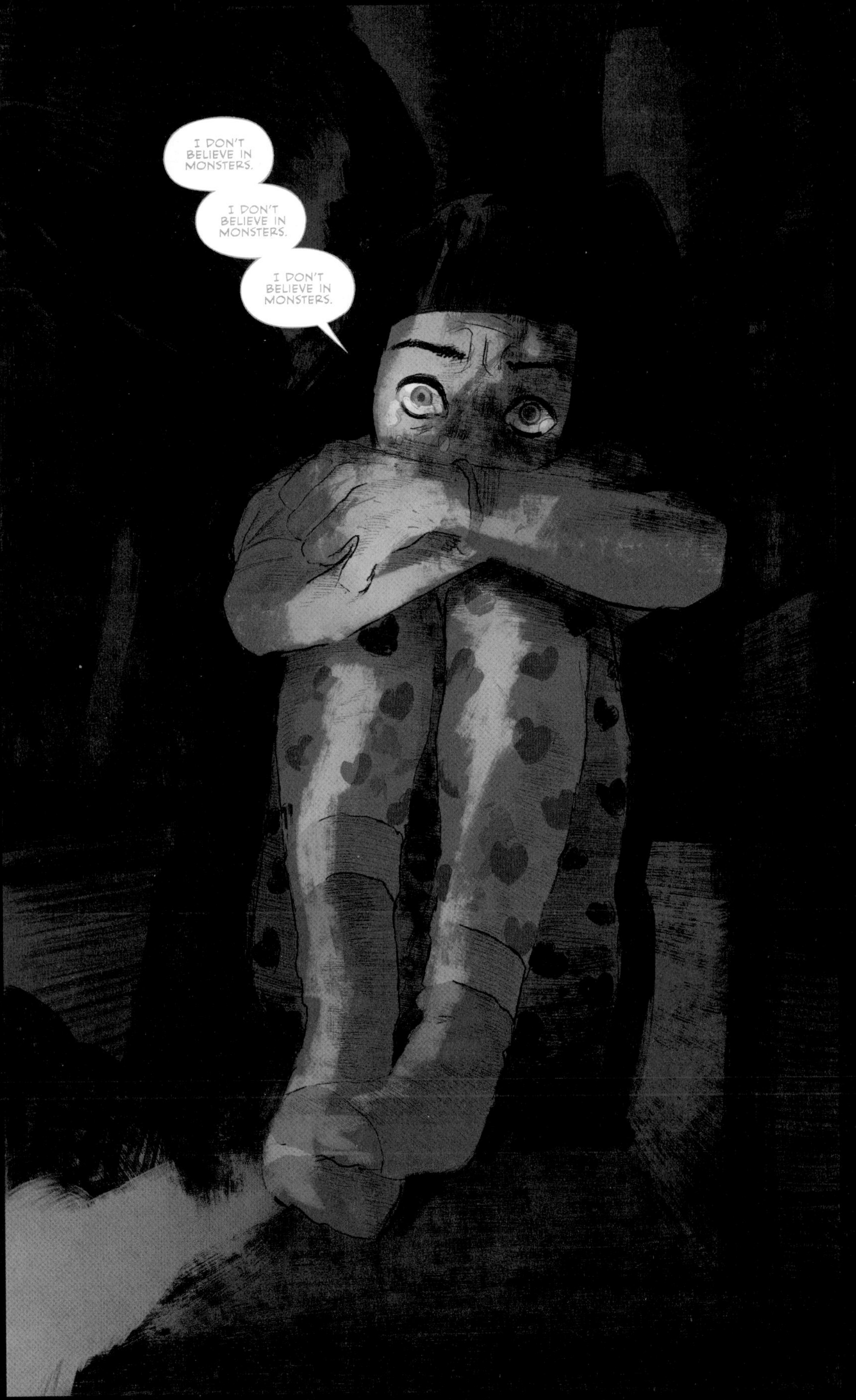
I DON'T BELIEVE IN MONSTERS.
I DON'T BELIEVE IN MONSTERS.
I DON'T BELIEVE IN MONSTERS.

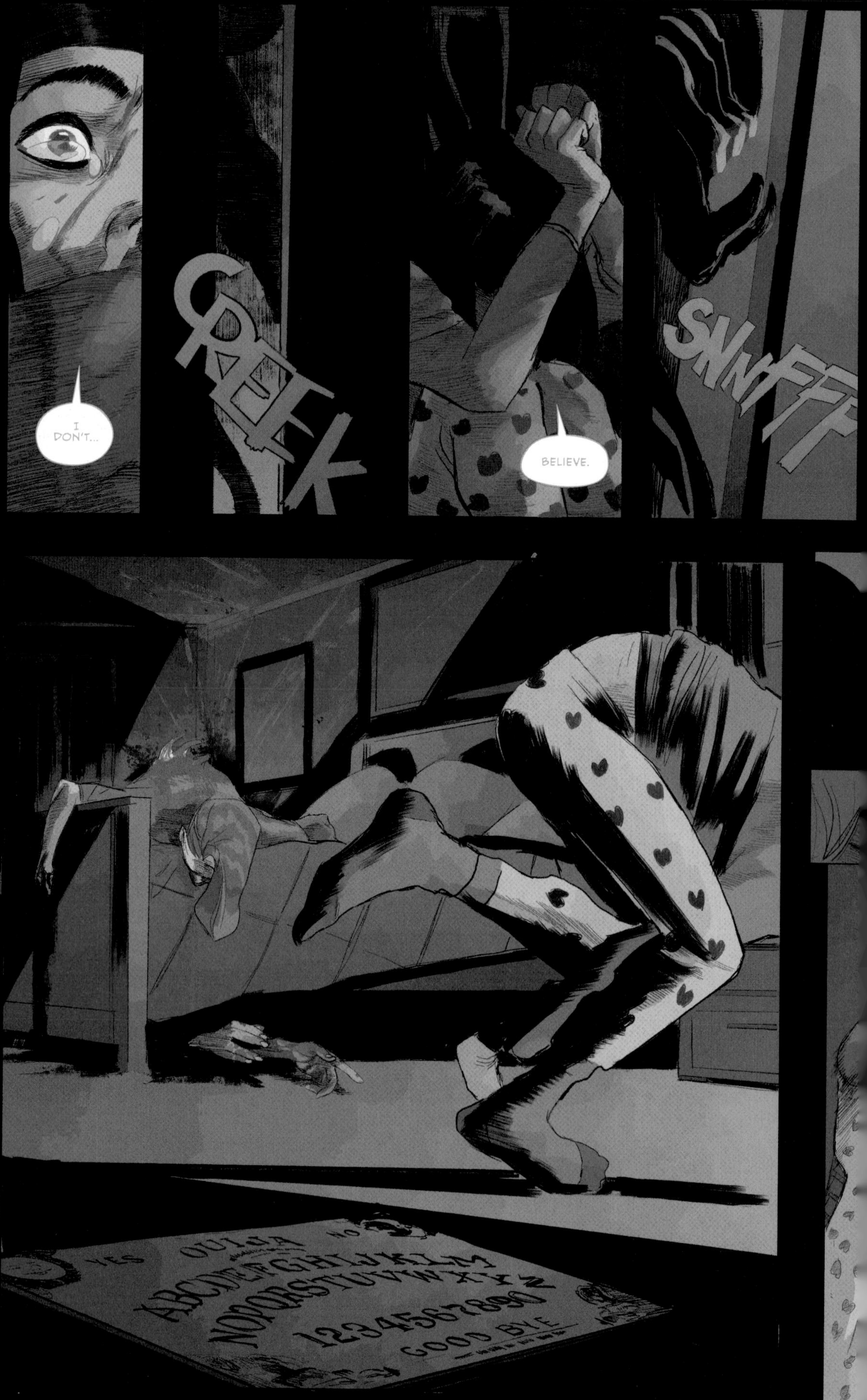
I DON'T...
CREEK
BELIEVE.
SNNFFF
YES
NO
OUIJA
ABCDEFGHIJKLM
NOPQRSTUVWXYZ
1234567890
GOOD BYE

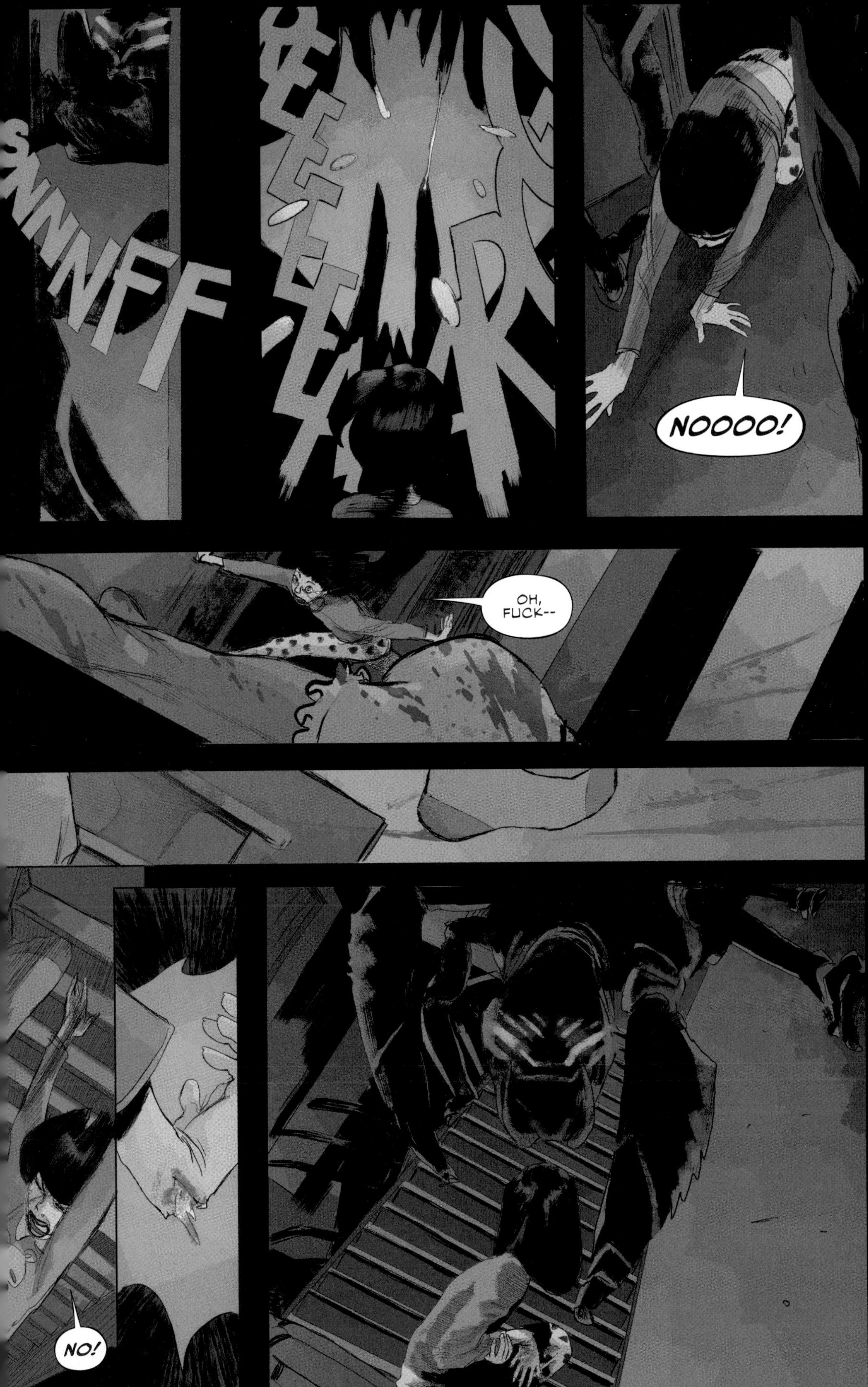
SNNNFF
NOOOO!
OH, FUCK--
NO!

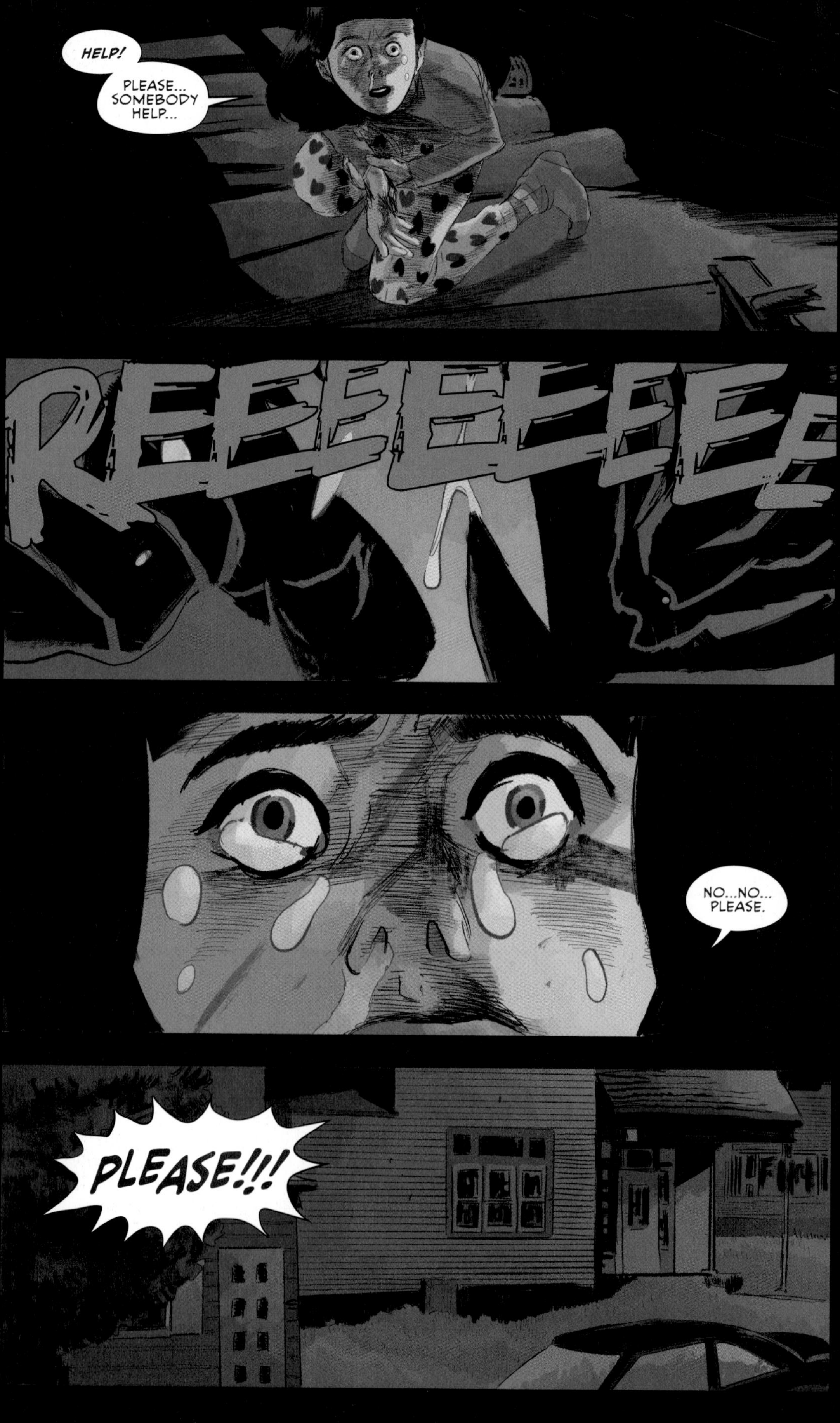
HELP!
PLEASE... SOMEBODY HELP...
REEEEEEEEEE
NO...NO... PLEASE.
PLEASE!!!

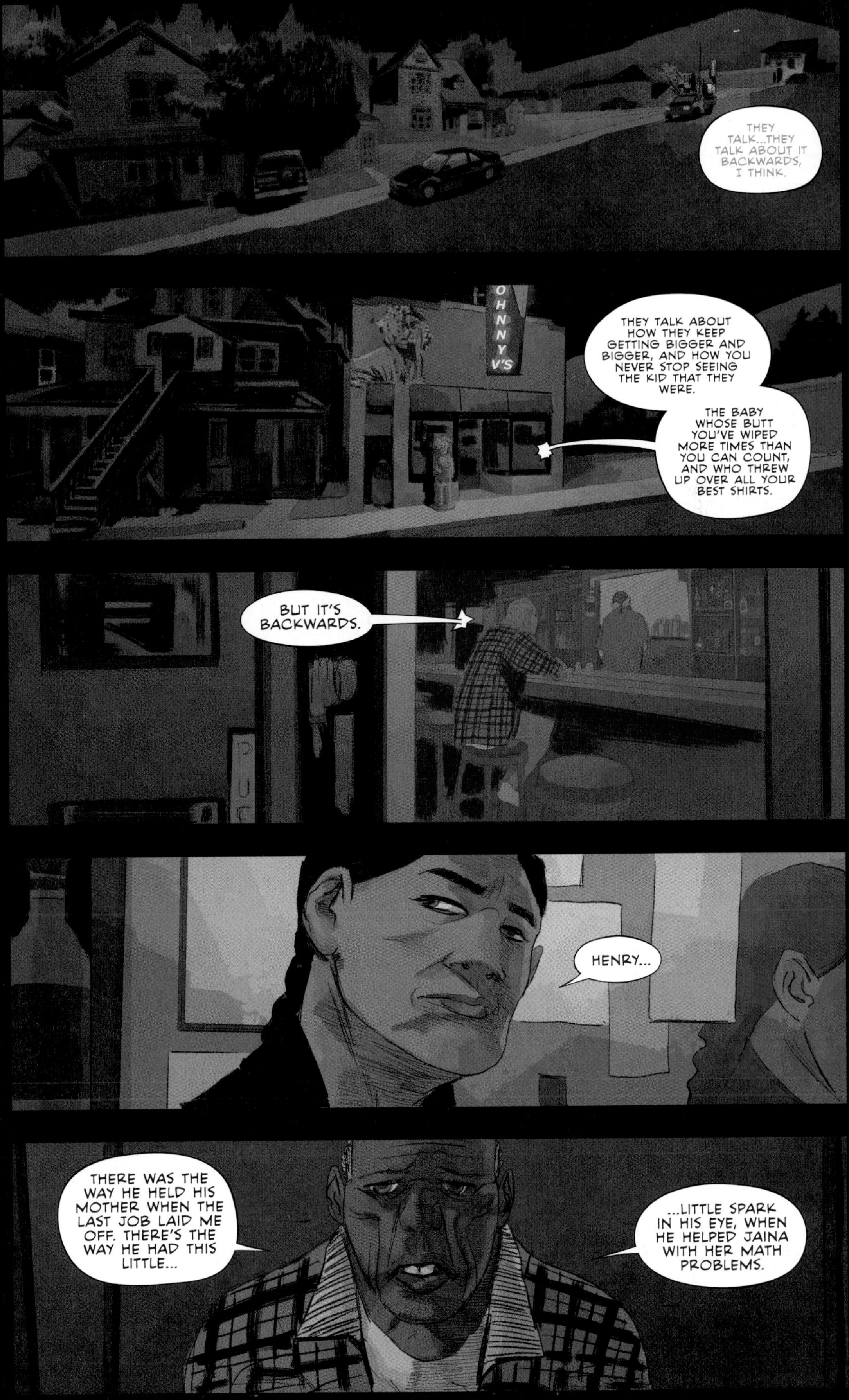
THEY TALK...THEY TALK ABOUT IT BACKWARDS, I THINK.
JOHNNY V'S
THEY TALK ABOUT HOW THEY KEEP GETTING BIGGER AND BIGGER, AND HOW YOU NEVER STOP SEEING THE KID THAT THEY WERE.
THE BABY WHOSE BUTT YOU'VE WIPED MORE TIMES THAN YOU CAN COUNT, AND WHO THREW UP OVER ALL YOUR BEST SHIRTS.
BUT IT'S BACKWARDS.
HENRY...
THERE WAS THE WAY HE HELD HIS MOTHER WHEN THE LAST JOB LAID ME OFF. THERE'S THE WAY HE HAD THIS LITTLE...
...LITTLE SPARK IN HIS EYE, WHEN HE HELPED JAINA WITH HER MATH PROBLEMS.

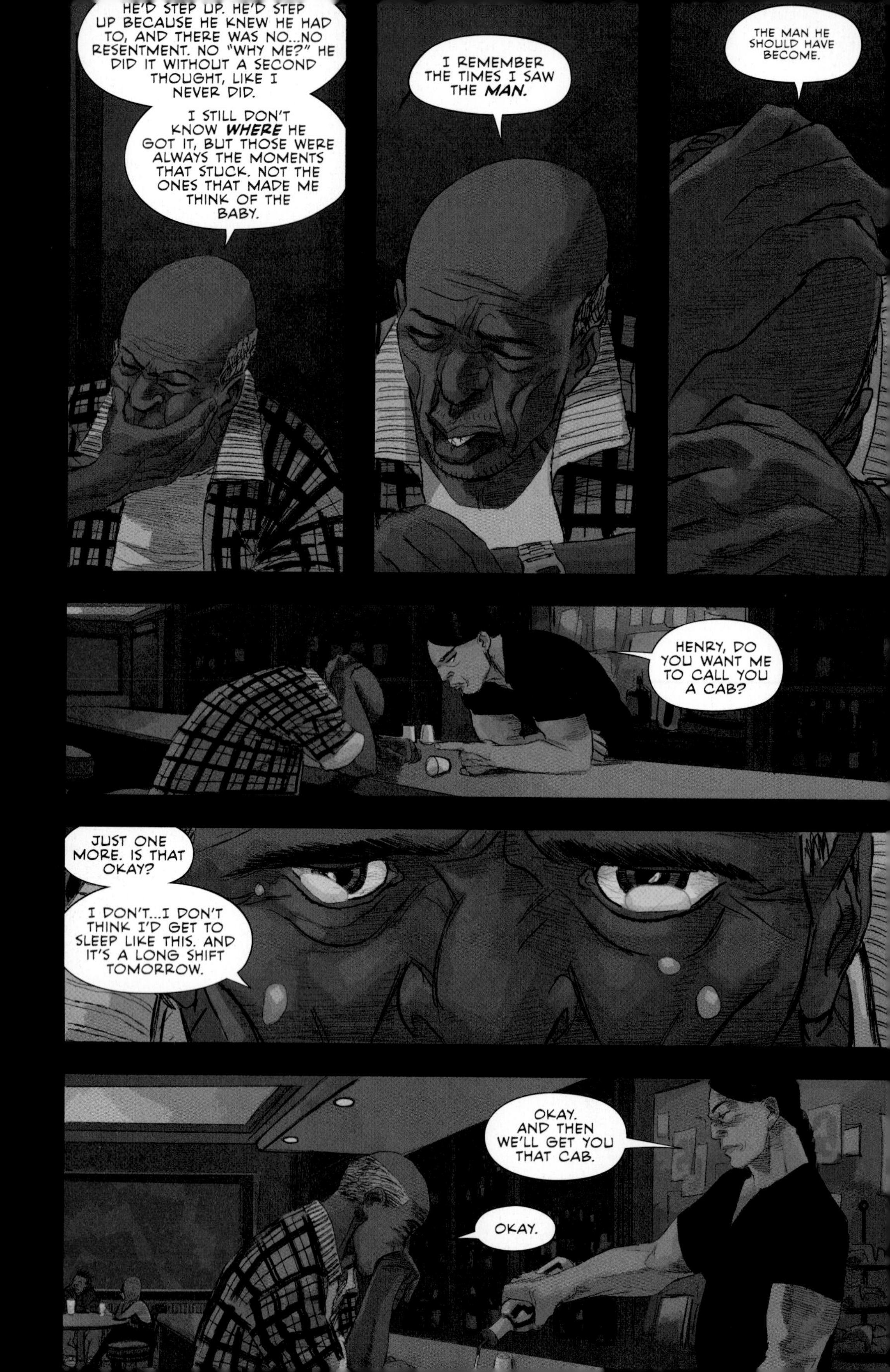

HE'D STEP UP. HE'D STEP UP BECAUSE HE KNEW HE HAD TO, AND THERE WAS NO...NO RESENTMENT. NO "WHY ME?" HE DID IT WITHOUT A SECOND THOUGHT, LIKE I NEVER DID.
I STILL DON'T KNOW WHERE HE GOT IT, BUT THOSE WERE ALWAYS THE MOMENTS THAT STUCK. NOT THE ONES THAT MADE ME THINK OF THE BABY.
I REMEMBER THE TIMES I SAW THE MAN.
THE MAN HE SHOULD HAVE BECOME.
HENRY, DO YOU WANT ME TO CALL YOU A CAB?
JUST ONE MORE. IS THAT OKAY?
I DON'T...I DON'T THINK I'D GET TO SLEEP LIKE THIS. AND IT'S A LONG SHIFT TOMORROW.
OKAY. AND THEN WE'LL GET YOU THAT CAB.
OKAY.

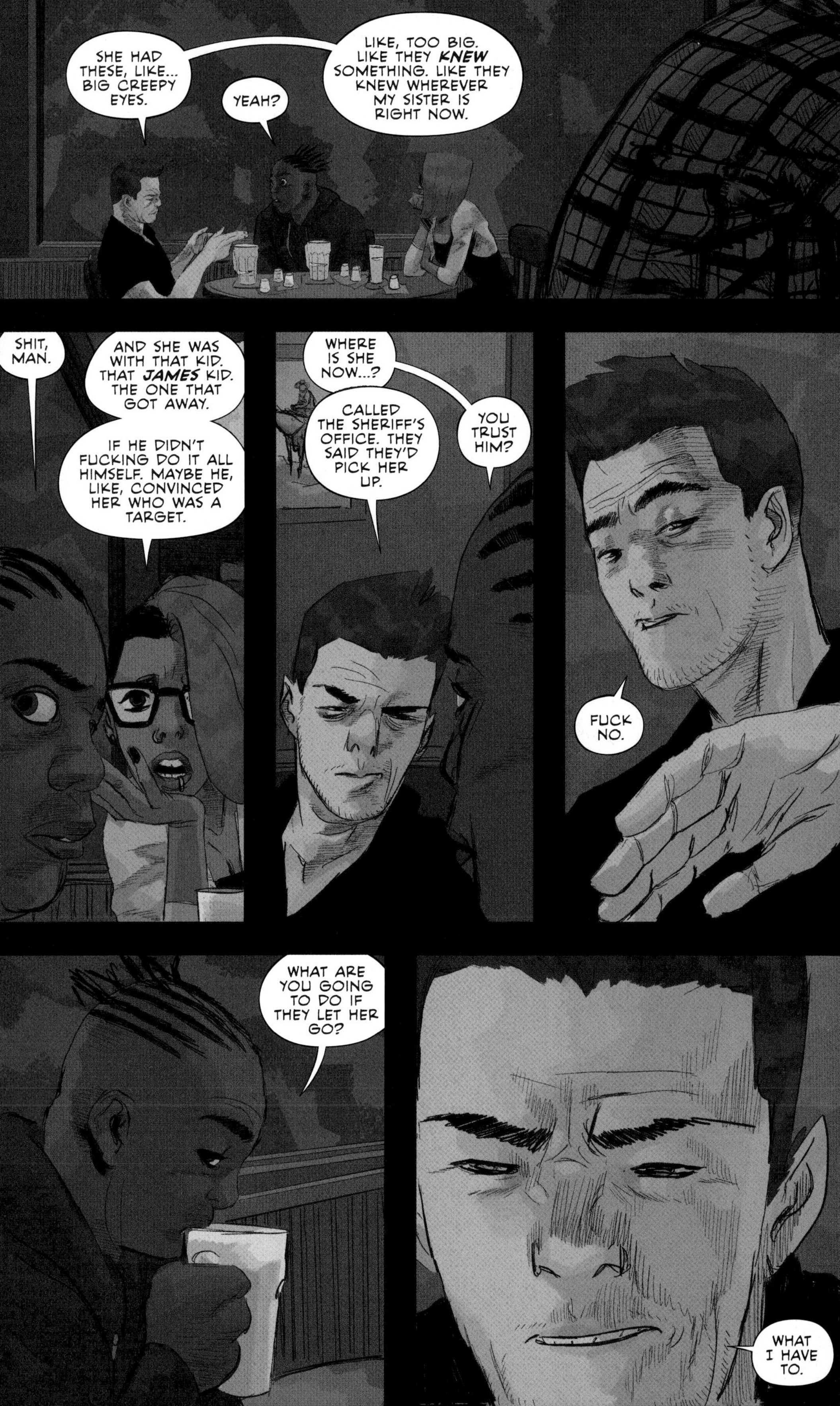
SHE HAD THESE, LIKE... BIG CREEPY EYES.
YEAH?
LIKE, TOO BIG. LIKE THEY KNEW SOMETHING. LIKE THEY KNEW WHEREVER MY SISTER IS RIGHT NOW.
SHIT, MAN.
AND SHE WAS WITH THAT KID. THAT JAMES KID. THE ONE THAT GOT AWAY.
IF HE DIDN'T FUCKING DO IT ALL HIMSELF. MAYBE HE, LIKE, CONVINCED HER WHO WAS A TARGET.
WHERE IS SHE NOW...?
CALLED THE SHERIFF'S OFFICE. THEY SAID THEY'D PICK HER UP.
YOU TRUST HIM?
FUCK NO.
WHAT ARE YOU GOING TO DO IF THEY LET HER GO?
WHAT I HAVE TO.

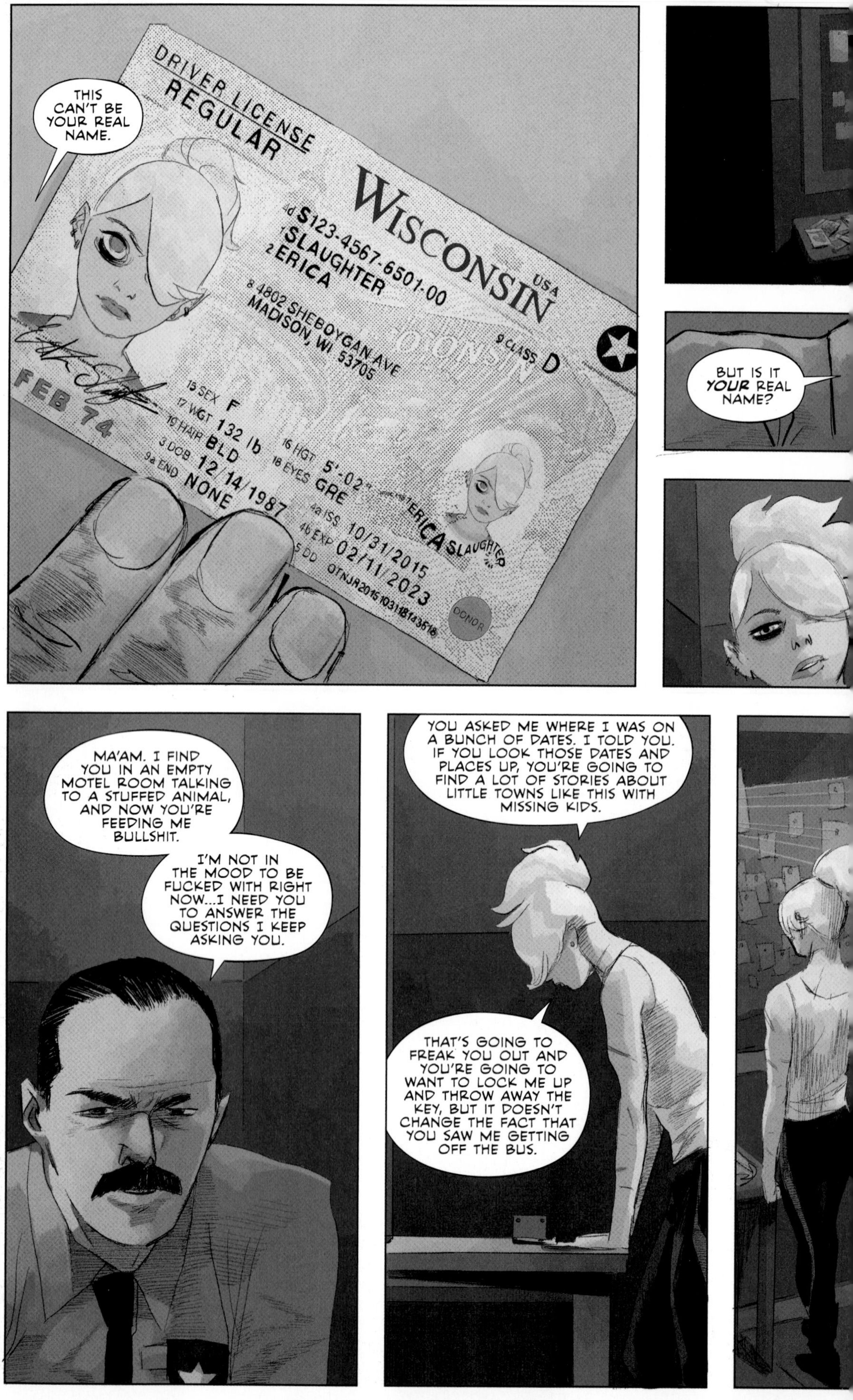
THIS CAN'T BE YOUR REAL NAME.
DRIVER LICENSE
REGULAR
WISCONSIN
USA
S123-4567-6501-00
SLAUGHTER
ERICA
4802 SHEBOYGAN AVE
MADISON, WI 53705
CLASS D
SEX F
WGT 132 lb
HAIR BLD
DOB 12/14/1987
END NONE
HGT 5'-02"
EYES GRE
ISS 10/31/2015
EXP 02/11/2023
FEB 74
ERICA SLAUGHTER
DONOR
BUT IS IT *YOUR* REAL NAME?
MA'AM. I FIND YOU IN AN EMPTY MOTEL ROOM TALKING TO A STUFFED ANIMAL, AND NOW YOU'RE FEEDING ME BULLSHIT.
I'M NOT IN THE MOOD TO BE FUCKED WITH RIGHT NOW...I NEED YOU TO ANSWER THE QUESTIONS I KEEP ASKING YOU.
YOU ASKED ME WHERE I WAS ON A BUNCH OF DATES. I TOLD YOU. IF YOU LOOK THOSE DATES AND PLACES UP, YOU'RE GOING TO FIND A LOT OF STORIES ABOUT LITTLE TOWNS LIKE THIS WITH MISSING KIDS.
THAT'S GOING TO FREAK YOU OUT AND YOU'RE GOING TO WANT TO LOCK ME UP AND THROW AWAY THE KEY, BUT IT DOESN'T CHANGE THE FACT THAT YOU SAW ME GETTING OFF THE BUS.

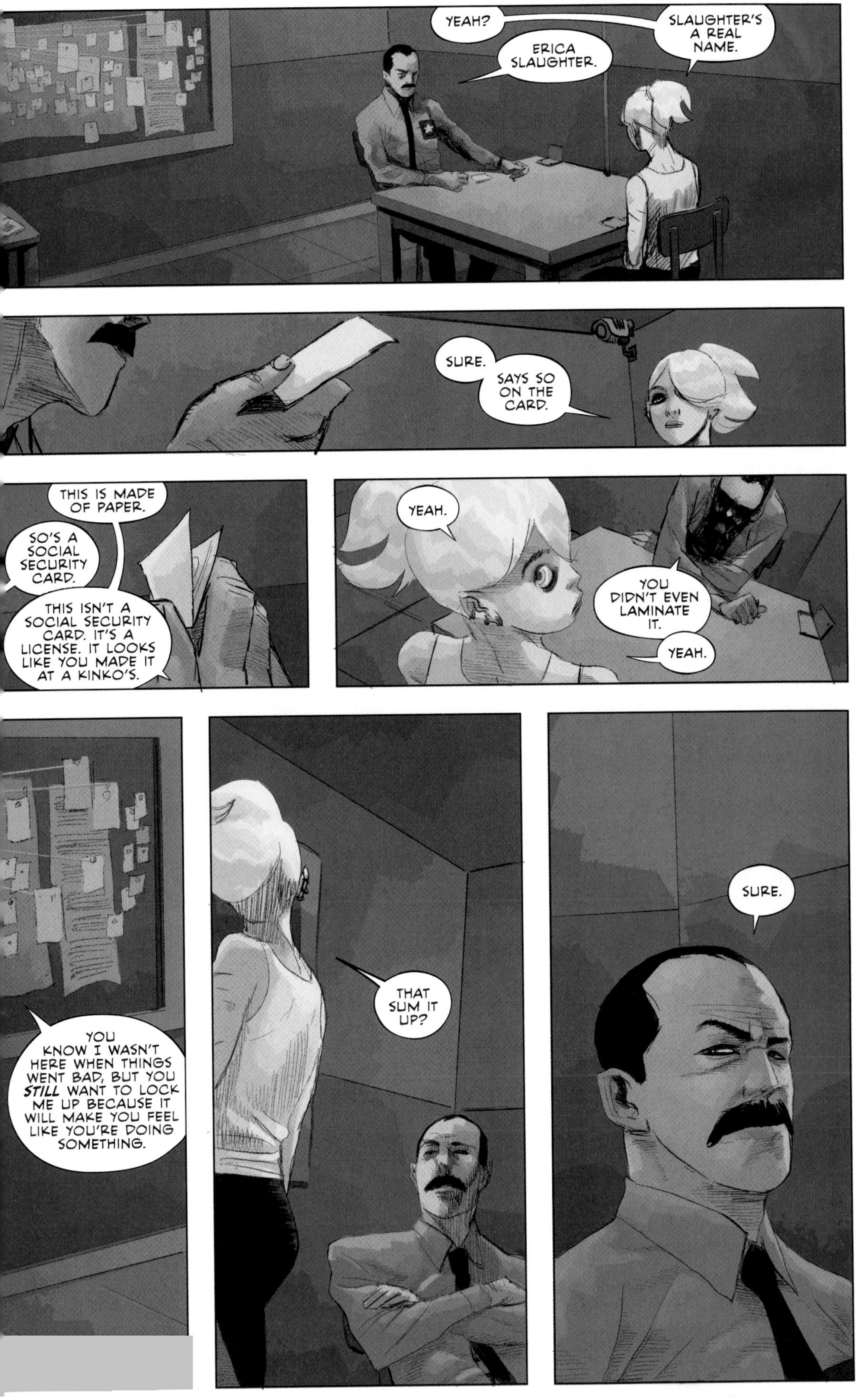
YEAH?
SLAUGHTER'S A REAL NAME.
ERICA SLAUGHTER.
SURE.
SAYS SO ON THE CARD.
THIS IS MADE OF PAPER.
SO'S A SOCIAL SECURITY CARD.
THIS ISN'T A SOCIAL SECURITY CARD. IT'S A LICENSE. IT LOOKS LIKE YOU MADE IT AT A KINKO'S.
YEAH.
YOU DIDN'T EVEN LAMINATE IT.
YEAH.
YOU KNOW I WASN'T HERE WHEN THINGS WENT BAD, BUT YOU STILL WANT TO LOCK ME UP BECAUSE IT WILL MAKE YOU FEEL LIKE YOU'RE DOING SOMETHING.
THAT SUM IT UP?
SURE.

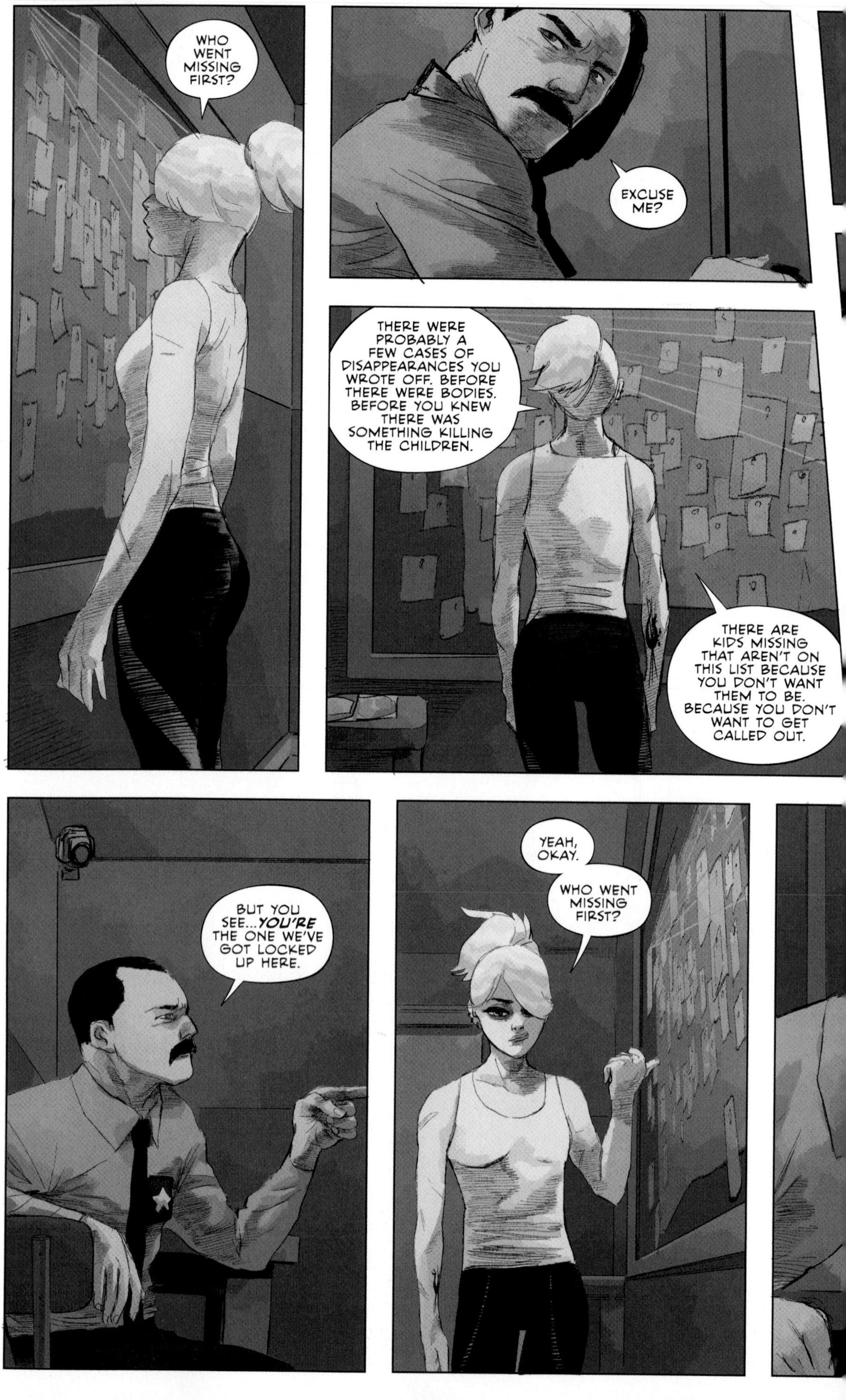
WHO WENT MISSING FIRST?
EXCUSE ME?
THERE WERE PROBABLY A FEW CASES OF DISAPPEARANCES YOU WROTE OFF. BEFORE THERE WERE BODIES. BEFORE YOU KNEW THERE WAS SOMETHING KILLING THE CHILDREN.
THERE ARE KIDS MISSING THAT AREN'T ON THIS LIST BECAUSE YOU DON'T WANT THEM TO BE. BECAUSE YOU DON'T WANT TO GET CALLED OUT.
BUT YOU SEE... *YOU'RE* THE ONE WE'VE GOT LOCKED UP HERE.
YEAH, OKAY.
WHO WENT MISSING FIRST?

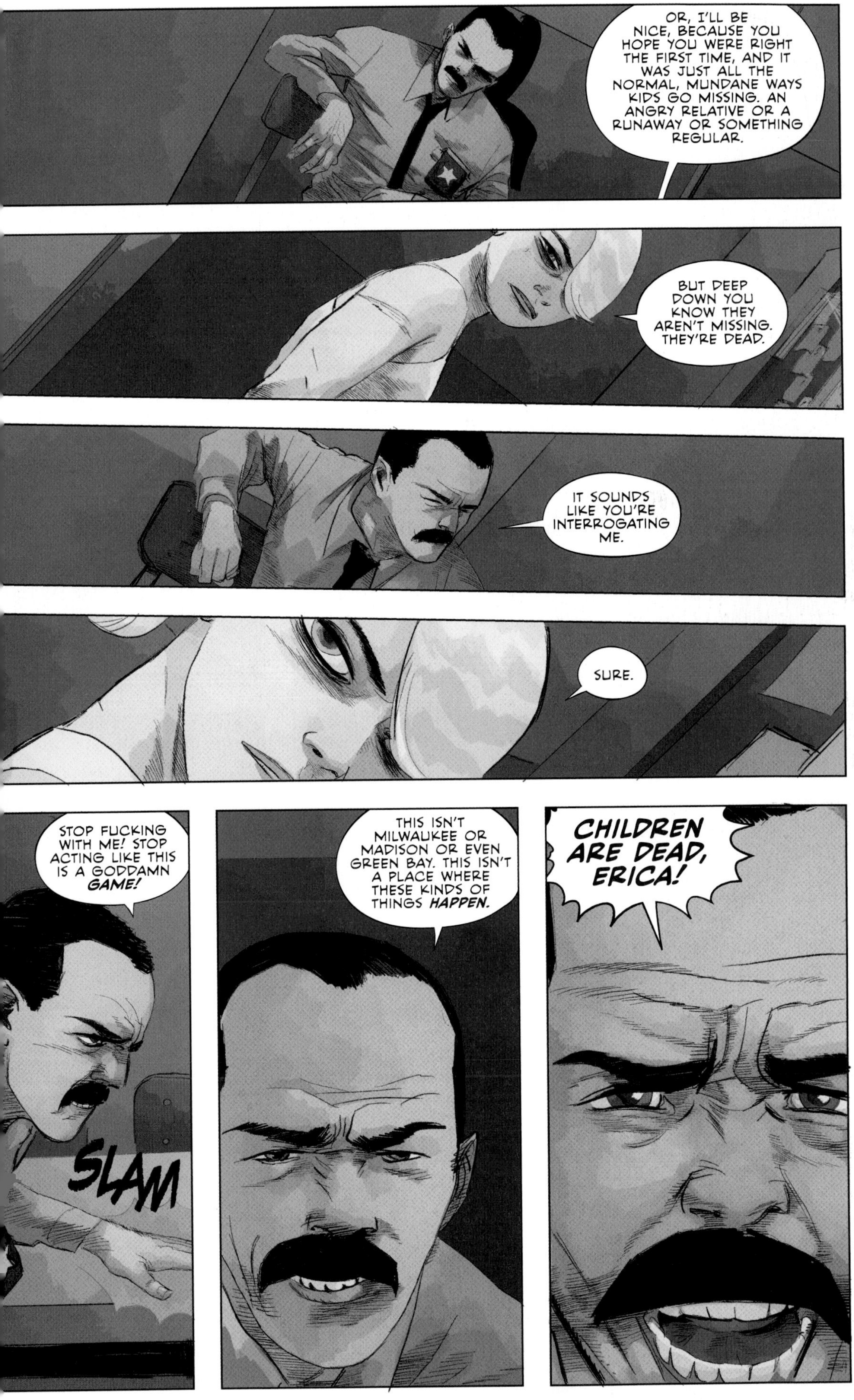
OR, I'LL BE NICE, BECAUSE YOU HOPE YOU WERE RIGHT THE FIRST TIME, AND IT WAS JUST ALL THE NORMAL, MUNDANE WAYS KIDS GO MISSING. AN ANGRY RELATIVE OR A RUNAWAY OR SOMETHING REGULAR.
BUT DEEP DOWN YOU KNOW THEY AREN'T MISSING. THEY'RE DEAD.
IT SOUNDS LIKE YOU'RE INTERROGATING ME.
SURE.
STOP FUCKING WITH ME! STOP ACTING LIKE THIS IS A GODDAMN GAME!
SLAM
THIS ISN'T MILWAUKEE OR MADISON OR EVEN GREEN BAY. THIS ISN'T A PLACE WHERE THESE KINDS OF THINGS HAPPEN.
CHILDREN ARE DEAD, ERICA!

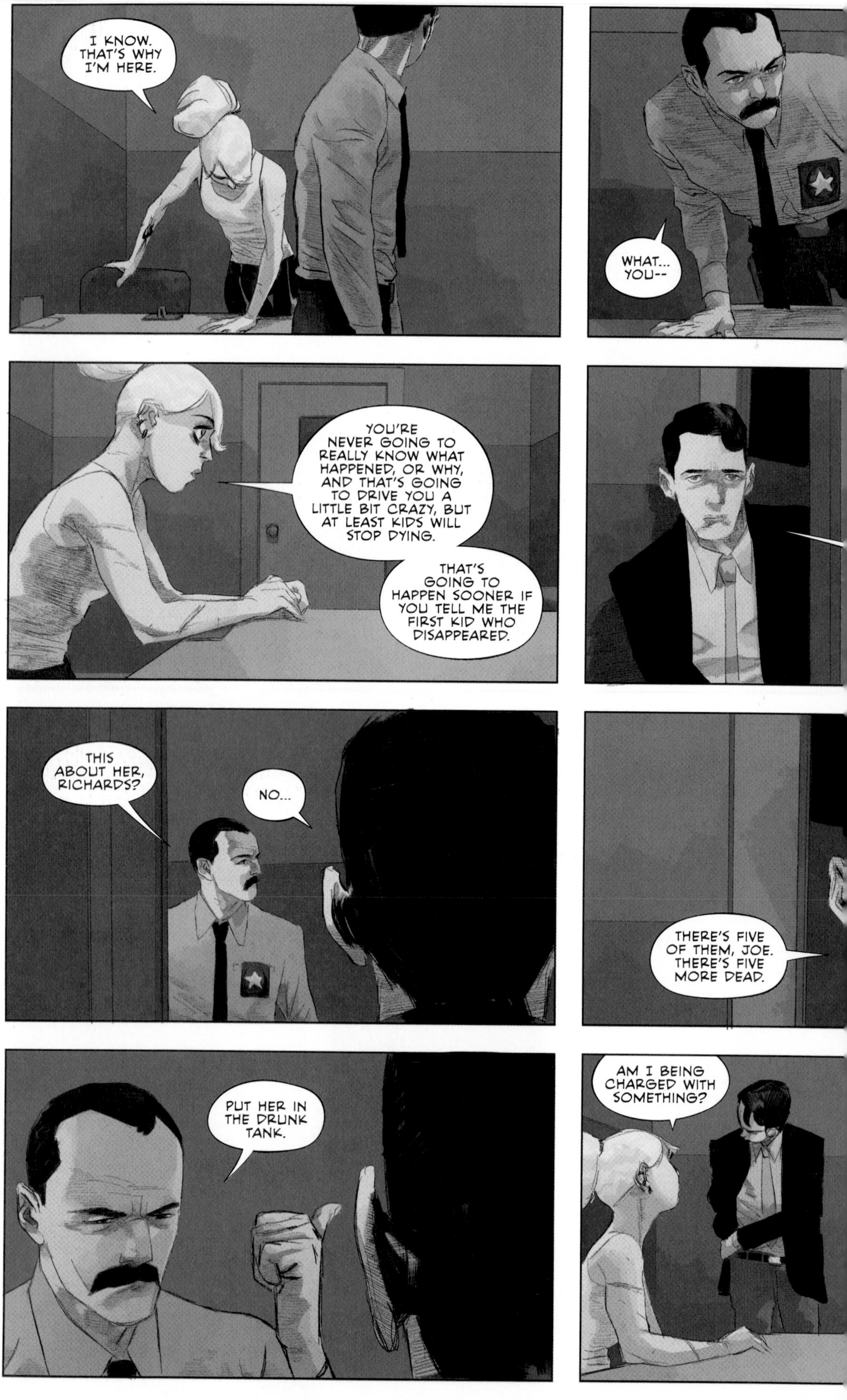
I KNOW. THAT'S WHY I'M HERE.
WHAT... YOU--
YOU'RE NEVER GOING TO REALLY KNOW WHAT HAPPENED, OR WHY, AND THAT'S GOING TO DRIVE YOU A LITTLE BIT CRAZY, BUT AT LEAST KIDS WILL STOP DYING.
THAT'S GOING TO HAPPEN SOONER IF YOU TELL ME THE FIRST KID WHO DISAPPEARED.
THIS ABOUT HER, RICHARDS?
NO...
THERE'S FIVE OF THEM, JOE. THERE'S FIVE MORE DEAD.
PUT HER IN THE DRUNK TANK.
AM I BEING CHARGED WITH SOMETHING?

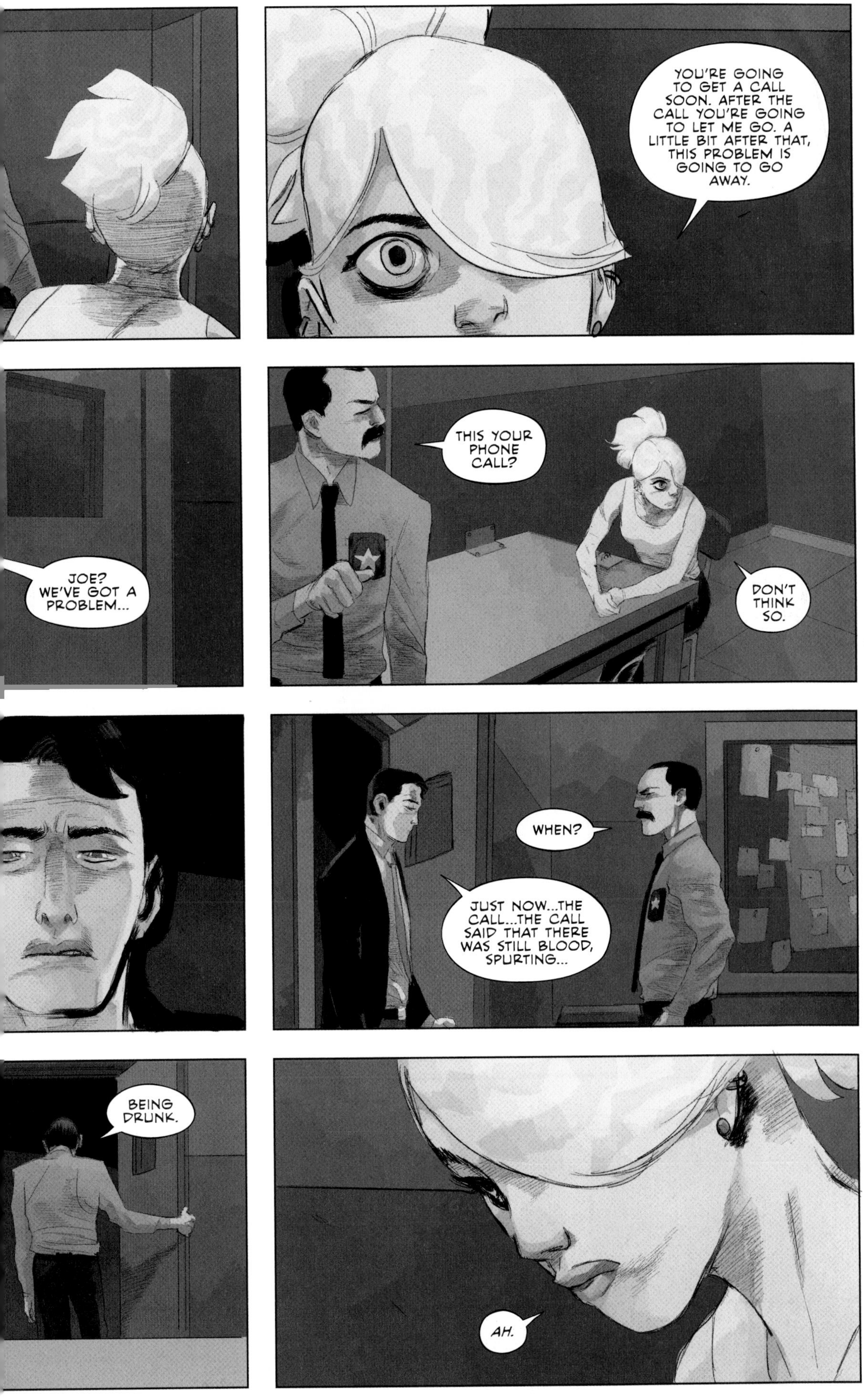
YOU'RE GOING TO GET A CALL SOON. AFTER THE CALL YOU'RE GOING TO LET ME GO. A LITTLE BIT AFTER THAT, THIS PROBLEM IS GOING TO GO AWAY.
JOE? WE'VE GOT A PROBLEM...
THIS YOUR PHONE CALL?
DON'T THINK SO.
WHEN?
JUST NOW...THE CALL...THE CALL SAID THAT THERE WAS STILL BLOOD, SPURTING...
BEING DRUNK.
AH.

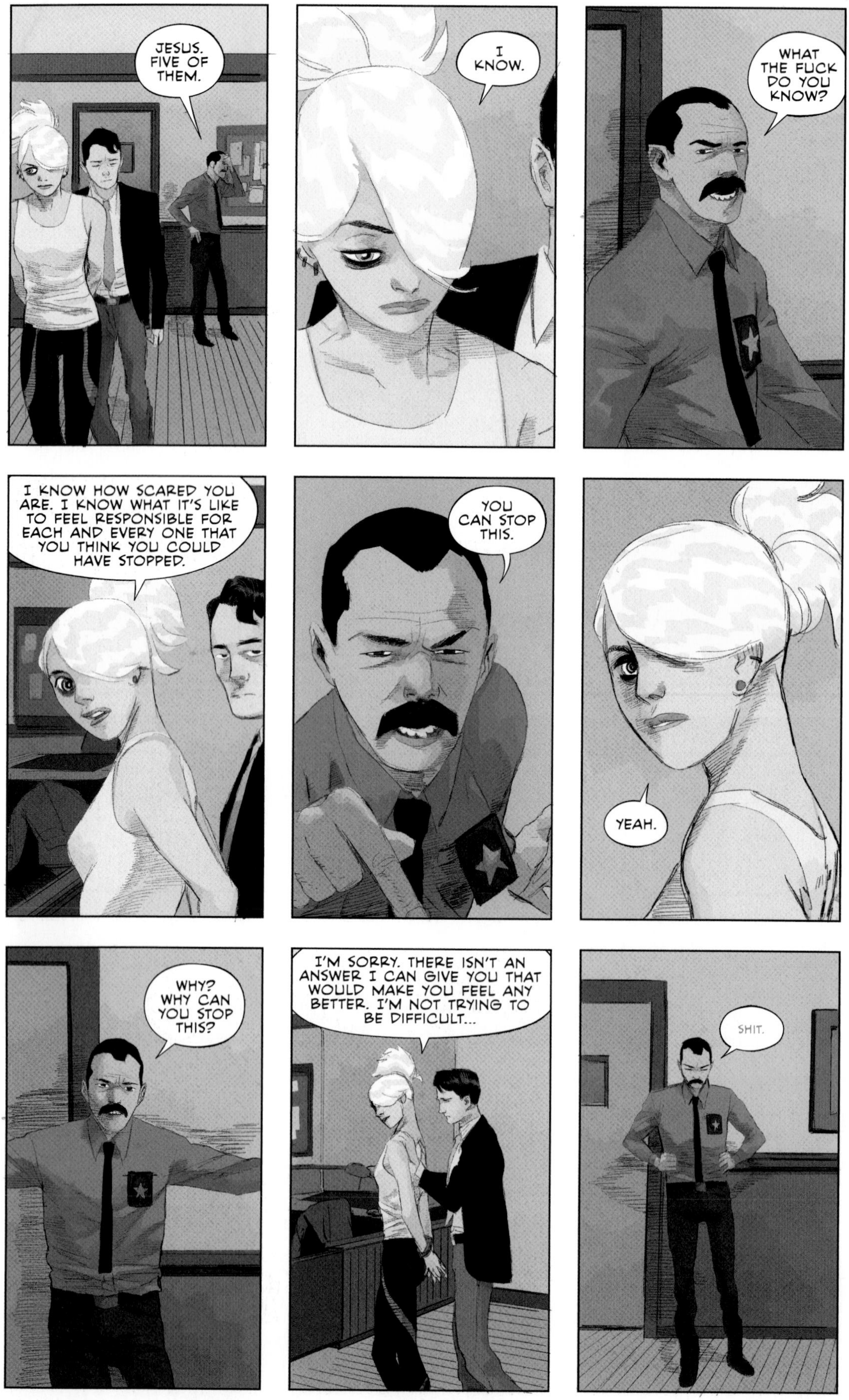
JESUS. FIVE OF THEM.
I KNOW.
WHAT THE FUCK DO YOU KNOW?
I KNOW HOW SCARED YOU ARE. I KNOW WHAT IT'S LIKE TO FEEL RESPONSIBLE FOR EACH AND EVERY ONE THAT YOU THINK YOU COULD HAVE STOPPED.
YOU CAN STOP THIS.
YEAH.
WHY? WHY CAN YOU STOP THIS?
I'M SORRY. THERE ISN'T AN ANSWER I CAN GIVE YOU THAT WOULD MAKE YOU FEEL ANY BETTER. I'M NOT TRYING TO BE DIFFICULT...
SHIT.

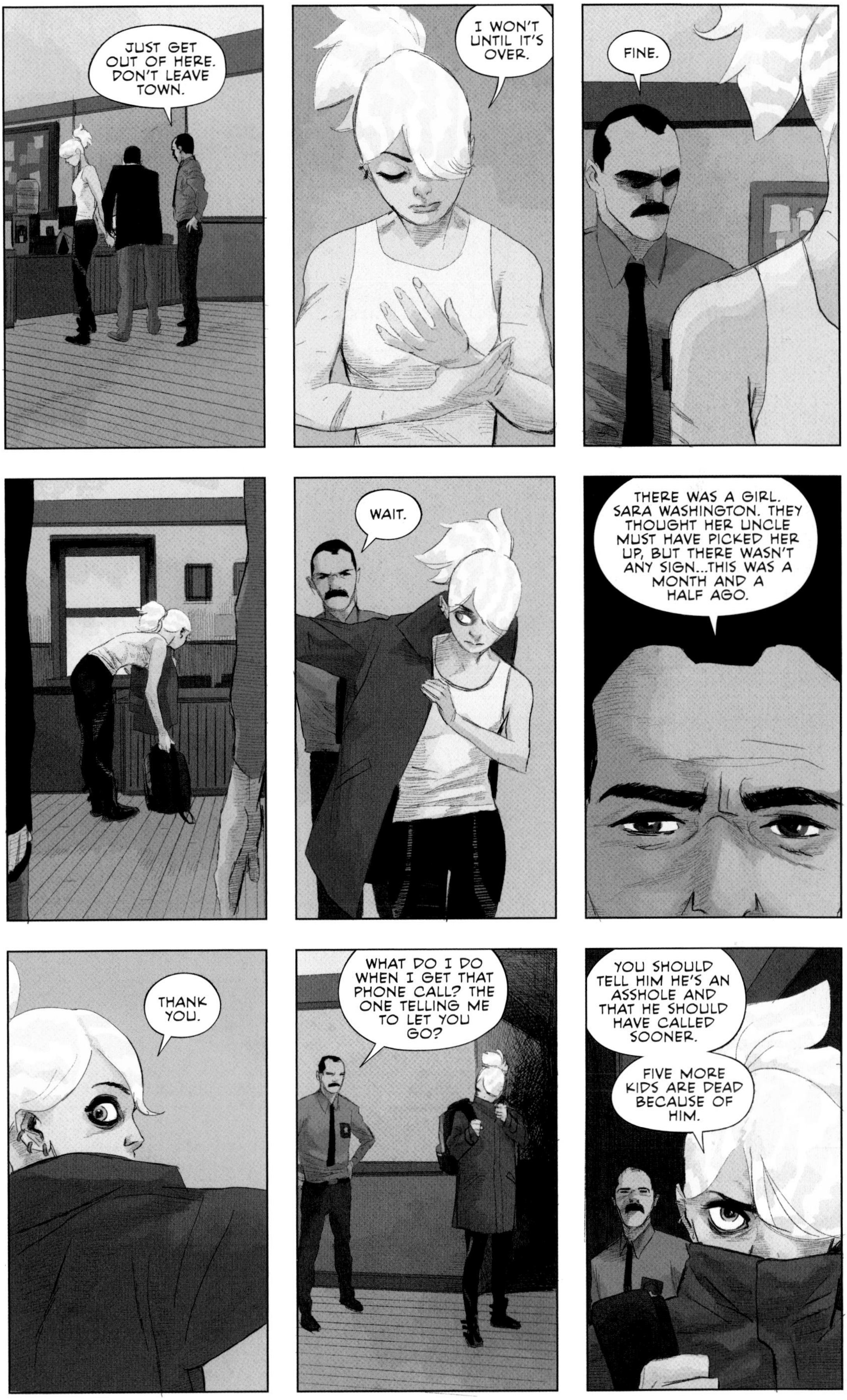
JUST GET OUT OF HERE. DON'T LEAVE TOWN.
I WON'T UNTIL IT'S OVER.
FINE.
WAIT.
THERE WAS A GIRL. SARA WASHINGTON. THEY THOUGHT HER UNCLE MUST HAVE PICKED HER UP, BUT THERE WASN'T ANY SIGN...THIS WAS A MONTH AND A HALF AGO.
THANK YOU.
WHAT DO I DO WHEN I GET THAT PHONE CALL? THE ONE TELLING ME TO LET YOU GO?
YOU SHOULD TELL HIM HE'S AN ASSHOLE AND THAT HE SHOULD HAVE CALLED SOONER.
FIVE MORE KIDS ARE DEAD BECAUSE OF HIM.

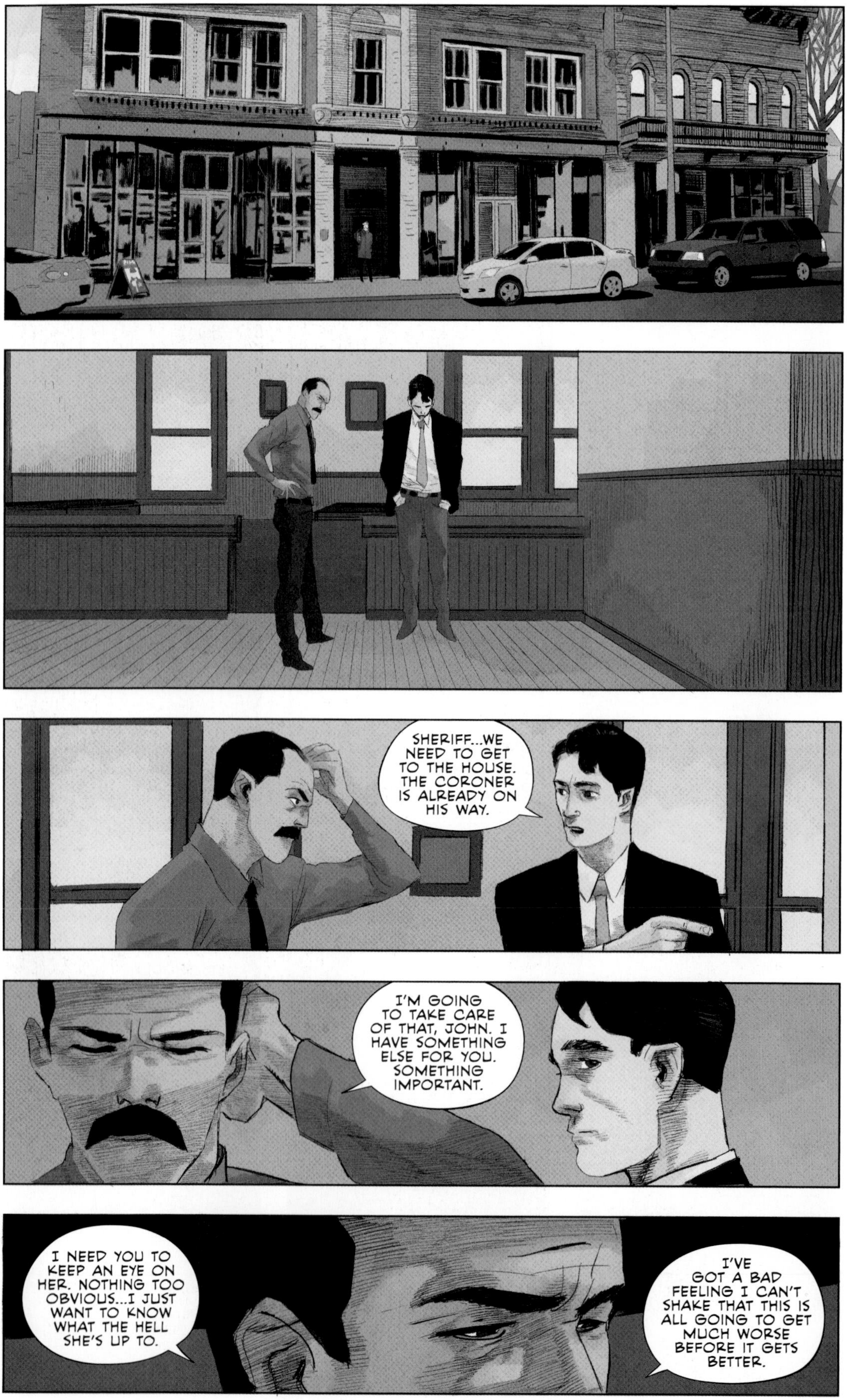
SHERIFF...WE NEED TO GET TO THE HOUSE. THE CORONER IS ALREADY ON HIS WAY.
I'M GOING TO TAKE CARE OF THAT, JOHN. I HAVE SOMETHING ELSE FOR YOU. SOMETHING IMPORTANT.
I NEED YOU TO KEEP AN EYE ON HER. NOTHING TOO OBVIOUS...I JUST WANT TO KNOW WHAT THE HELL SHE'S UP TO.
I'VE GOT A BAD FEELING I CAN'T SHAKE THAT THIS IS ALL GOING TO GET MUCH WORSE BEFORE IT GETS BETTER.

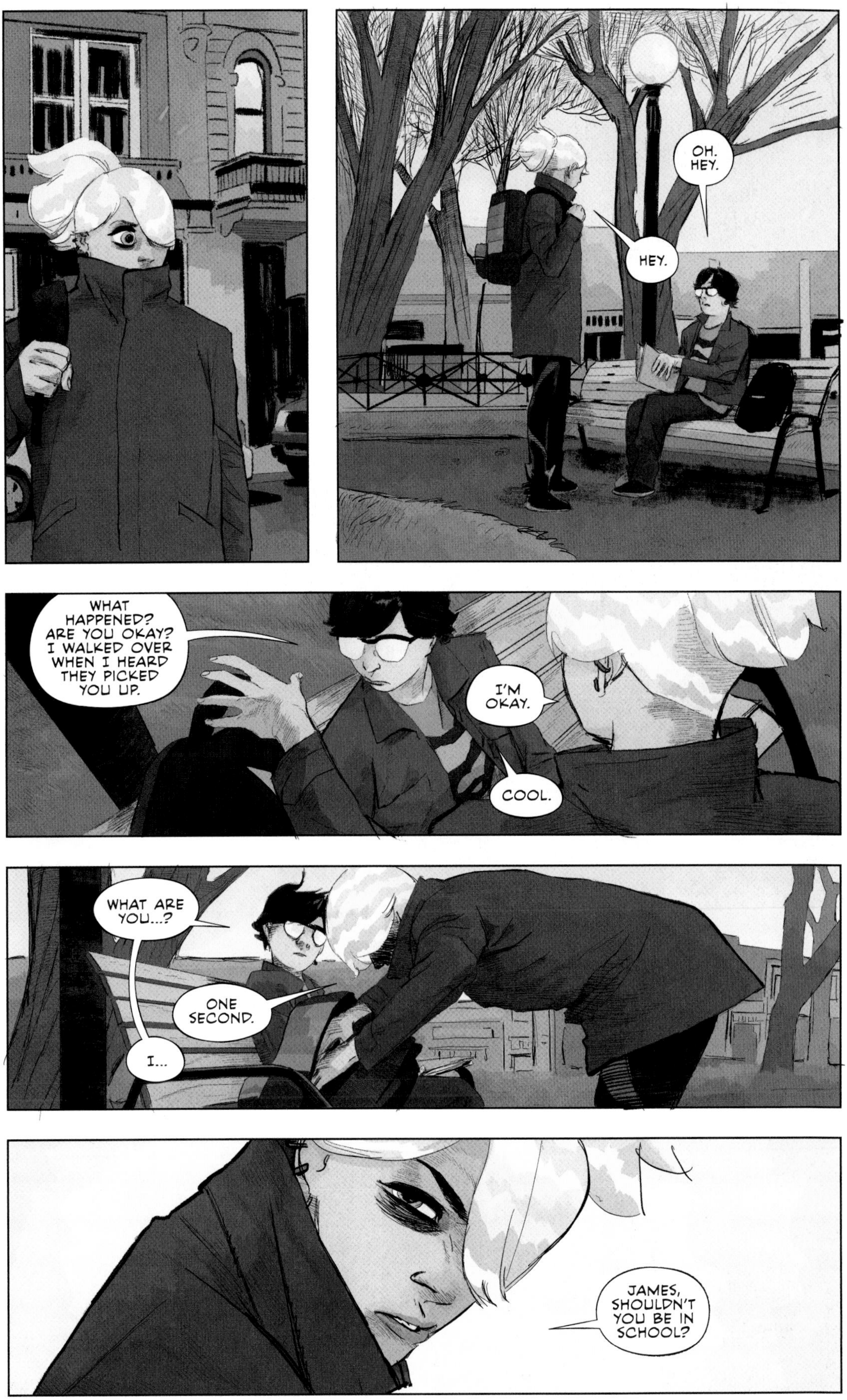
OH. HEY.
HEY.
WHAT HAPPENED? ARE YOU OKAY? I WALKED OVER WHEN I HEARD THEY PICKED YOU UP.
I'M OKAY.
COOL.
WHAT ARE YOU...?
ONE SECOND.
I...
JAMES, SHOULDN'T YOU BE IN SCHOOL?

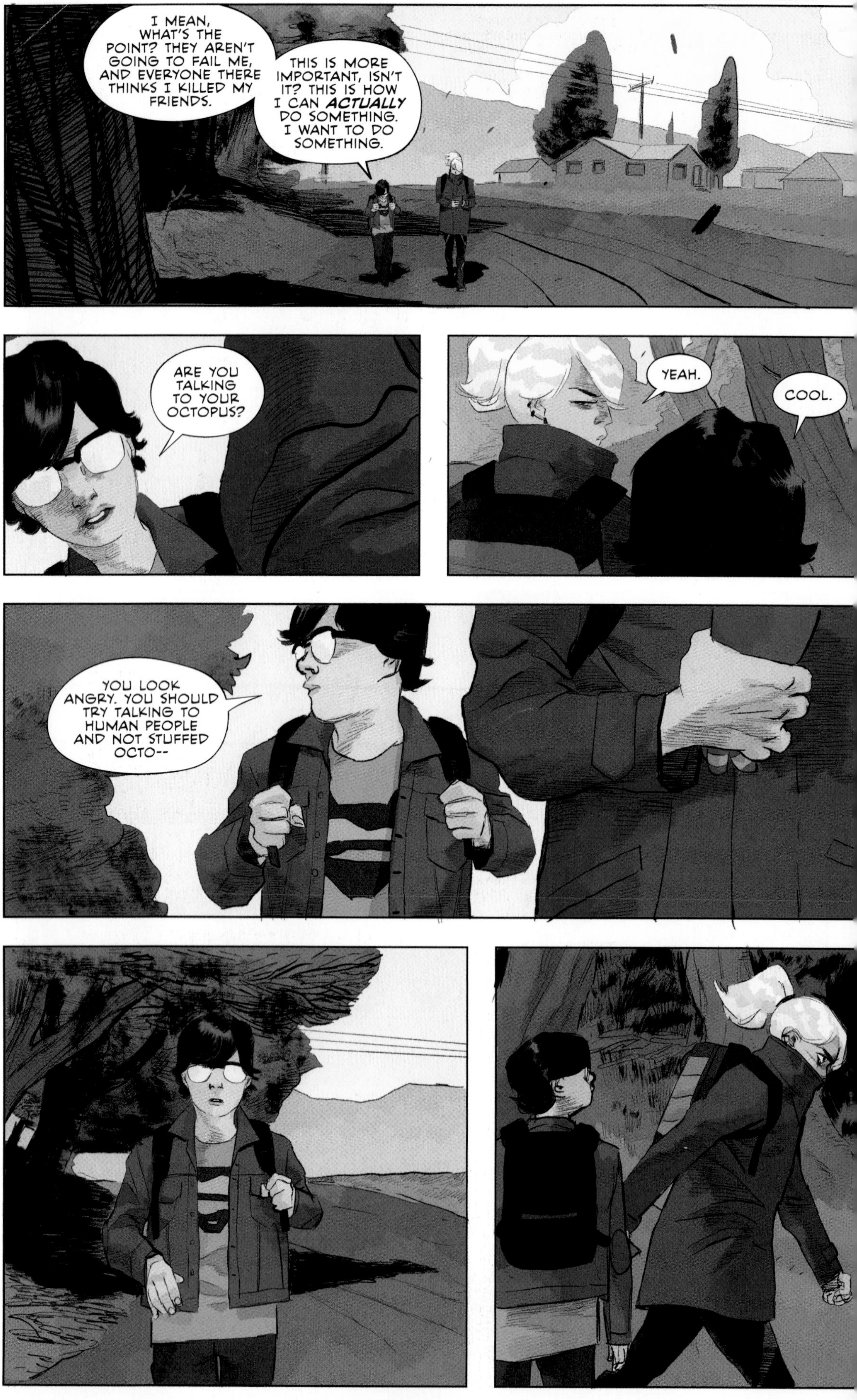
I MEAN, WHAT'S THE POINT? THEY AREN'T GOING TO FAIL ME, AND EVERYONE THERE THINKS I KILLED MY FRIENDS.
THIS IS MORE IMPORTANT, ISN'T IT? THIS IS HOW I CAN ACTUALLY DO SOMETHING. I WANT TO DO SOMETHING.
ARE YOU TALKING TO YOUR OCTOPUS?
YEAH.
COOL.
YOU LOOK ANGRY. YOU SHOULD TRY TALKING TO HUMAN PEOPLE AND NOT STUFFED OCTO--

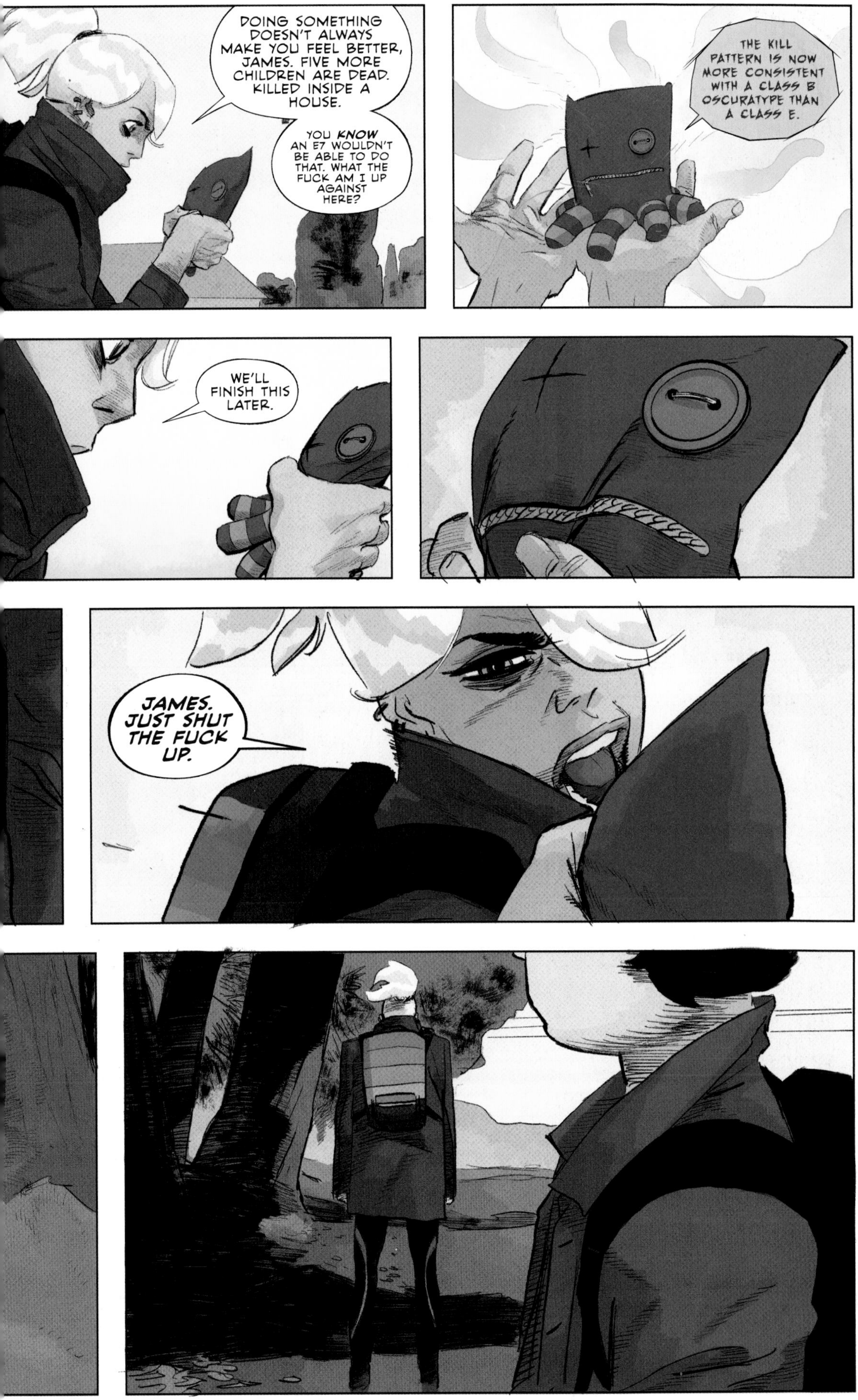
DOING SOMETHING DOESN'T ALWAYS MAKE YOU FEEL BETTER, JAMES. FIVE MORE CHILDREN ARE DEAD. KILLED INSIDE A HOUSE.
YOU KNOW AN E7 WOULDN'T BE ABLE TO DO THAT. WHAT THE FUCK AM I UP AGAINST HERE?
THE KILL PATTERN IS NOW MORE CONSISTENT WITH A CLASS B OSCURATYPE THAN A CLASS E.
WE'LL FINISH THIS LATER.
JAMES. JUST SHUT THE FUCK UP.

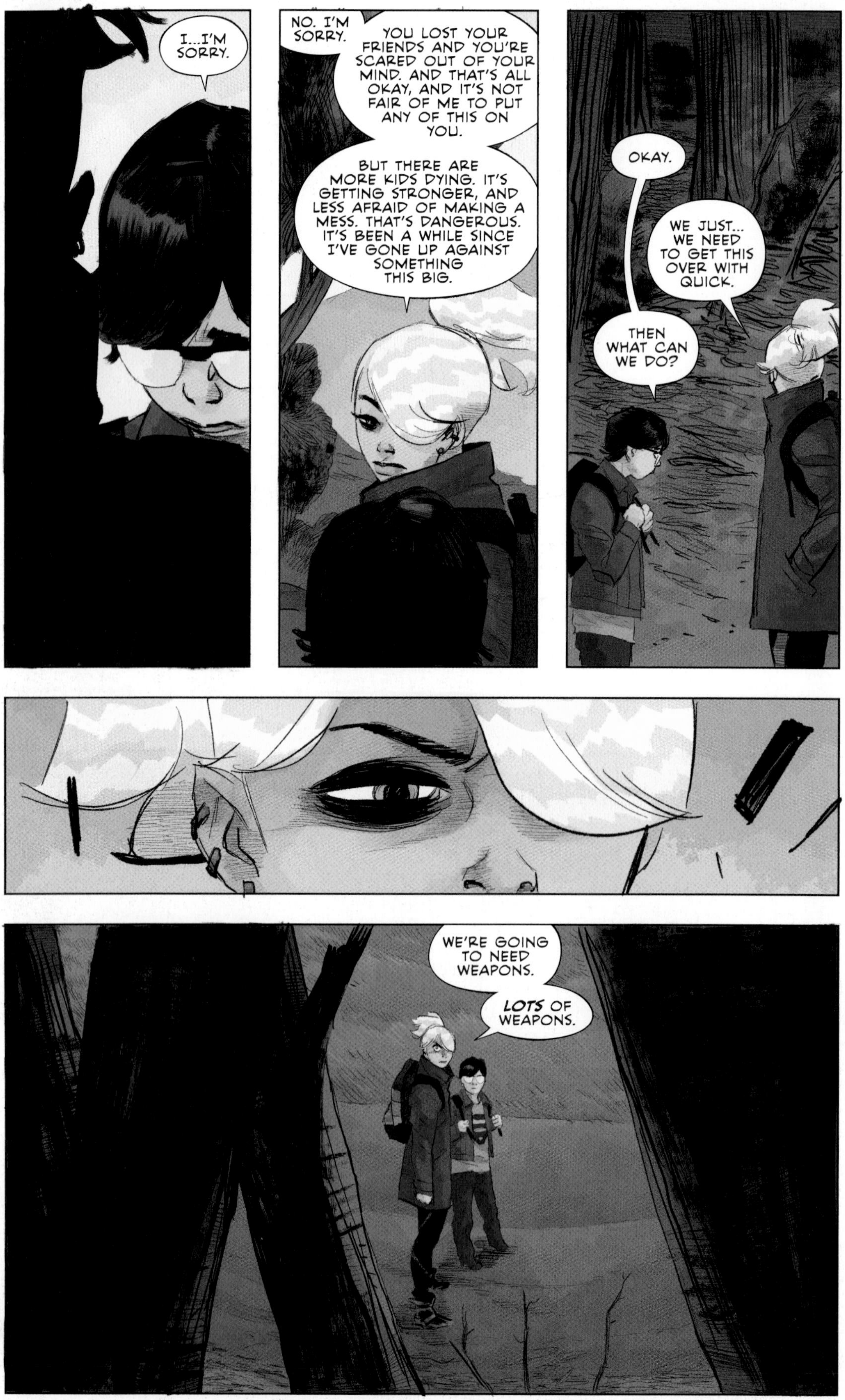
I...I'M SORRY.
NO. I'M SORRY.
YOU LOST YOUR FRIENDS AND YOU'RE SCARED OUT OF YOUR MIND. AND THAT'S ALL OKAY, AND IT'S NOT FAIR OF ME TO PUT ANY OF THIS ON YOU.
BUT THERE ARE MORE KIDS DYING. IT'S GETTING STRONGER, AND LESS AFRAID OF MAKING A MESS. THAT'S DANGEROUS. IT'S BEEN A WHILE SINCE I'VE GONE UP AGAINST SOMETHING THIS BIG.
OKAY.
THEN WHAT CAN WE DO?
WE JUST... WE NEED TO GET THIS OVER WITH QUICK.
WE'RE GOING TO NEED WEAPONS.
LOTS OF WEAPONS.

CHAPTER
FOUR

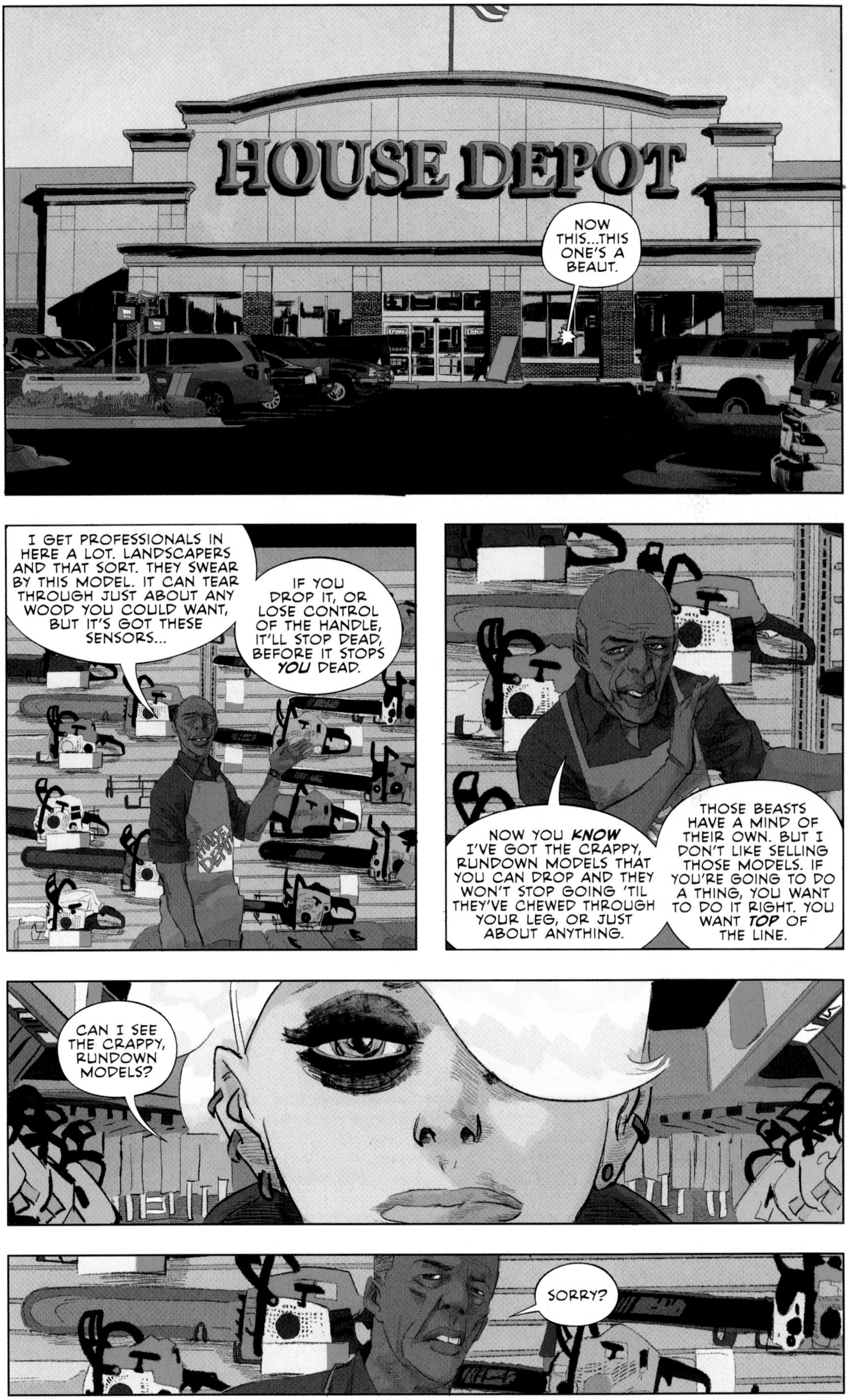
HOUSE DEPOT
NOW THIS...THIS ONE'S A BEAUT.
I GET PROFESSIONALS IN HERE A LOT. LANDSCAPERS AND THAT SORT. THEY SWEAR BY THIS MODEL. IT CAN TEAR THROUGH JUST ABOUT ANY WOOD YOU COULD WANT, BUT IT'S GOT THESE SENSORS...
IF YOU DROP IT, OR LOSE CONTROL OF THE HANDLE, IT'LL STOP DEAD, BEFORE IT STOPS *YOU* DEAD.
HOUSE DEPOT
NOW YOU *KNOW* I'VE GOT THE CRAPPY, RUNDOWN MODELS THAT YOU CAN DROP AND THEY WON'T STOP GOING 'TIL THEY'VE CHEWED THROUGH YOUR LEG, OR JUST ABOUT ANYTHING.
THOSE BEASTS HAVE A MIND OF THEIR OWN. BUT I DON'T LIKE SELLING THOSE MODELS. IF YOU'RE GOING TO DO A THING, YOU WANT TO DO IT RIGHT. YOU WANT *TOP* OF THE LINE.
CAN I SEE THE CRAPPY, RUNDOWN MODELS?
SORRY?

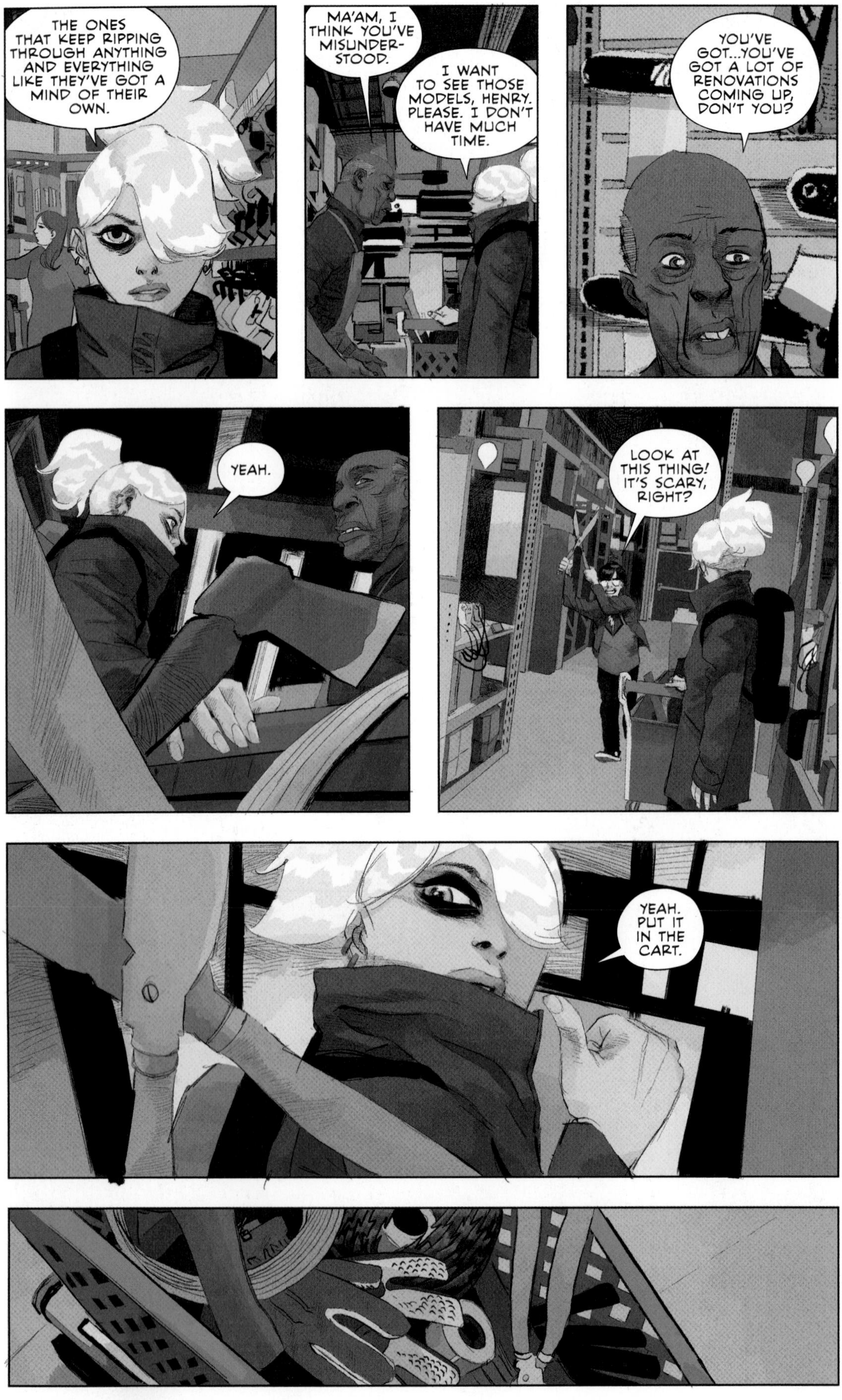
THE ONES THAT KEEP RIPPING THROUGH ANYTHING AND EVERYTHING LIKE THEY'VE GOT A MIND OF THEIR OWN.
MA'AM, I THINK YOU'VE MISUNDERSTOOD.
I WANT TO SEE THOSE MODELS, HENRY. PLEASE. I DON'T HAVE MUCH TIME.
YOU'VE GOT...YOU'VE GOT A LOT OF RENOVATIONS COMING UP, DON'T YOU?
YEAH.
LOOK AT THIS THING! IT'S SCARY, RIGHT?
YEAH. PUT IT IN THE CART.

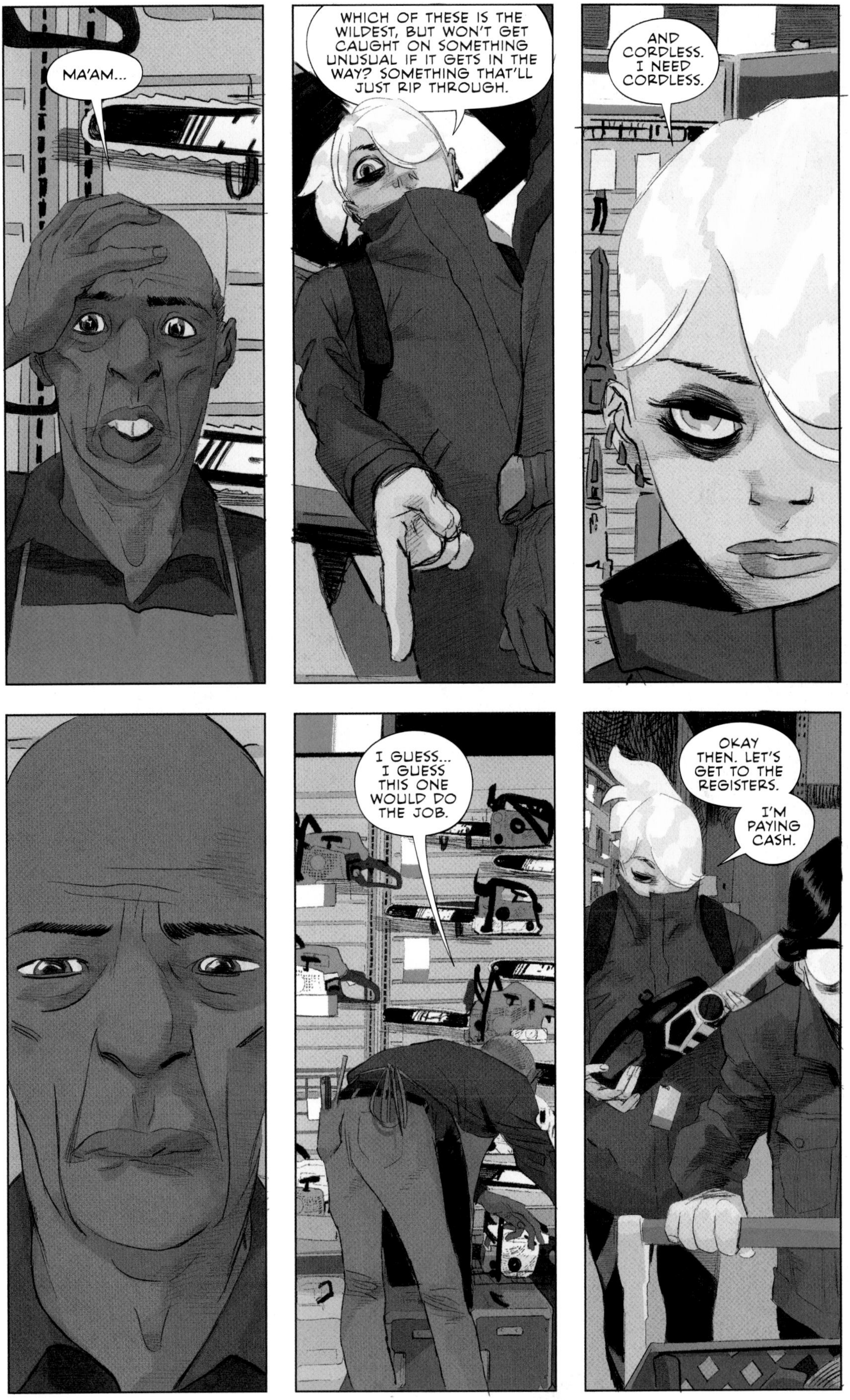
MA'AM...
WHICH OF THESE IS THE WILDEST, BUT WON'T GET CAUGHT ON SOMETHING UNUSUAL IF IT GETS IN THE WAY? SOMETHING THAT'LL JUST RIP THROUGH.
AND CORDLESS. I NEED CORDLESS.
I GUESS... I GUESS THIS ONE WOULD DO THE JOB.
OKAY THEN. LET'S GET TO THE REGISTERS.
I'M PAYING CASH.

DAD, YOU IN HERE?

DAD. IT'S TOMMY.

OH.

HOW'S YOUR MOTHER?

CALL HER IF YOU REALLY WANT TO KNOW.

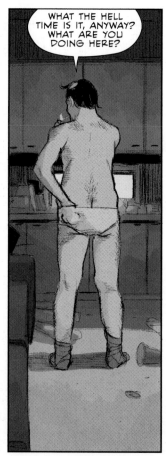

WHAT THE HELL TIME IS IT, ANYWAY? WHAT ARE YOU DOING HERE?

IS THERE... IS THERE NEWS...?

IS SOPHIE...

DID THEY FIND HER BODY?

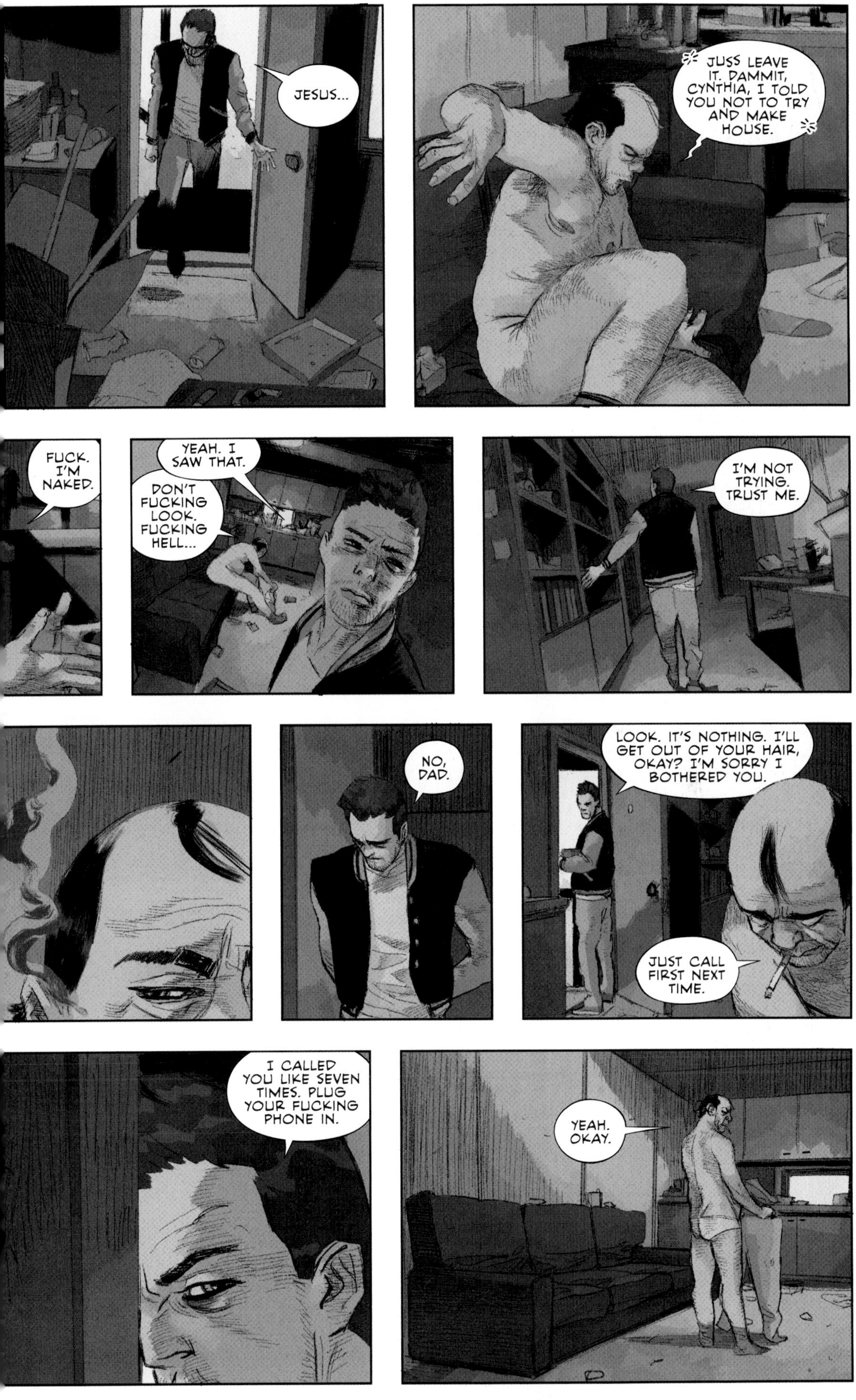
JESUS...
JUSS LEAVE IT. DAMMIT, CYNTHIA, I TOLD YOU NOT TO TRY AND MAKE HOUSE.
FUCK. I'M NAKED.
YEAH. I SAW THAT.
DON'T FUCKING LOOK. FUCKING HELL...
I'M NOT TRYING. TRUST ME.
NO, DAD.
LOOK. IT'S NOTHING. I'LL GET OUT OF YOUR HAIR, OKAY? I'M SORRY I BOTHERED YOU.
JUST CALL FIRST NEXT TIME.
I CALLED YOU LIKE SEVEN TIMES. PLUG YOUR FUCKING PHONE IN.
YEAH. OKAY.

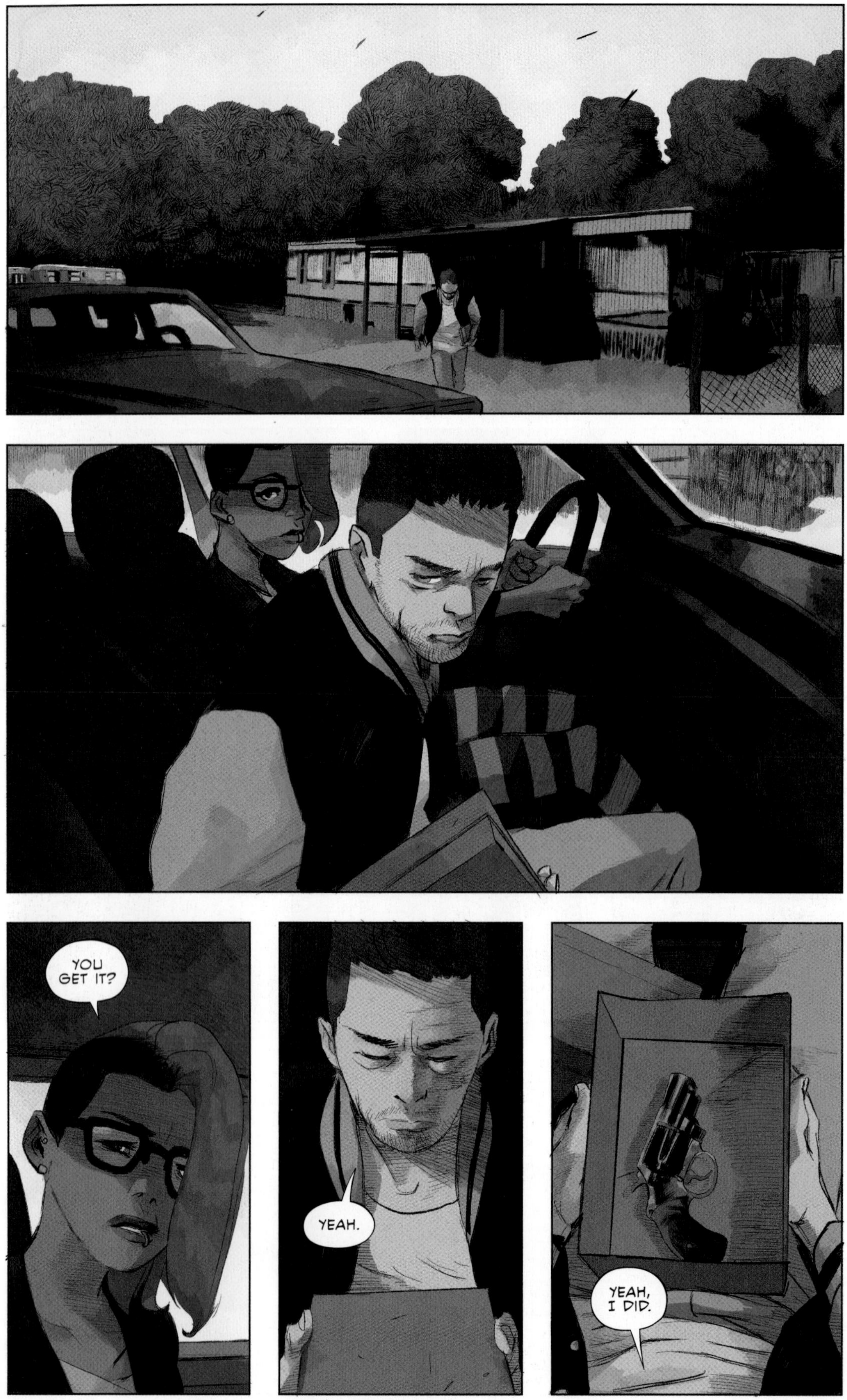
YOU GET IT?
YEAH.
YEAH, I DID.

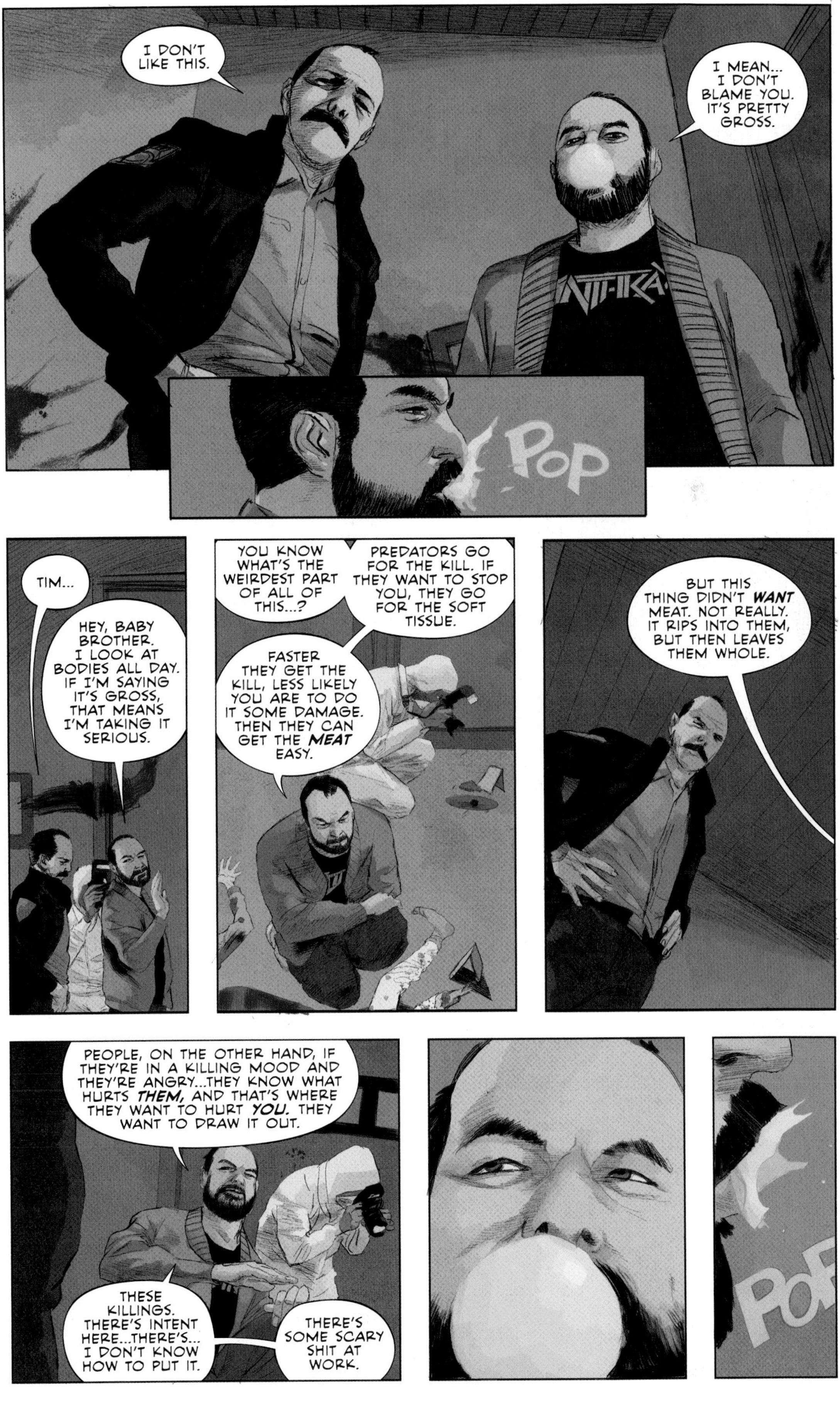
I DON'T LIKE THIS.
I MEAN... I DON'T BLAME YOU. IT'S PRETTY GROSS.
POP
TIM...
HEY, BABY BROTHER. I LOOK AT BODIES ALL DAY. IF I'M SAYING IT'S GROSS, THAT MEANS I'M TAKING IT SERIOUS.
YOU KNOW WHAT'S THE WEIRDEST PART OF ALL OF THIS...?
PREDATORS GO FOR THE KILL. IF THEY WANT TO STOP YOU, THEY GO FOR THE SOFT TISSUE.
FASTER THEY GET THE KILL, LESS LIKELY YOU ARE TO DO IT SOME DAMAGE. THEN THEY CAN GET THE *MEAT* EASY.
BUT THIS THING DIDN'T *WANT* MEAT. NOT REALLY. IT RIPS INTO THEM, BUT THEN LEAVES THEM WHOLE.
PEOPLE, ON THE OTHER HAND, IF THEY'RE IN A KILLING MOOD AND THEY'RE ANGRY...THEY KNOW WHAT HURTS *THEM,* AND THAT'S WHERE THEY WANT TO HURT *YOU.* THEY WANT TO DRAW IT OUT.
THESE KILLINGS. THERE'S INTENT HERE...THERE'S... I DON'T KNOW HOW TO PUT IT.
THERE'S SOME SCARY SHIT AT WORK.

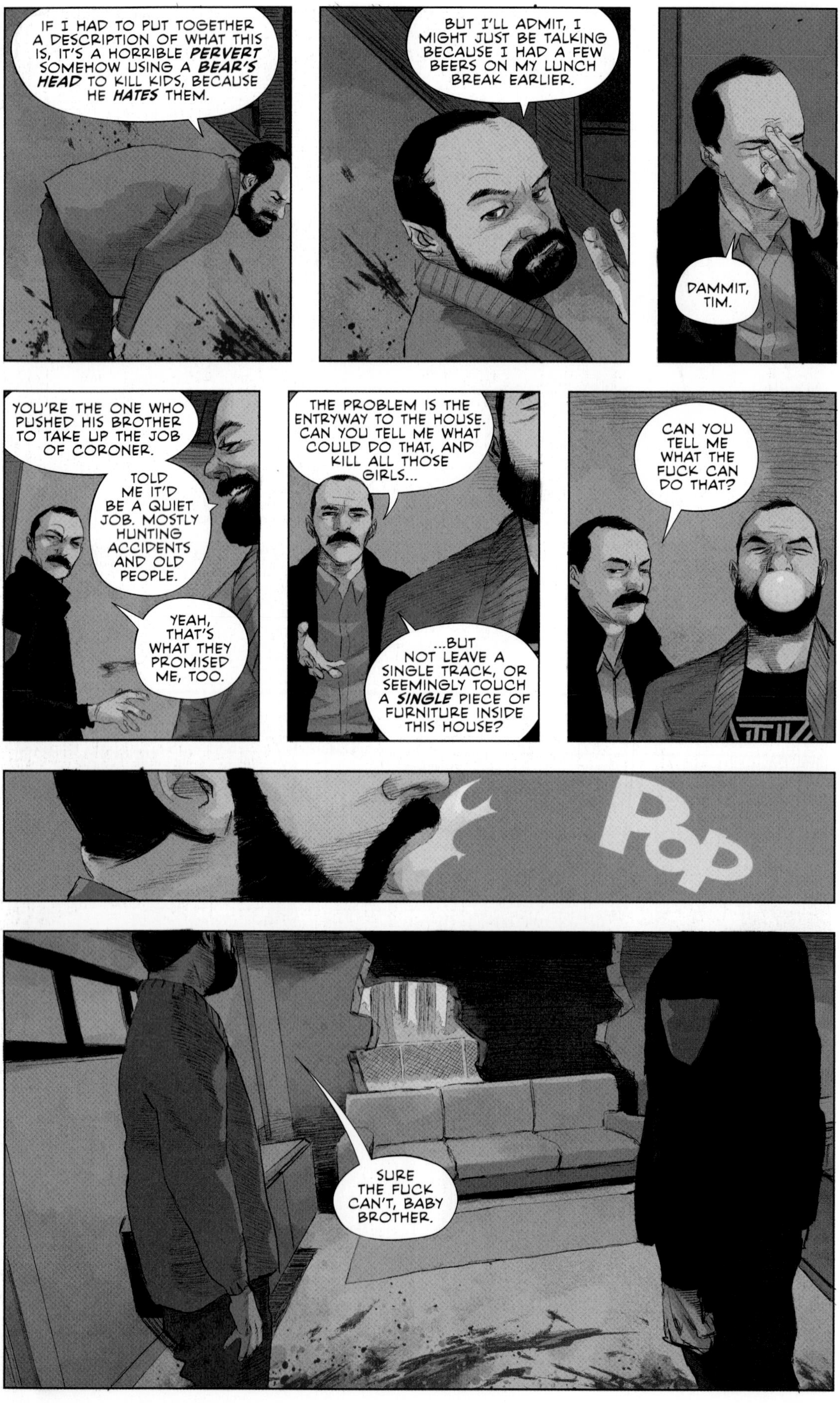
IF I HAD TO PUT TOGETHER A DESCRIPTION OF WHAT THIS IS, IT'S A HORRIBLE PERVERT SOMEHOW USING A BEAR'S HEAD TO KILL KIDS, BECAUSE HE HATES THEM.
BUT I'LL ADMIT, I MIGHT JUST BE TALKING BECAUSE I HAD A FEW BEERS ON MY LUNCH BREAK EARLIER.
DAMMIT, TIM.
YOU'RE THE ONE WHO PUSHED HIS BROTHER TO TAKE UP THE JOB OF CORONER.
TOLD ME IT'D BE A QUIET JOB. MOSTLY HUNTING ACCIDENTS AND OLD PEOPLE.
YEAH, THAT'S WHAT THEY PROMISED ME, TOO.
THE PROBLEM IS THE ENTRYWAY TO THE HOUSE. CAN YOU TELL ME WHAT COULD DO THAT, AND KILL ALL THOSE GIRLS...
...BUT NOT LEAVE A SINGLE TRACK, OR SEEMINGLY TOUCH A SINGLE PIECE OF FURNITURE INSIDE THIS HOUSE?
CAN YOU TELL ME WHAT THE FUCK CAN DO THAT?
POP
SURE THE FUCK CAN'T, BABY BROTHER.

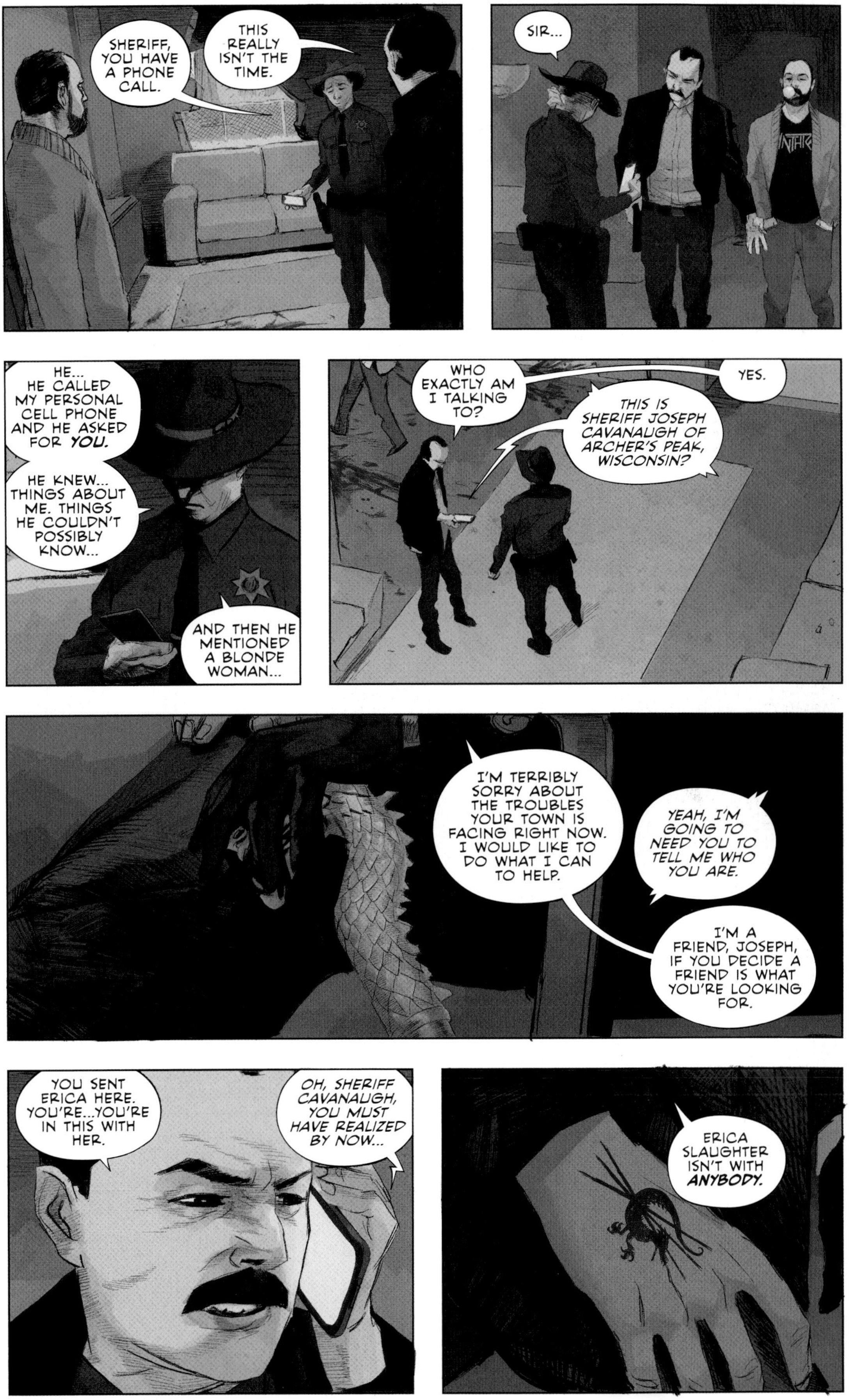
SHERIFF, YOU HAVE A PHONE CALL.
THIS REALLY ISN'T THE TIME.
SIR...
HE... HE CALLED MY PERSONAL CELL PHONE AND HE ASKED FOR *YOU.*
HE KNEW... THINGS ABOUT ME. THINGS HE COULDN'T POSSIBLY KNOW...
AND THEN HE MENTIONED A BLONDE WOMAN...
WHO EXACTLY AM I TALKING TO?
THIS IS SHERIFF JOSEPH CAVANAUGH OF ARCHER'S PEAK, WISCONSIN?
YES.
I'M TERRIBLY SORRY ABOUT THE TROUBLES YOUR TOWN IS FACING RIGHT NOW. I WOULD LIKE TO DO WHAT I CAN TO HELP.
YEAH, I'M GOING TO NEED YOU TO TELL ME WHO YOU ARE.
I'M A FRIEND, JOSEPH, IF YOU DECIDE A FRIEND IS WHAT YOU'RE LOOKING FOR.
YOU SENT ERICA HERE. YOU'RE...YOU'RE IN THIS WITH HER.
OH, SHERIFF CAVANAUGH, YOU MUST HAVE REALIZED BY NOW...
ERICA SLAUGHTER ISN'T WITH ***ANYBODY.***

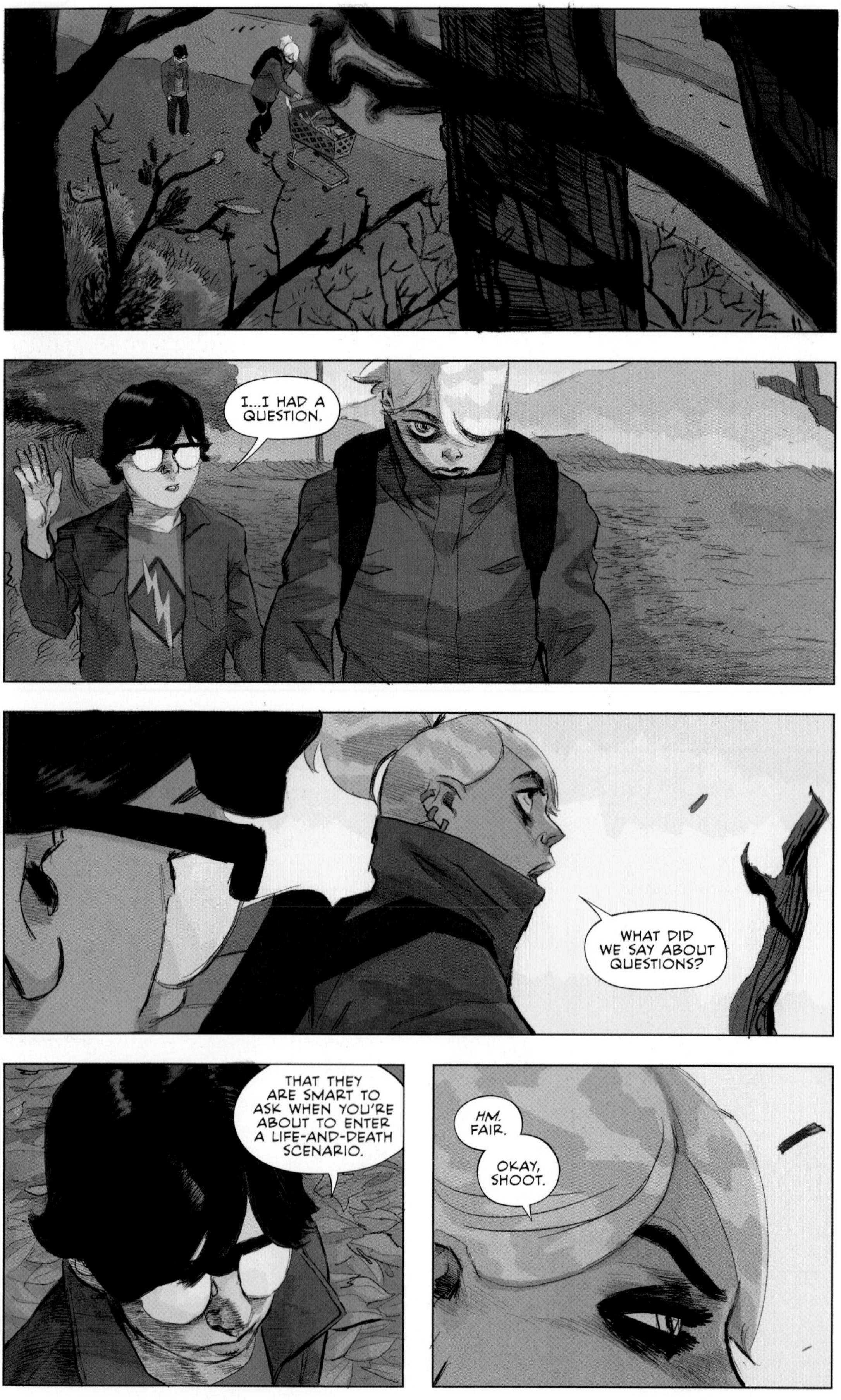
I...I HAD A QUESTION.
WHAT DID WE SAY ABOUT QUESTIONS?
THAT THEY ARE SMART TO ASK WHEN YOU'RE ABOUT TO ENTER A LIFE-AND-DEATH SCENARIO.
HM. FAIR.
OKAY, SHOOT.

WHAT ARE MONSTERS?

THEY'RE BIG SCARY THINGS THAT EAT CHILDREN.

OKAY.

WHAT, DID YOU THINK THERE WAS A BIGGER ANSWER THAN THAT?

I MEAN, YEAH. OF COURSE. THERE *HAS* TO BE A BIGGER ANSWER THAN THAT.

MONSTERS AREN'T *REAL.*

OF COURSE THEY ARE. YOU'VE SEEN ONE OF THEM. IT ATE YOUR FRIENDS.

BUT WHY...*WHY* DID IT EAT MY FRIENDS?

BECAUSE THEY COULD SEE IT. BECAUSE THEY BELIEVED IN IT.

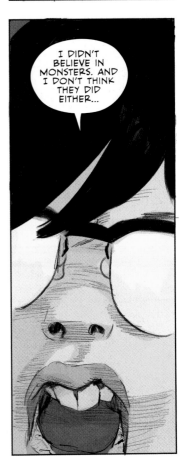

I DIDN'T BELIEVE IN MONSTERS. AND I DON'T THINK THEY DID EITHER...

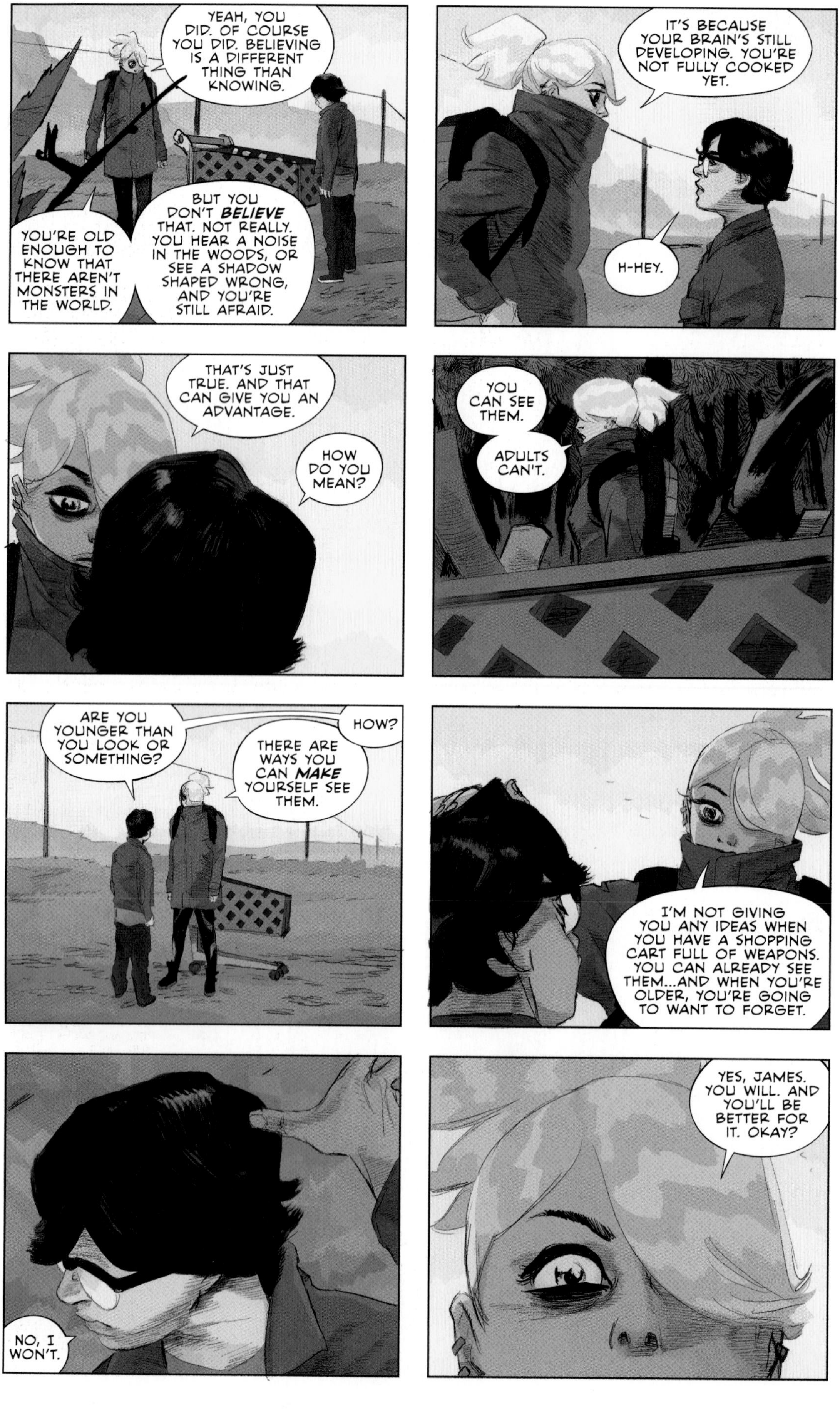
YEAH, YOU DID. OF COURSE YOU DID. BELIEVING IS A DIFFERENT THING THAN KNOWING.
YOU'RE OLD ENOUGH TO KNOW THAT THERE AREN'T MONSTERS IN THE WORLD.
BUT YOU DON'T **BELIEVE** THAT. NOT REALLY. YOU HEAR A NOISE IN THE WOODS, OR SEE A SHADOW SHAPED WRONG, AND YOU'RE STILL AFRAID.
IT'S BECAUSE YOUR BRAIN'S STILL DEVELOPING. YOU'RE NOT FULLY COOKED YET.
H-HEY.
THAT'S JUST TRUE. AND THAT CAN GIVE YOU AN ADVANTAGE.
HOW DO YOU MEAN?
YOU CAN SEE THEM.
ADULTS CAN'T.
ARE YOU YOUNGER THAN YOU LOOK OR SOMETHING?
HOW?
THERE ARE WAYS YOU CAN **MAKE** YOURSELF SEE THEM.
I'M NOT GIVING YOU ANY IDEAS WHEN YOU HAVE A SHOPPING CART FULL OF WEAPONS. YOU CAN ALREADY SEE THEM...AND WHEN YOU'RE OLDER, YOU'RE GOING TO WANT TO FORGET.
NO, I WON'T.
YES, JAMES. YOU WILL. AND YOU'LL BE BETTER FOR IT. OKAY?

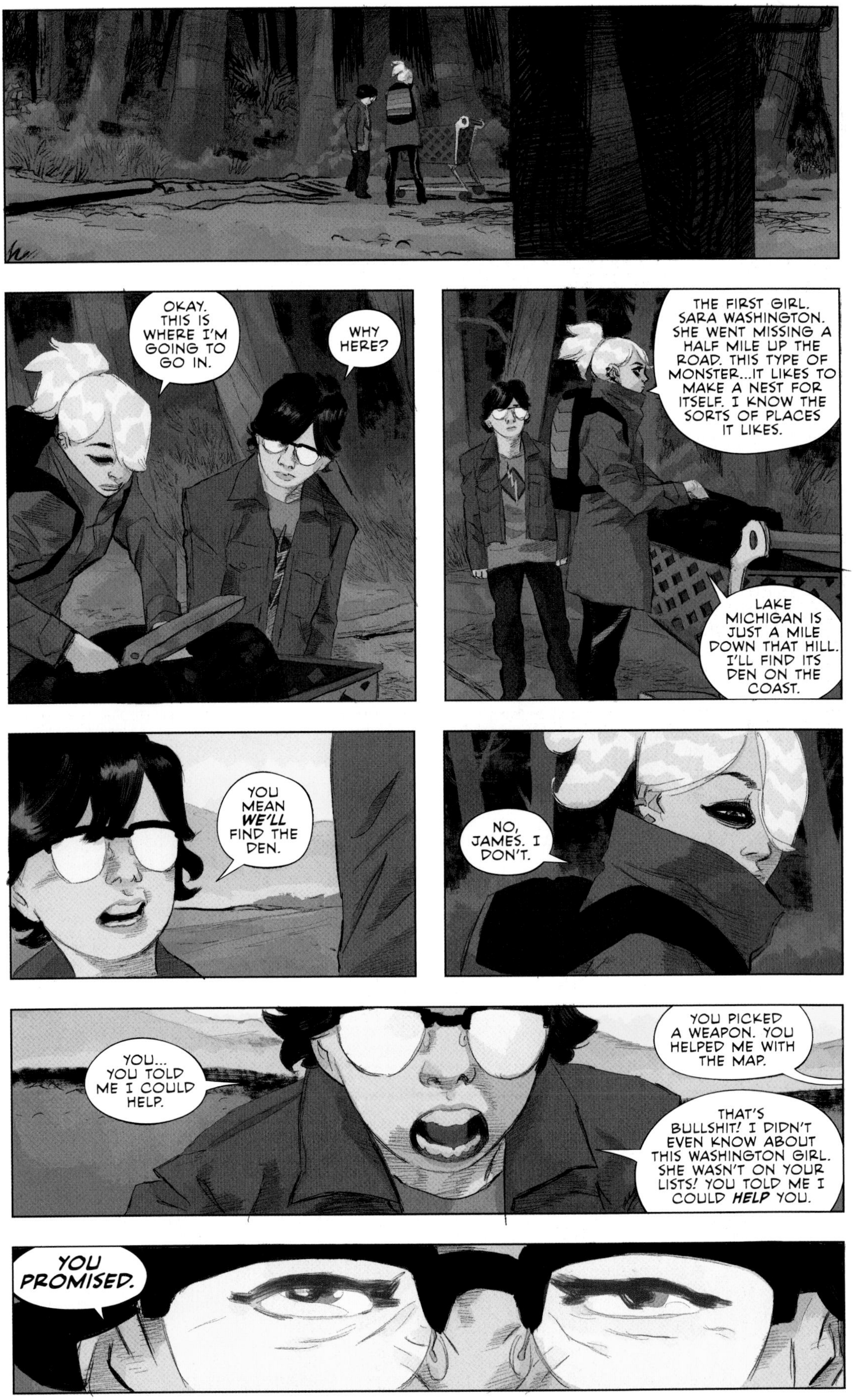
OKAY. THIS IS WHERE I'M GOING TO GO IN.
WHY HERE?
THE FIRST GIRL. SARA WASHINGTON. SHE WENT MISSING A HALF MILE UP THE ROAD. THIS TYPE OF MONSTER...IT LIKES TO MAKE A NEST FOR ITSELF. I KNOW THE SORTS OF PLACES IT LIKES.
LAKE MICHIGAN IS JUST A MILE DOWN THAT HILL. I'LL FIND ITS DEN ON THE COAST.
YOU MEAN WE'LL FIND THE DEN.
NO, JAMES. I DON'T.
YOU... YOU TOLD ME I COULD HELP.
YOU PICKED A WEAPON. YOU HELPED ME WITH THE MAP.
THAT'S BULLSHIT! I DIDN'T EVEN KNOW ABOUT THIS WASHINGTON GIRL. SHE WASN'T ON YOUR LISTS! YOU TOLD ME I COULD HELP YOU.
YOU PROMISED.

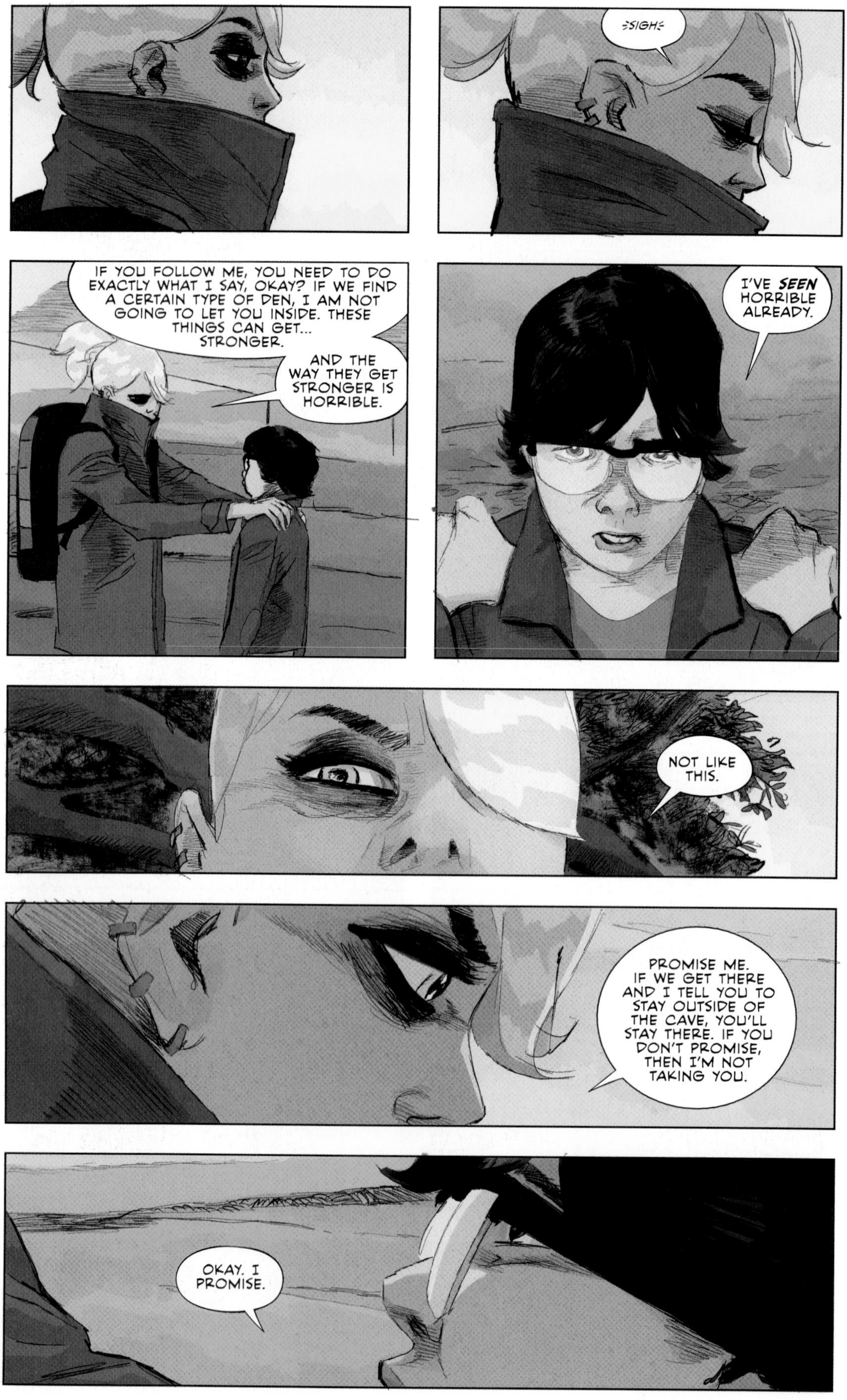

=SIGH=
IF YOU FOLLOW ME, YOU NEED TO DO EXACTLY WHAT I SAY, OKAY? IF WE FIND A CERTAIN TYPE OF DEN, I AM NOT GOING TO LET YOU INSIDE. THESE THINGS CAN GET... STRONGER.
AND THE WAY THEY GET STRONGER IS HORRIBLE.
I'VE SEEN HORRIBLE ALREADY.
NOT LIKE THIS.
PROMISE ME. IF WE GET THERE AND I TELL YOU TO STAY OUTSIDE OF THE CAVE, YOU'LL STAY THERE. IF YOU DON'T PROMISE, THEN I'M NOT TAKING YOU.
OKAY. I PROMISE.

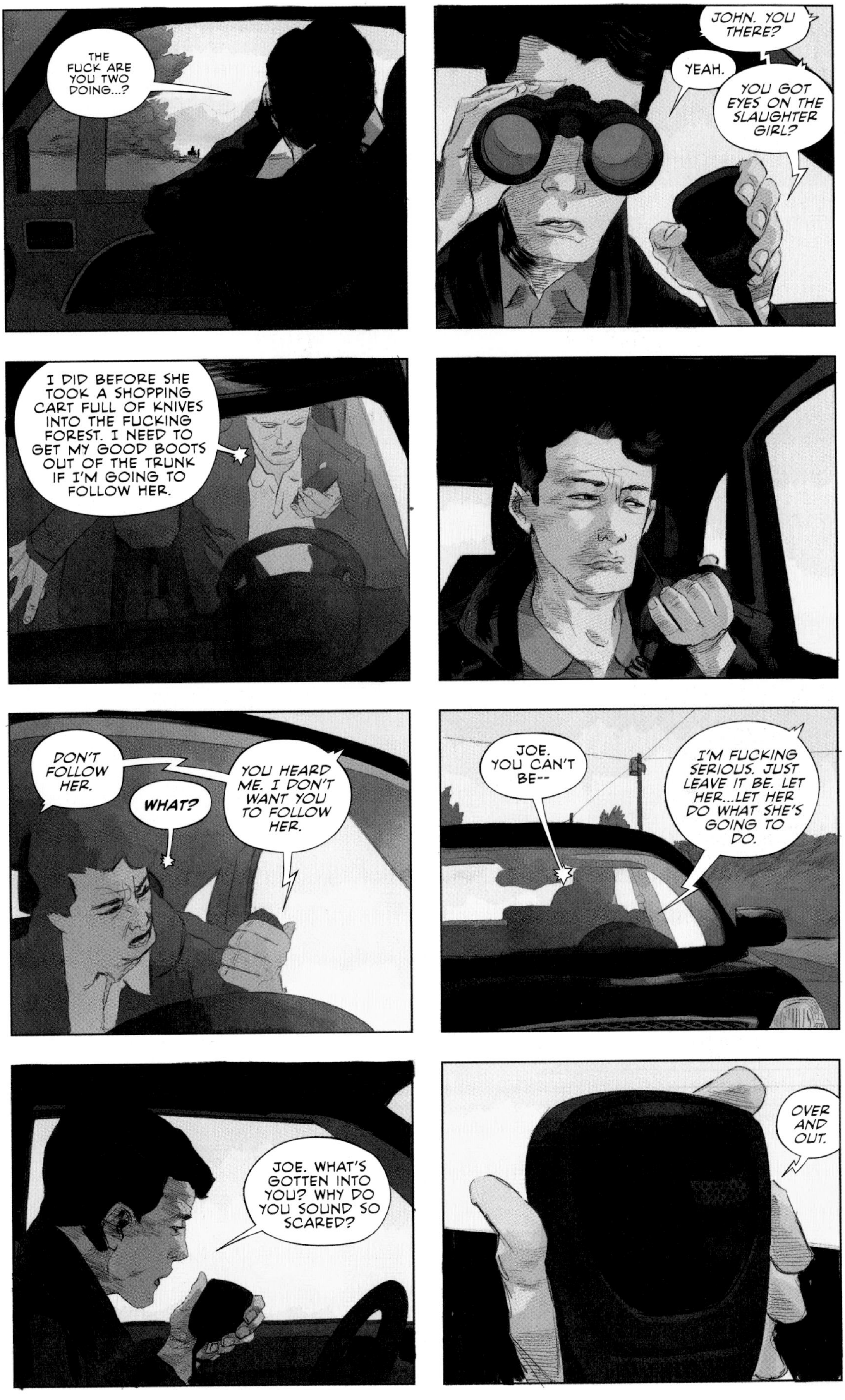
THE FUCK ARE YOU TWO DOING...?
JOHN. YOU THERE?
YEAH.
YOU GOT EYES ON THE SLAUGHTER GIRL?
I DID BEFORE SHE TOOK A SHOPPING CART FULL OF KNIVES INTO THE FUCKING FOREST. I NEED TO GET MY GOOD BOOTS OUT OF THE TRUNK IF I'M GOING TO FOLLOW HER.
DON'T FOLLOW HER.
WHAT?
YOU HEARD ME. I DON'T WANT YOU TO FOLLOW HER.
JOE. YOU CAN'T BE--
I'M FUCKING SERIOUS. JUST LEAVE IT BE. LET HER...LET HER DO WHAT SHE'S GOING TO DO.
JOE. WHAT'S GOTTEN INTO YOU? WHY DO YOU SOUND SO SCARED?
OVER AND OUT.

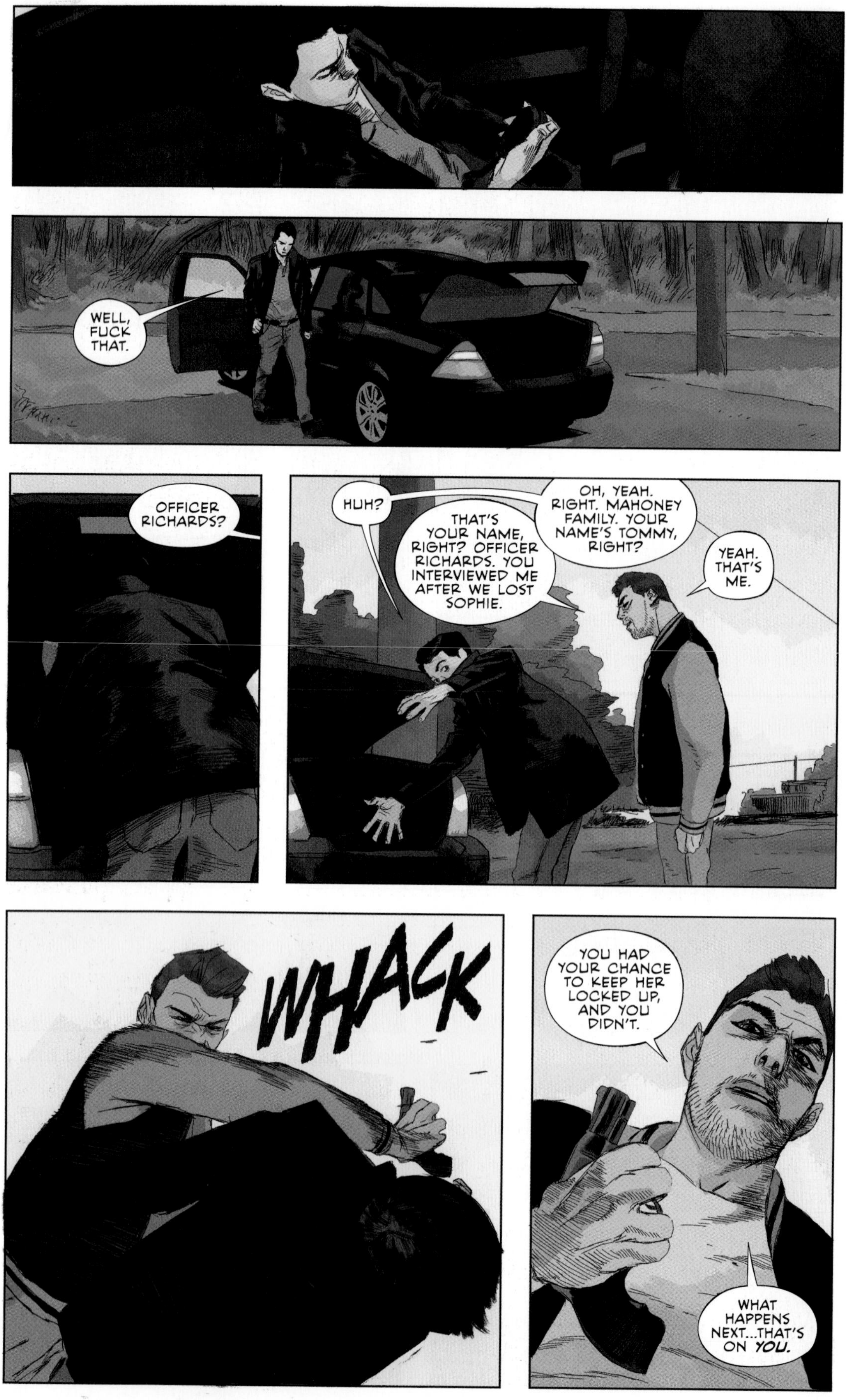
WELL, FUCK THAT.
OFFICER RICHARDS?
HUH?
THAT'S YOUR NAME, RIGHT? OFFICER RICHARDS. YOU INTERVIEWED ME AFTER WE LOST SOPHIE.
OH, YEAH. RIGHT. MAHONEY FAMILY. YOUR NAME'S TOMMY, RIGHT?
YEAH. THAT'S ME.
WHACK
YOU HAD YOUR CHANCE TO KEEP HER LOCKED UP, AND YOU DIDN'T.
WHAT HAPPENS NEXT...THAT'S ON YOU.

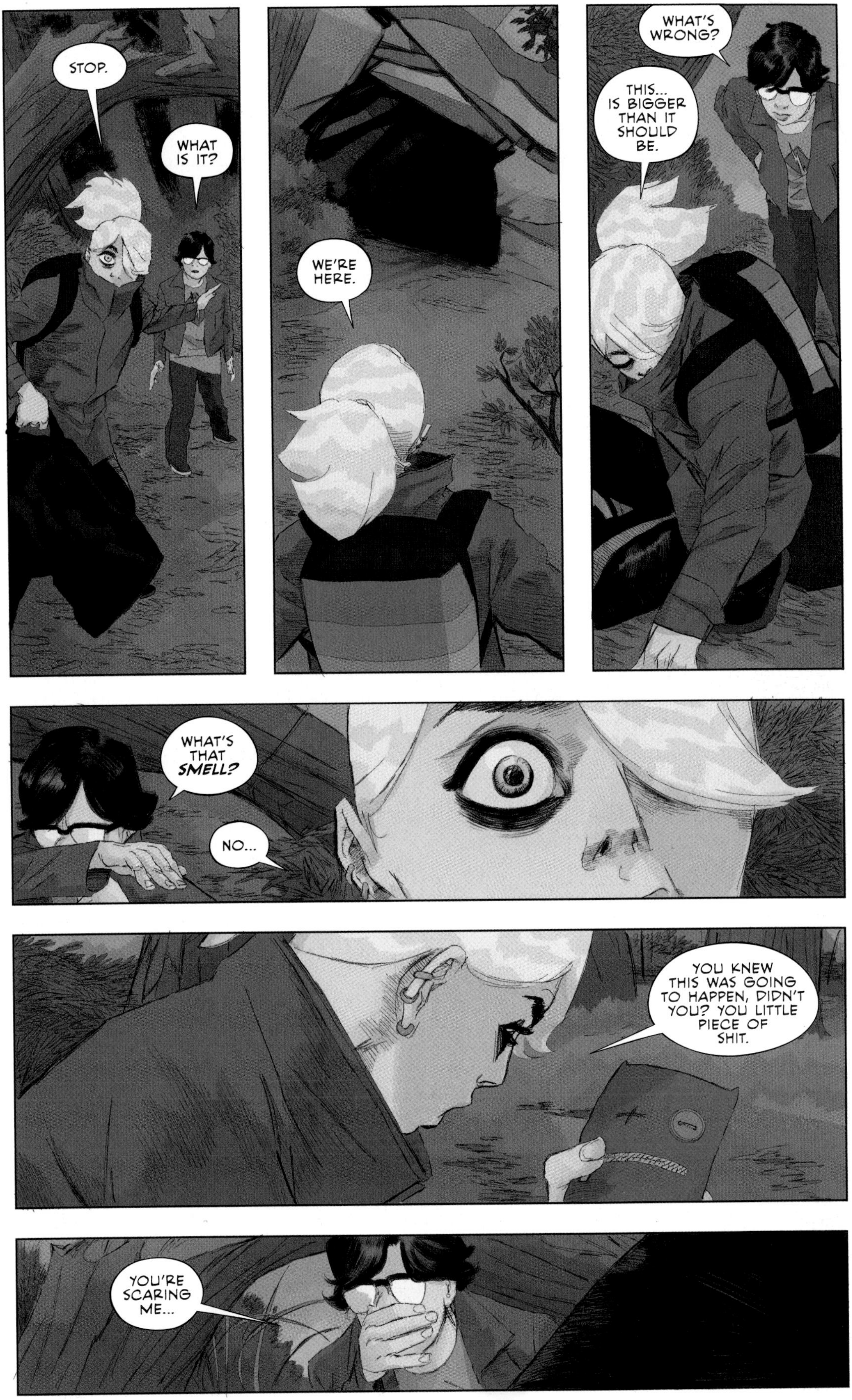
STOP.
WHAT IS IT?
WE'RE HERE.
WHAT'S WRONG?
THIS... IS BIGGER THAN IT SHOULD BE.
WHAT'S THAT *SMELL?*
NO...
YOU KNEW THIS WAS GOING TO HAPPEN, DIDN'T YOU? YOU LITTLE PIECE OF SHIT.
YOU'RE SCARING ME...

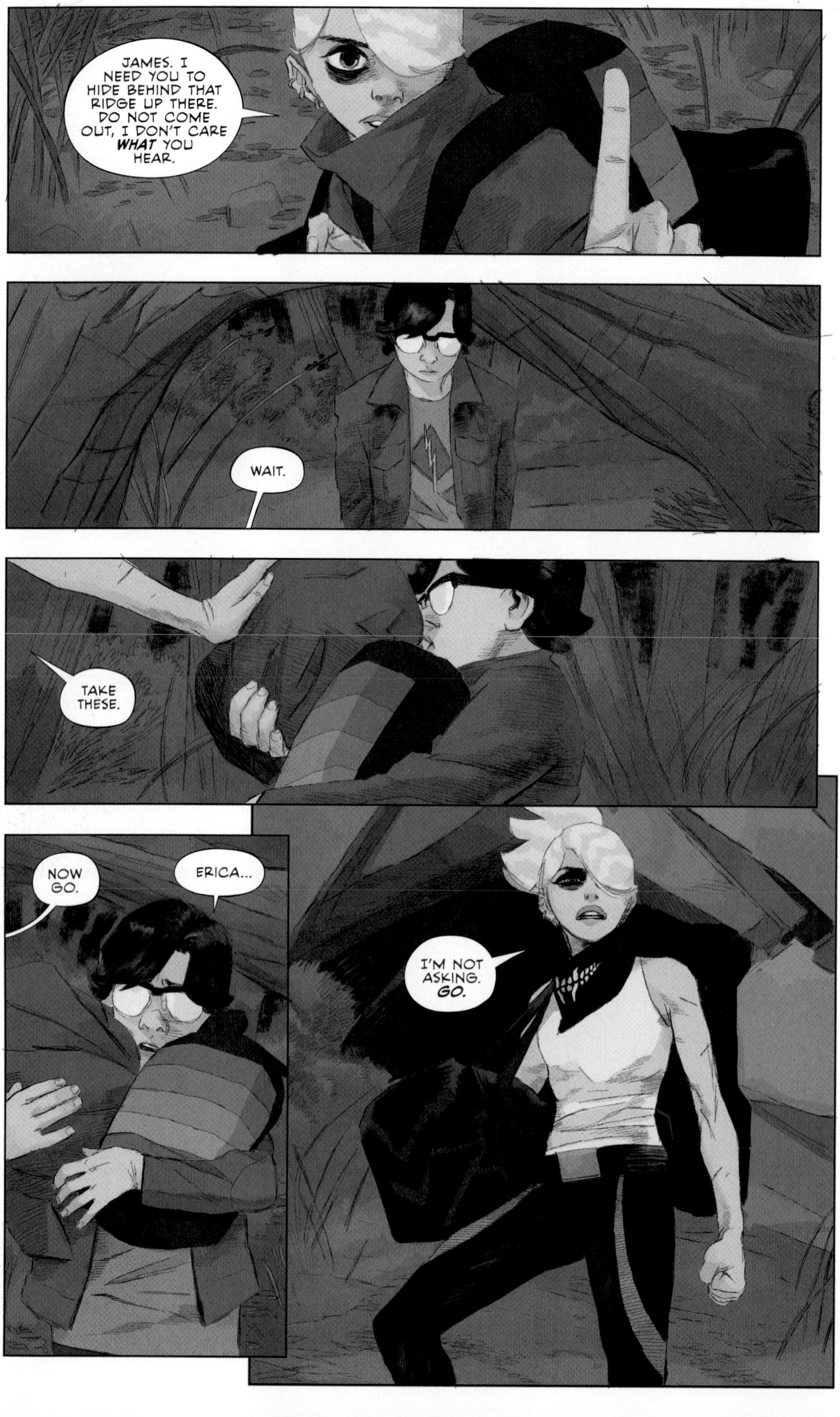
JAMES. I NEED YOU TO HIDE BEHIND THAT RIDGE UP THERE. DO NOT COME OUT, I DON'T CARE **WHAT** YOU HEAR.
WAIT.
TAKE THESE.
ERICA...
NOW GO.
I'M NOT ASKING. **GO.**

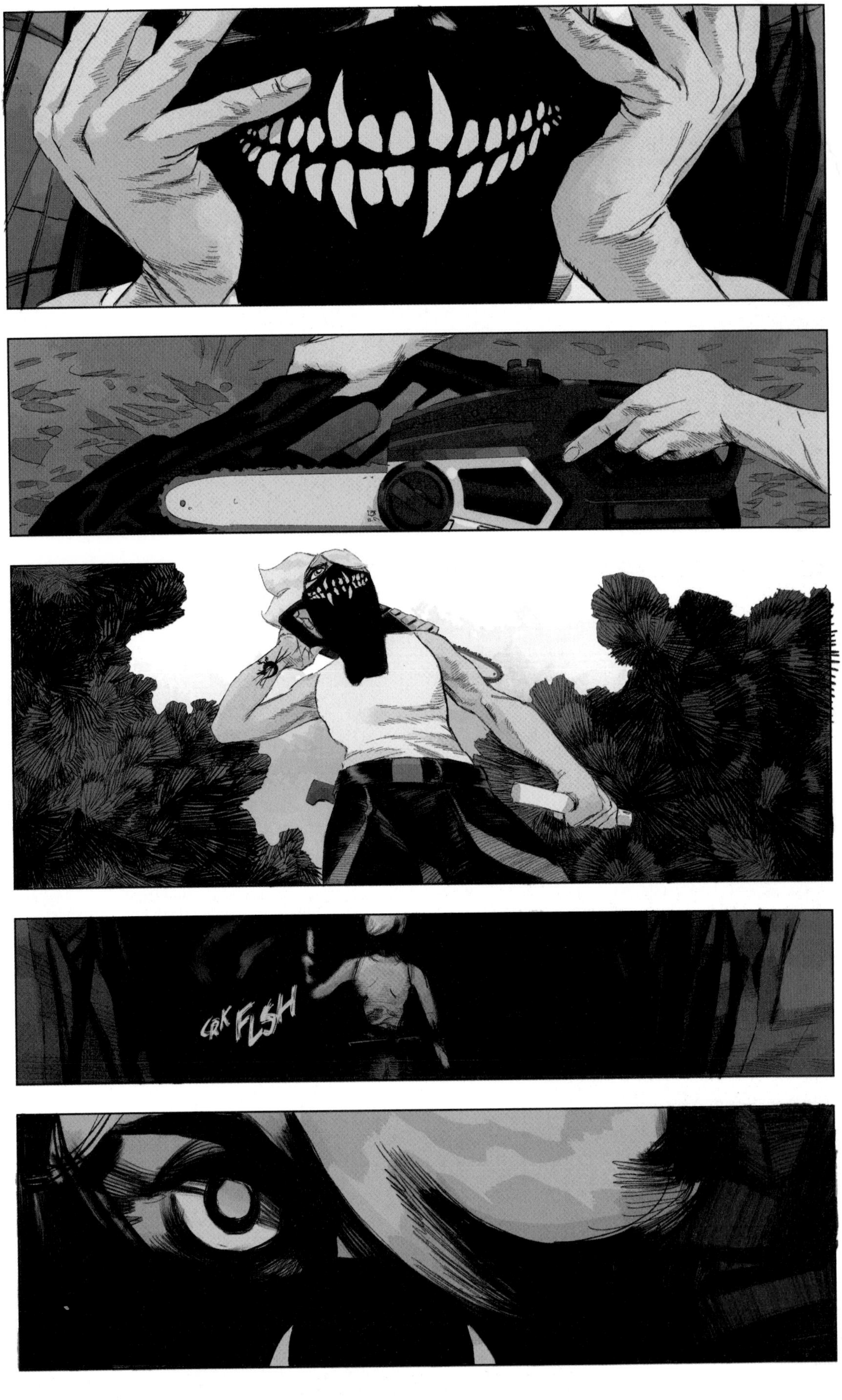
CRK FLSH

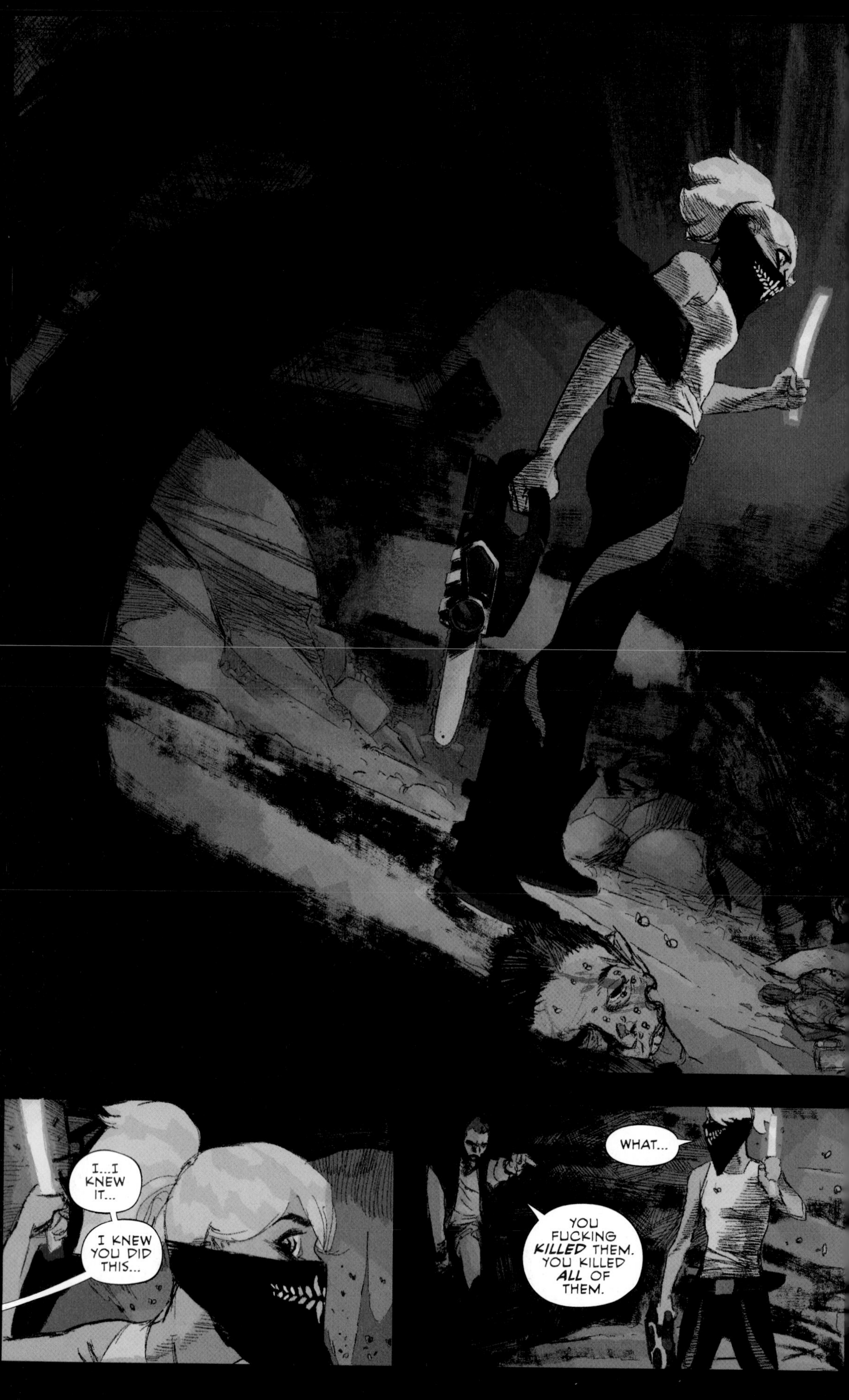
I...I KNEW IT...
I KNEW YOU DID THIS...
WHAT...
YOU FUCKING KILLED THEM. YOU KILLED ALL OF THEM.

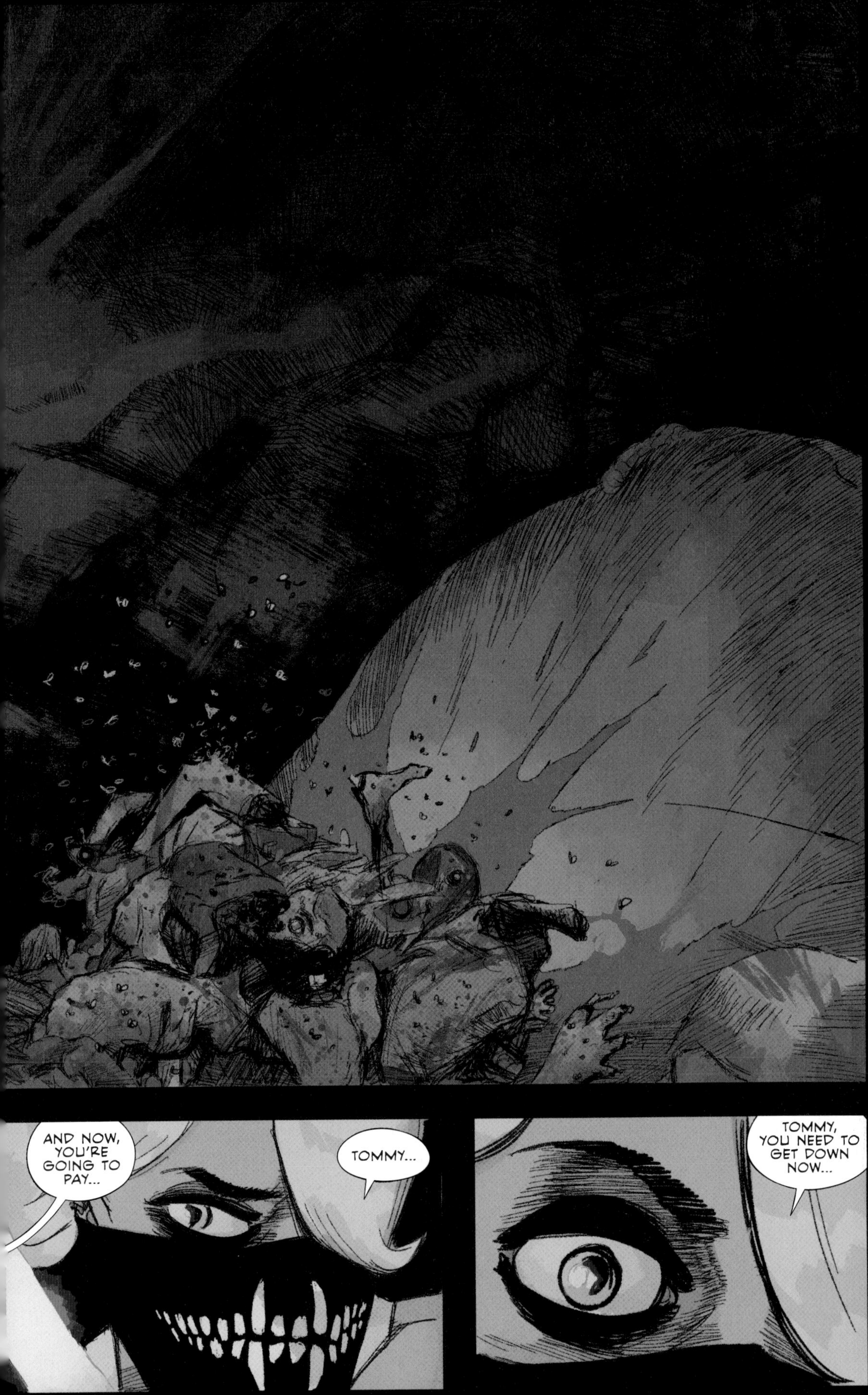
AND NOW, YOU'RE GOING TO PAY...
TOMMY...
TOMMY, YOU NEED TO GET DOWN NOW...

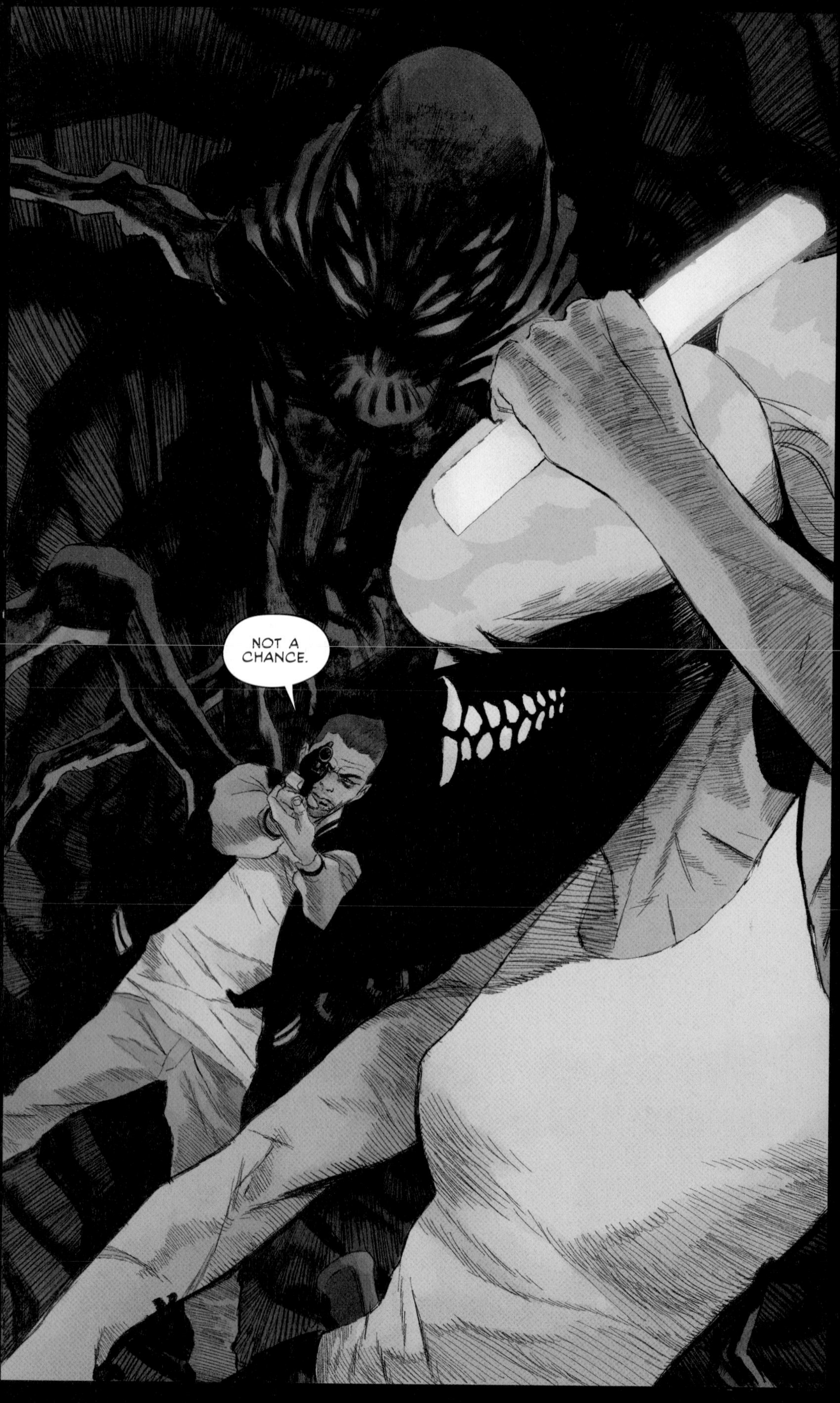
NOT A CHANCE.

CHAPTER
FIVE

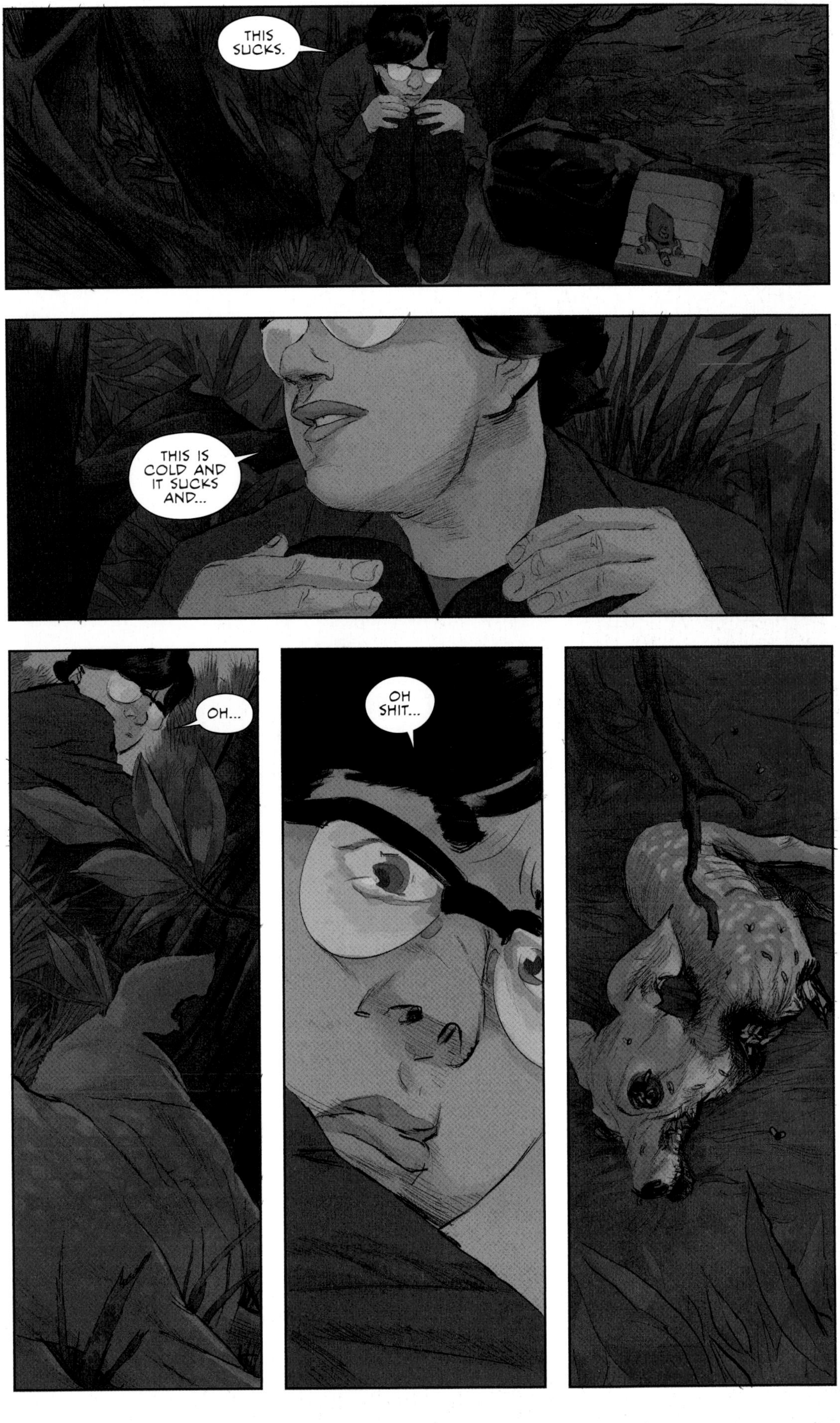
THIS SUCKS.
THIS IS COLD AND IT SUCKS AND...
OH...
OH SHIT...

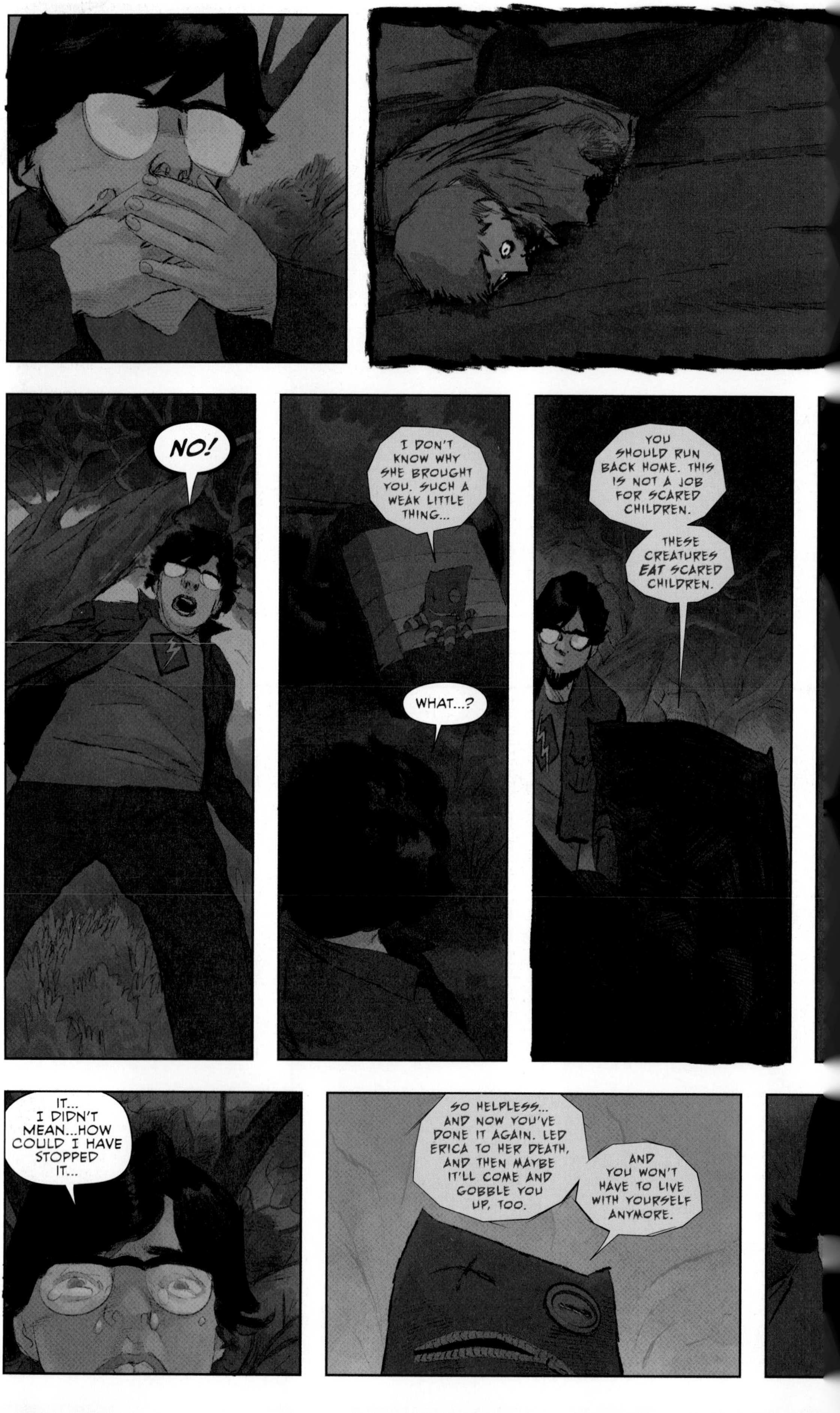
NO!
I DON'T KNOW WHY SHE BROUGHT YOU. SUCH A WEAK LITTLE THING...
WHAT...?
YOU SHOULD RUN BACK HOME. THIS IS NOT A JOB FOR SCARED CHILDREN.
THESE CREATURES EAT SCARED CHILDREN.
IT... I DIDN'T MEAN...HOW COULD I HAVE STOPPED IT...
SO HELPLESS... AND NOW YOU'VE DONE IT AGAIN. LED ERICA TO HER DEATH, AND THEN MAYBE IT'LL COME AND GOBBLE YOU UP, TOO.
AND YOU WON'T HAVE TO LIVE WITH YOURSELF ANYMORE.

NO.

I'M...I'M NOT *AFRAID!* AND YOU'RE... YOU'RE NOT REAL.

YES, THAT'S RIGHT. I'M NOT REAL. THIS IS ALL A NIGHTMARE. A NIGHTMARE THAT GUTTED YOUR FRIENDS. IT'S EASIER TO THINK THAT WAY, YES?

SO YOU DON'T HAVE TO FACE THAT YOU LED THEM DOWN INTO THE DARK WOODS LATE AT NIGHT, TO THEIR DEATHS.

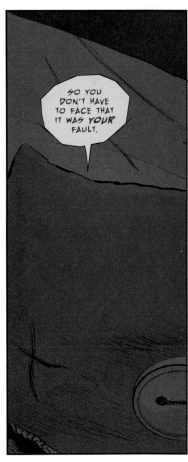

SO YOU DON'T HAVE TO FACE THAT IT WAS *YOUR* FAULT.

THAT'S NOT WHAT I WANT!

THEN *DO* SOMETHING ABOUT IT.

YOU HAVE THE WEAPONS SHE DOESN'T. YOU HAVE THE MEANS TO HELP.

IF YOU DON'T WANT ERICA TO DIE, NOW IS THE TIME TO *ACT.*

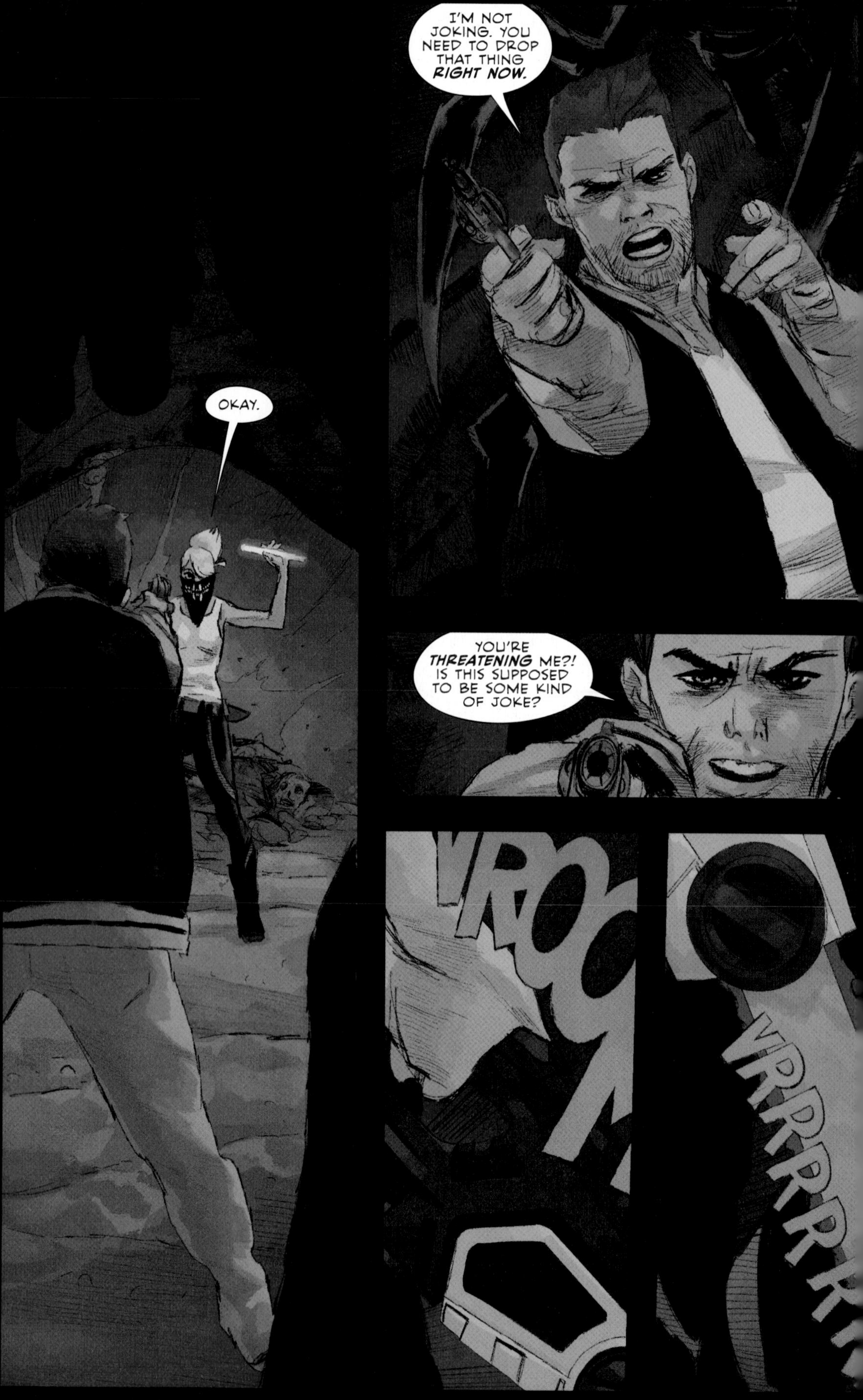
OKAY.
I'M NOT JOKING. YOU NEED TO DROP THAT THING RIGHT NOW.
YOU'RE THREATENING ME?! IS THIS SUPPOSED TO BE SOME KIND OF JOKE?
VROO
VRRRRRR

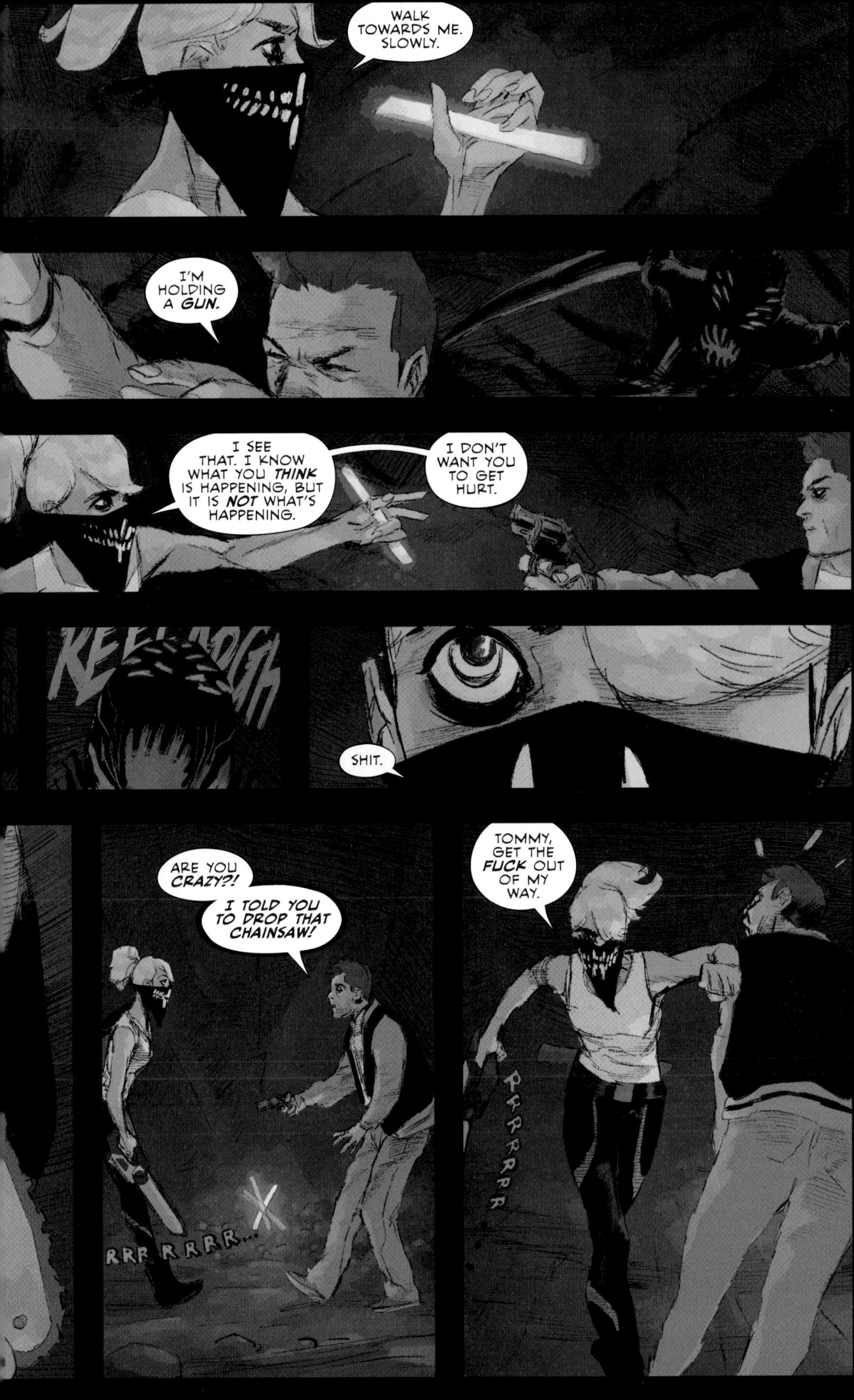
WALK TOWARDS ME. SLOWLY.
I'M HOLDING A GUN.
I SEE THAT. I KNOW WHAT YOU THINK IS HAPPENING, BUT IT IS NOT WHAT'S HAPPENING.
I DON'T WANT YOU TO GET HURT.
SHIT.
ARE YOU CRAZY?!
I TOLD YOU TO DROP THAT CHAINSAW!
RRRRRRR...
TOMMY, GET THE FUCK OUT OF MY WAY.
RRRRRRRR

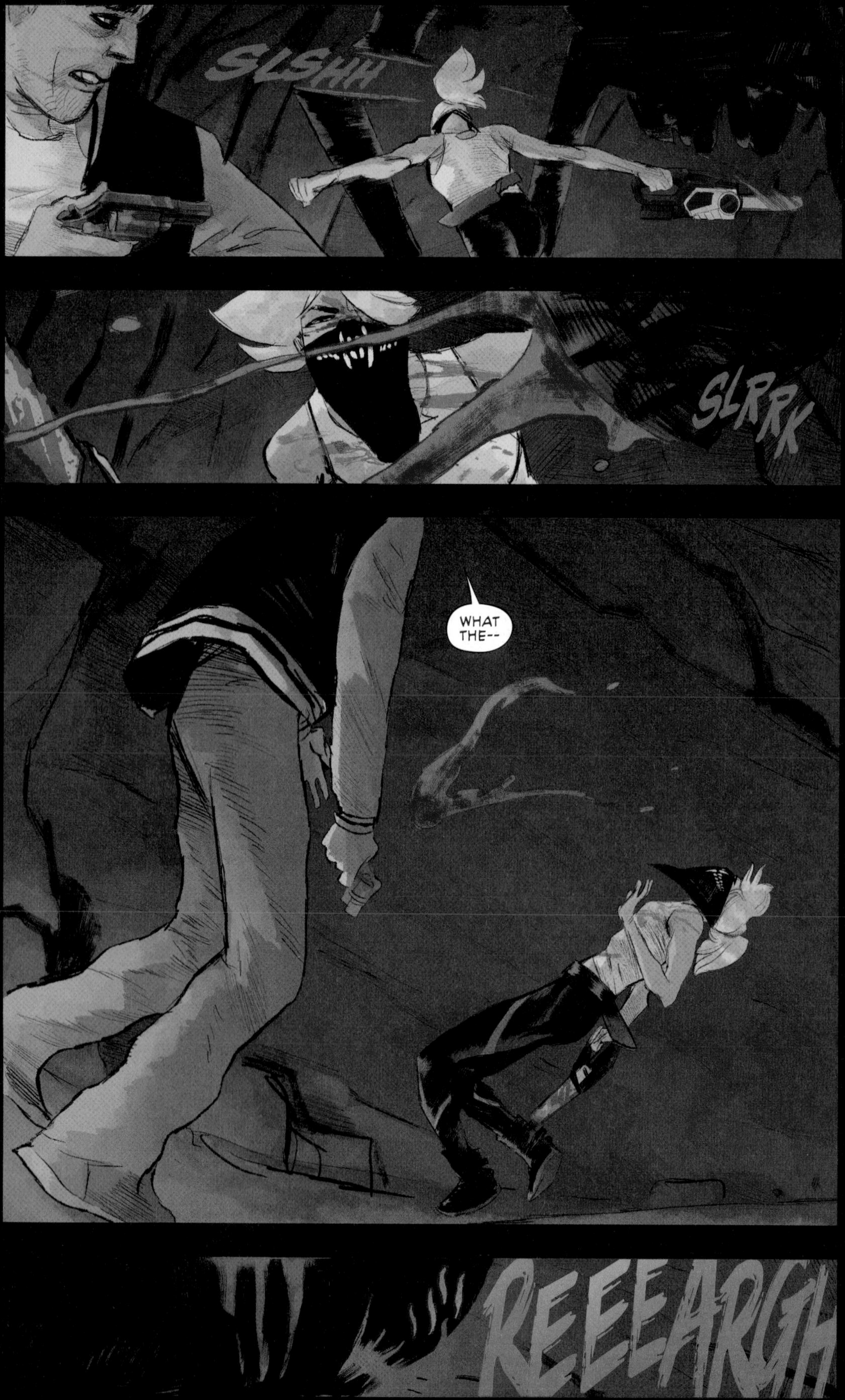
SLSHH
SLRRK
WHAT THE--
REEEARGH

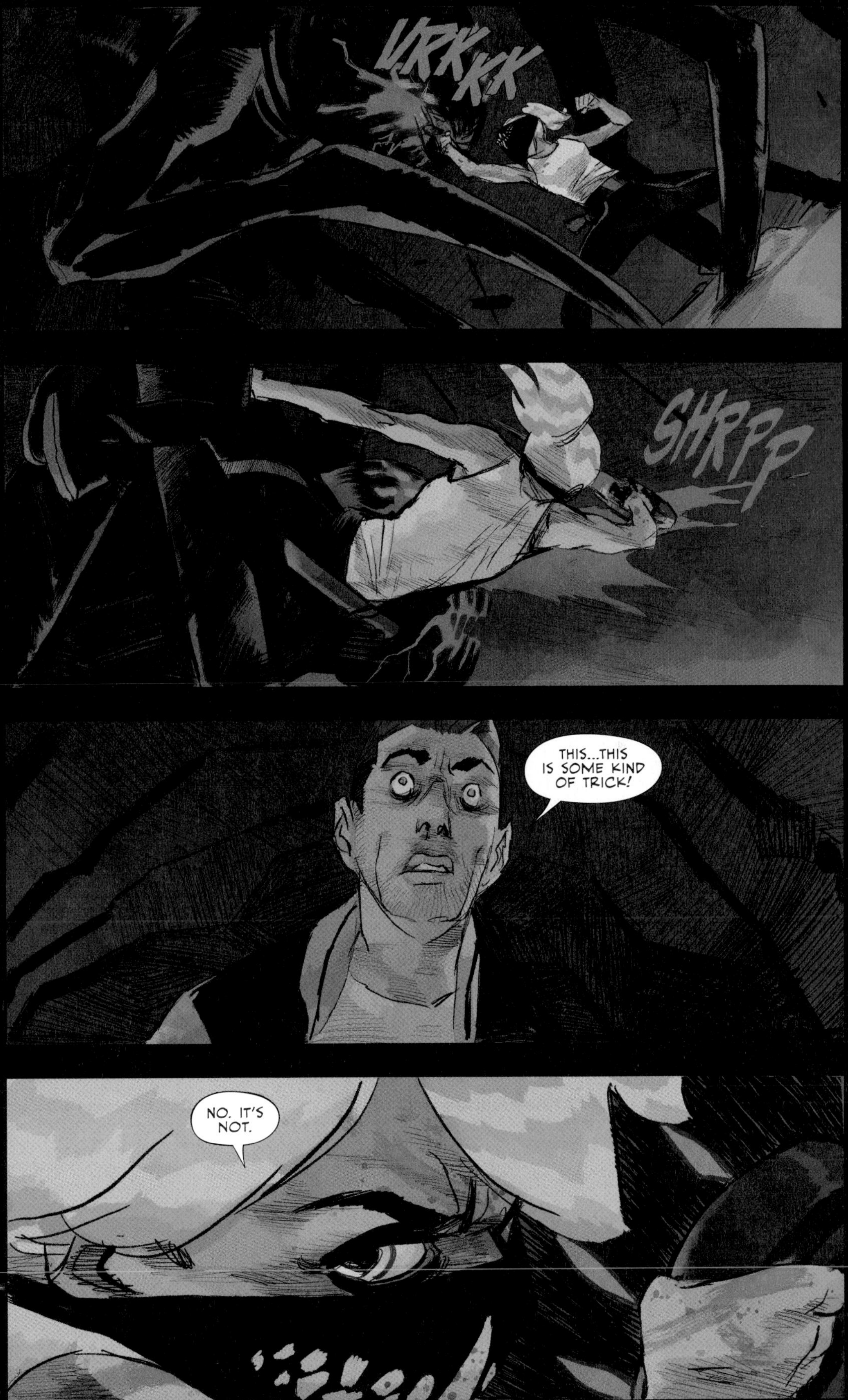
URKKK
SHRPP
THIS...THIS IS SOME KIND OF TRICK!
NO. IT'S NOT.

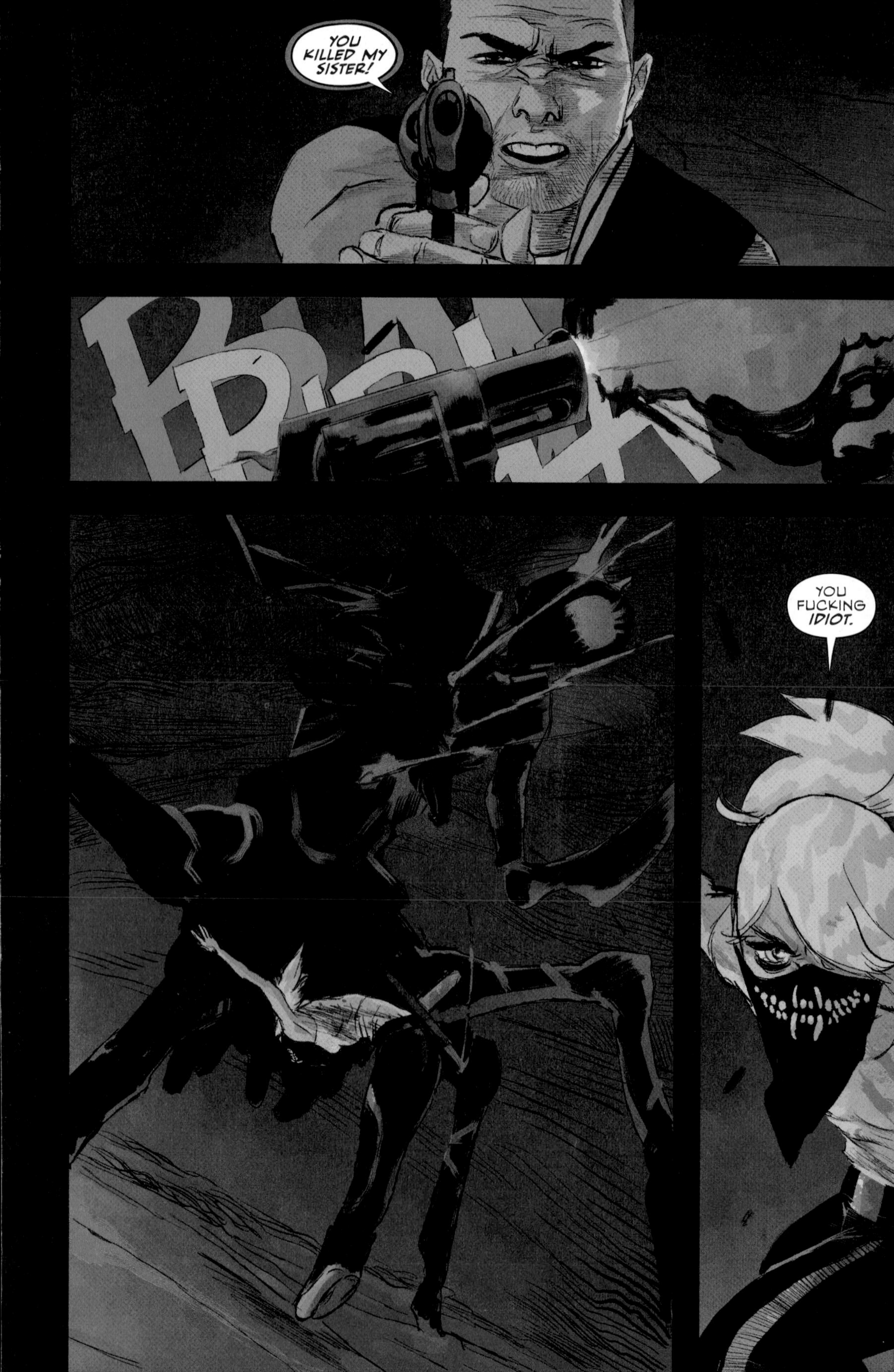
YOU KILLED MY SISTER!
YOU FUCKING *IDIOT.*

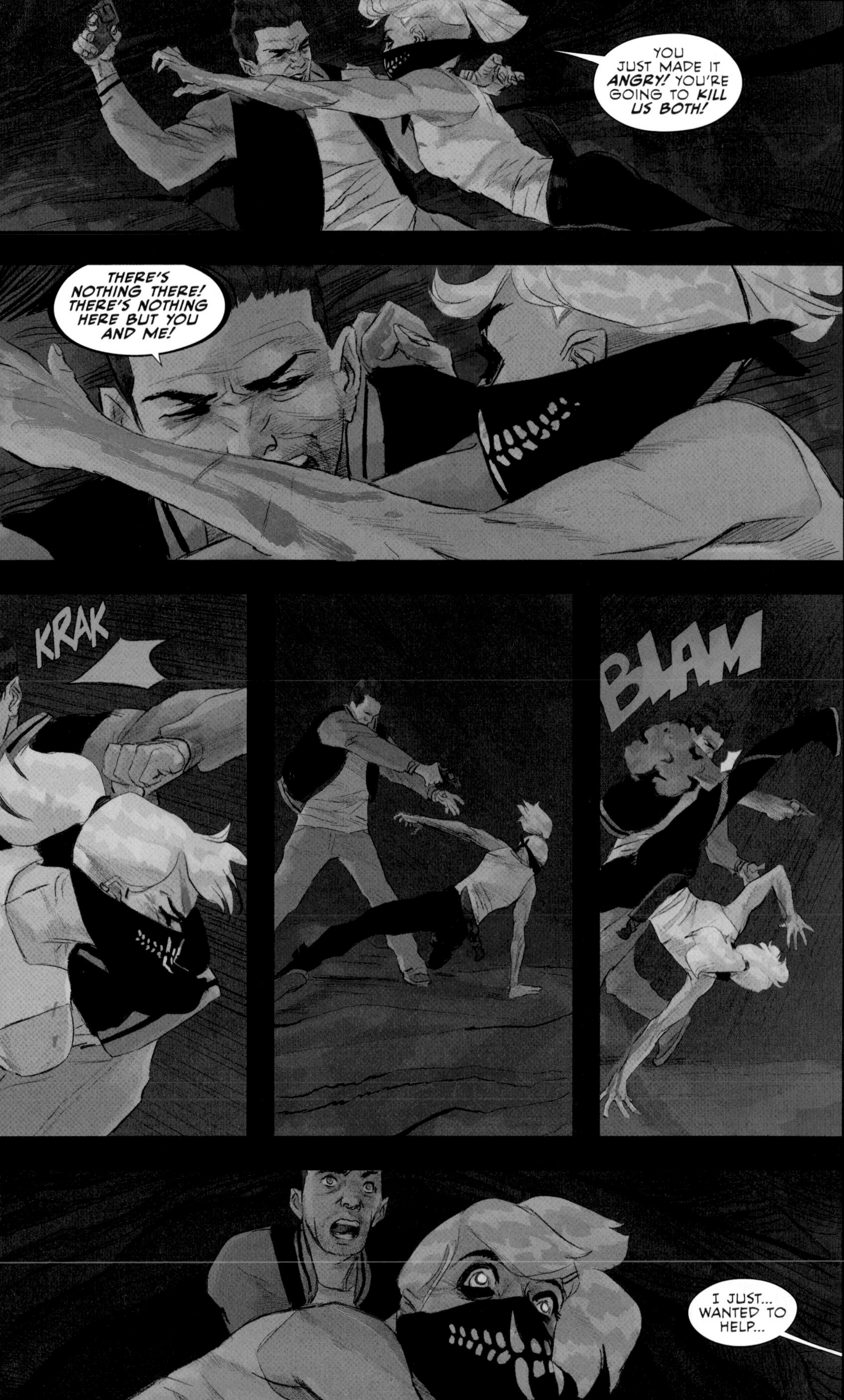
YOU JUST MADE IT ANGRY! YOU'RE GOING TO KILL US BOTH!
THERE'S NOTHING THERE! THERE'S NOTHING HERE BUT YOU AND ME!
KRAK
BLAM
I JUST... WANTED TO HELP...

THOK

OH, WOW. IT HURTS...SO MUCH...

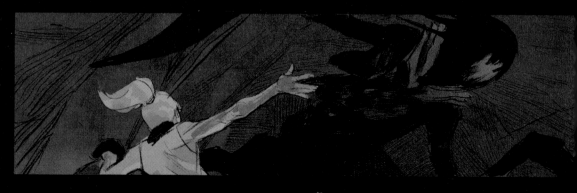

I'VE BEEN SHOT.

NO!

I DIDN'T... I DIDN'T MEAN...

SNNFF

TUNK

I NEED YOUR JACKET. TRY NOT TO SCREAM.

...HUH...?

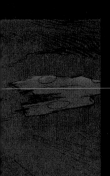

I KNOW YOU'RE IN A LOT OF PAIN RIGHT NOW, BUT I NEED YOU TO STAY QUIET. IF YOU STAY QUIET, I CAN KEEP YOU ALIVE.

O... OKAY.

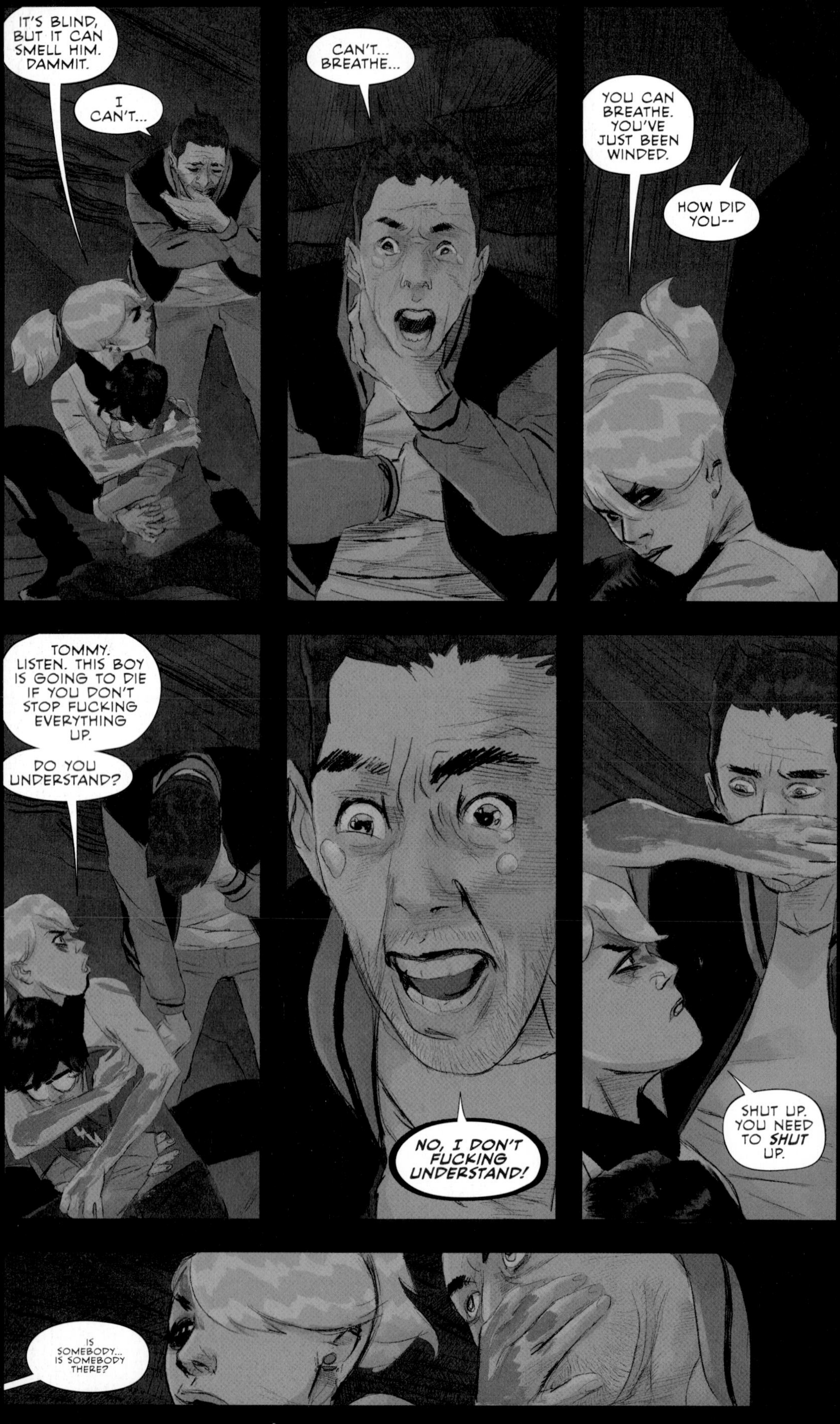
IT'S BLIND, BUT IT CAN SMELL HIM. DAMMIT.
I CAN'T...
CAN'T... BREATHE...
YOU CAN BREATHE. YOU'VE JUST BEEN WINDED.
HOW DID YOU--
TOMMY. LISTEN. THIS BOY IS GOING TO DIE IF YOU DON'T STOP FUCKING EVERYTHING UP.
DO YOU UNDERSTAND?
NO, I DON'T FUCKING UNDERSTAND!
SHUT UP. YOU NEED TO SHUT UP.
IS SOMEBODY... IS SOMEBODY THERE?

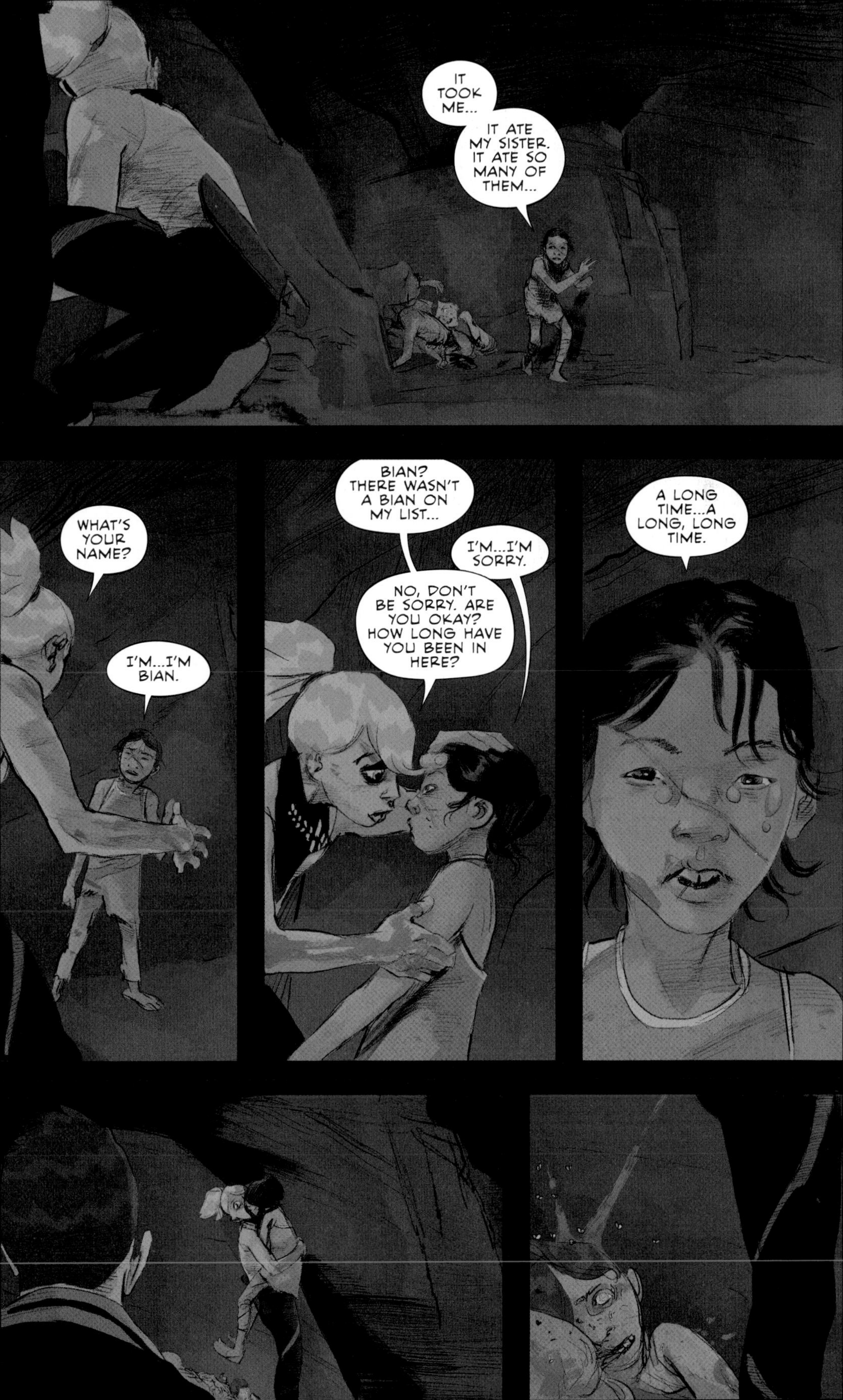
IT TOOK ME...
IT ATE MY SISTER. IT ATE SO MANY OF THEM...
WHAT'S YOUR NAME?
I'M...I'M BIAN.
BIAN? THERE WASN'T A BIAN ON MY LIST...
I'M...I'M SORRY.
NO, DON'T BE SORRY. ARE YOU OKAY? HOW LONG HAVE YOU BEEN IN HERE?
A LONG TIME...A LONG, LONG TIME.

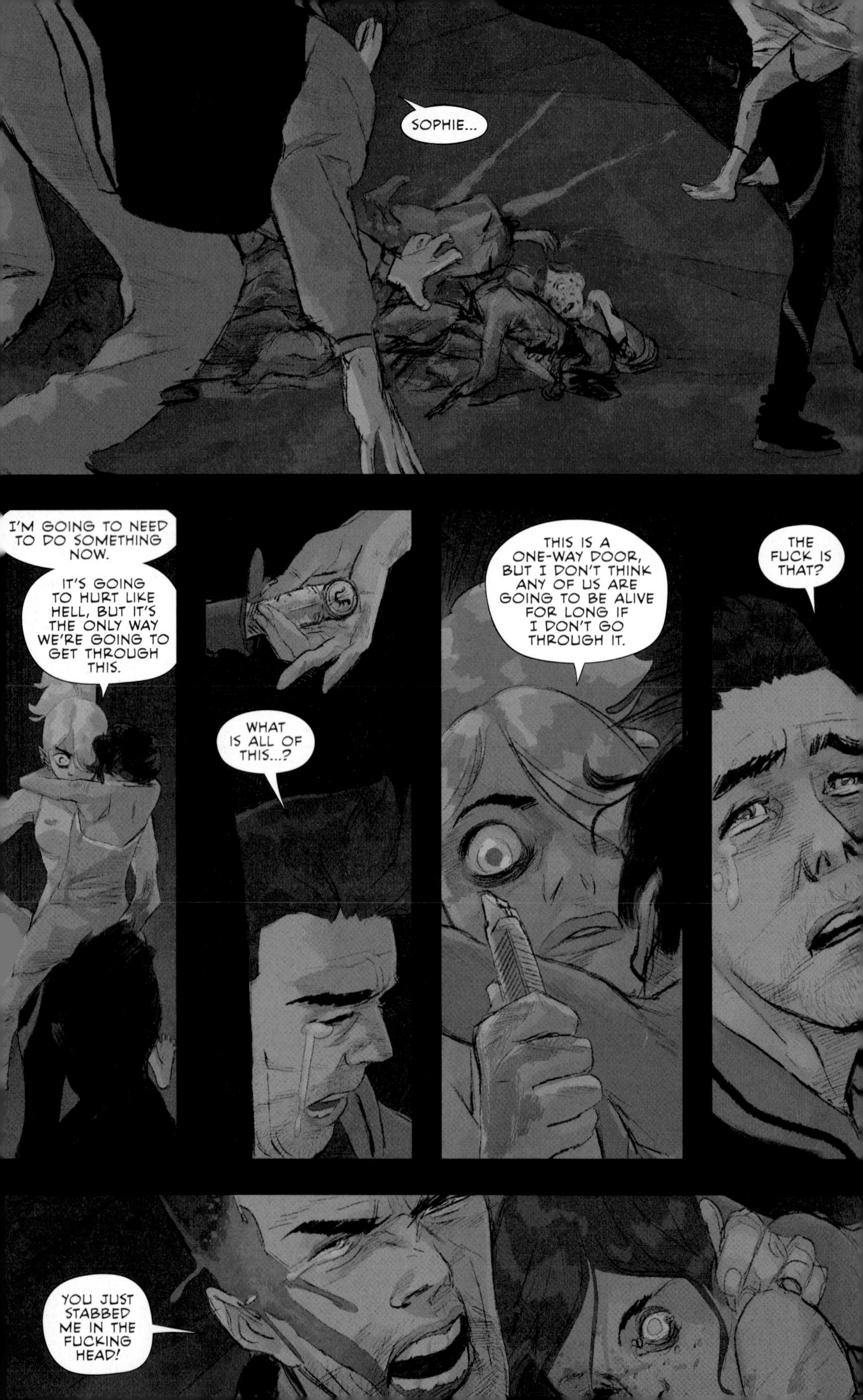
SOPHIE...
I'M GOING TO NEED TO DO SOMETHING NOW.
IT'S GOING TO HURT LIKE HELL, BUT IT'S THE ONLY WAY WE'RE GOING TO GET THROUGH THIS.
WHAT IS ALL OF THIS...?
THIS IS A ONE-WAY DOOR, BUT I DON'T THINK ANY OF US ARE GOING TO BE ALIVE FOR LONG IF I DON'T GO THROUGH IT.
THE FUCK IS THAT?
YOU JUST STABBED ME IN THE FUCKING HEAD!

OH GOD, SOPHIE...
I'M SORRY, I'M SO SORRY...
TOMMY. WE'RE RUNNING OUT OF TIME.
IT'S **HORDE GOLD** FROM THE **HOUSE OF SLAUGHTER.**
I NEED YOU TO SEE.
WHAT ARE YOU--
WHAC
WHAT DID YOU...?
I'M SORRY.

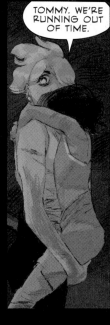

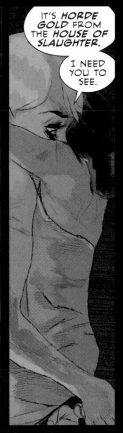

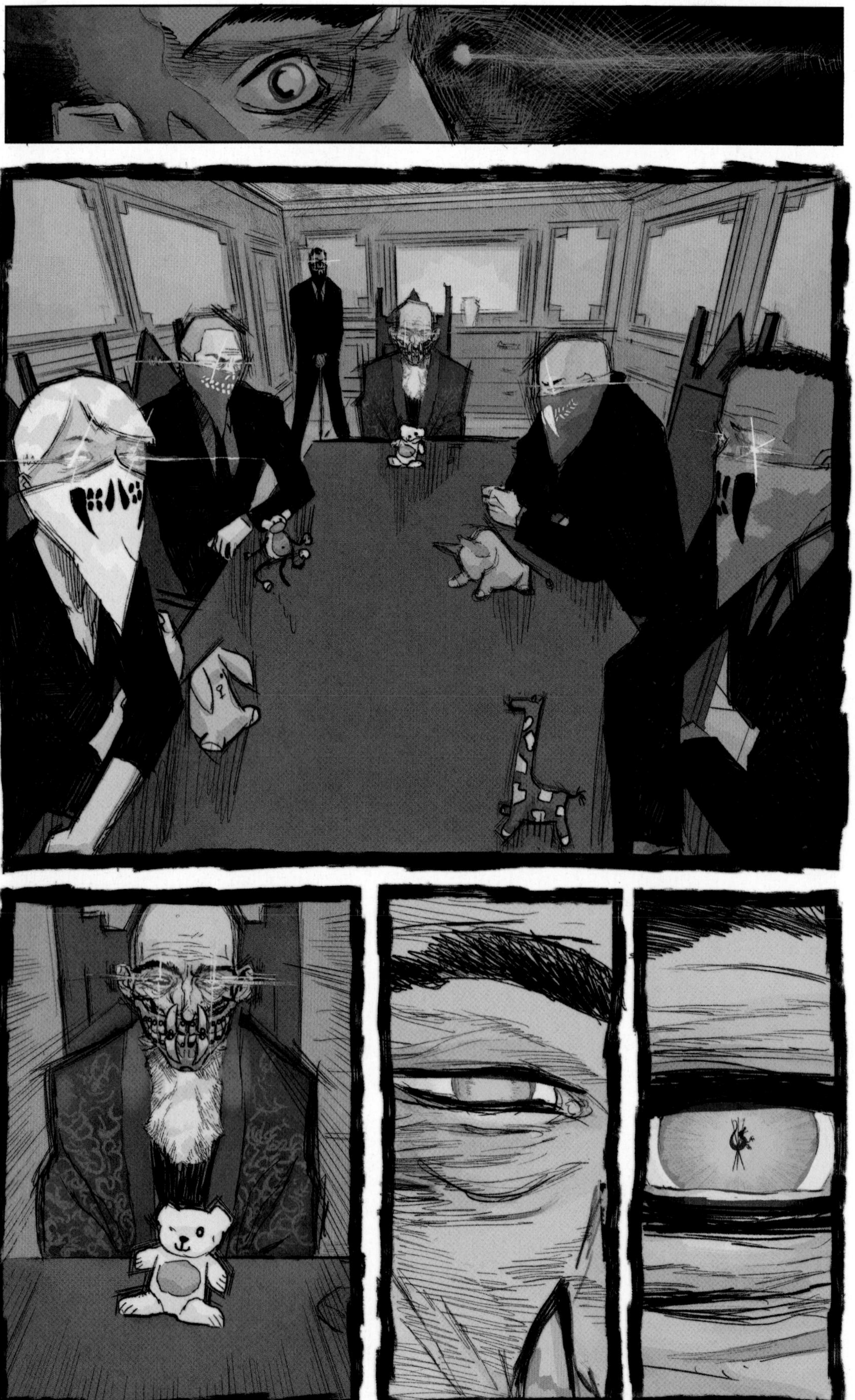

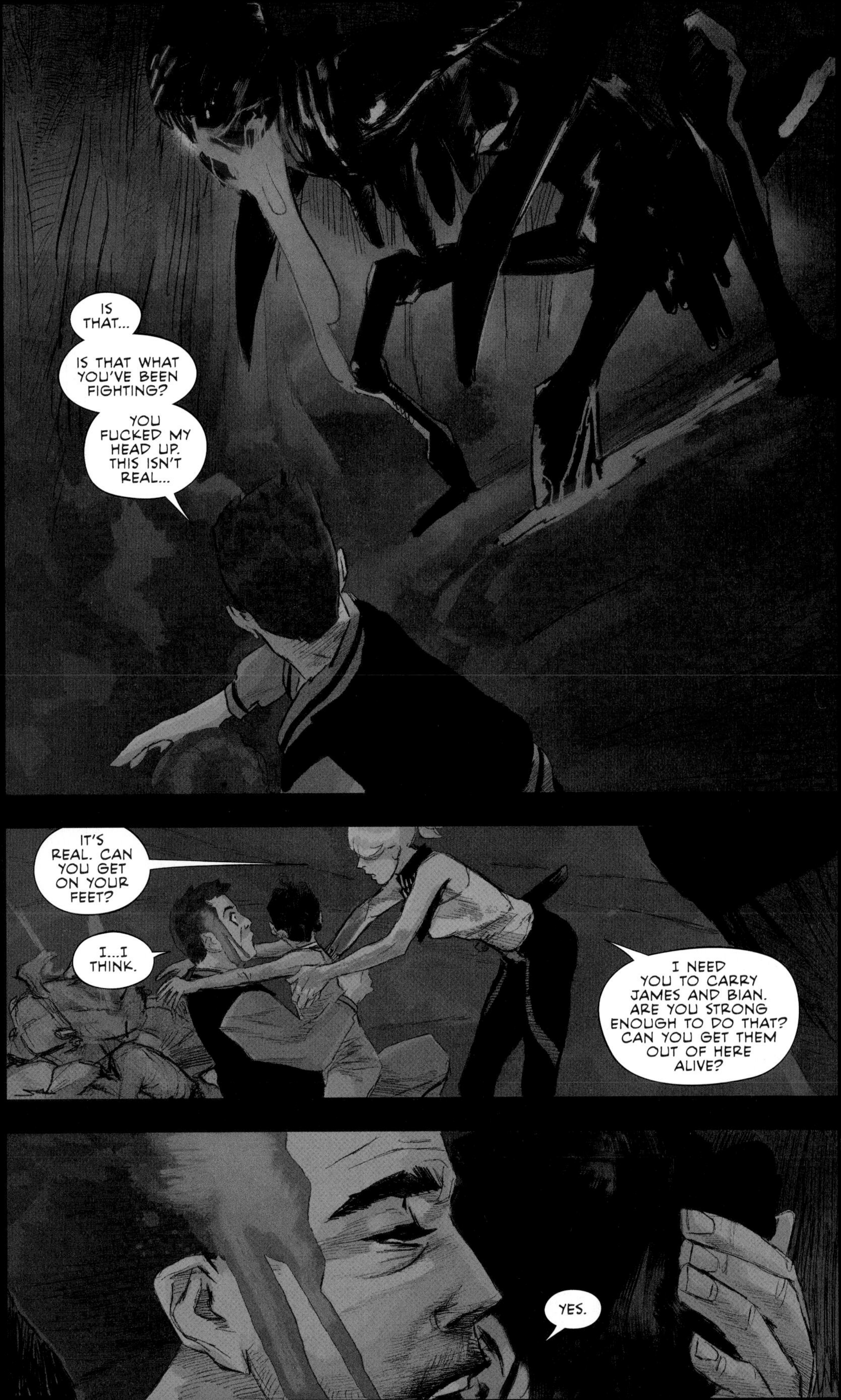
IS THAT...
IS THAT WHAT YOU'VE BEEN FIGHTING?
YOU FUCKED MY HEAD UP. THIS ISN'T REAL...
IT'S REAL. CAN YOU GET ON YOUR FEET?
I...I THINK.
I NEED YOU TO CARRY JAMES AND BIAN. ARE YOU STRONG ENOUGH TO DO THAT? CAN YOU GET THEM OUT OF HERE ALIVE?
YES.

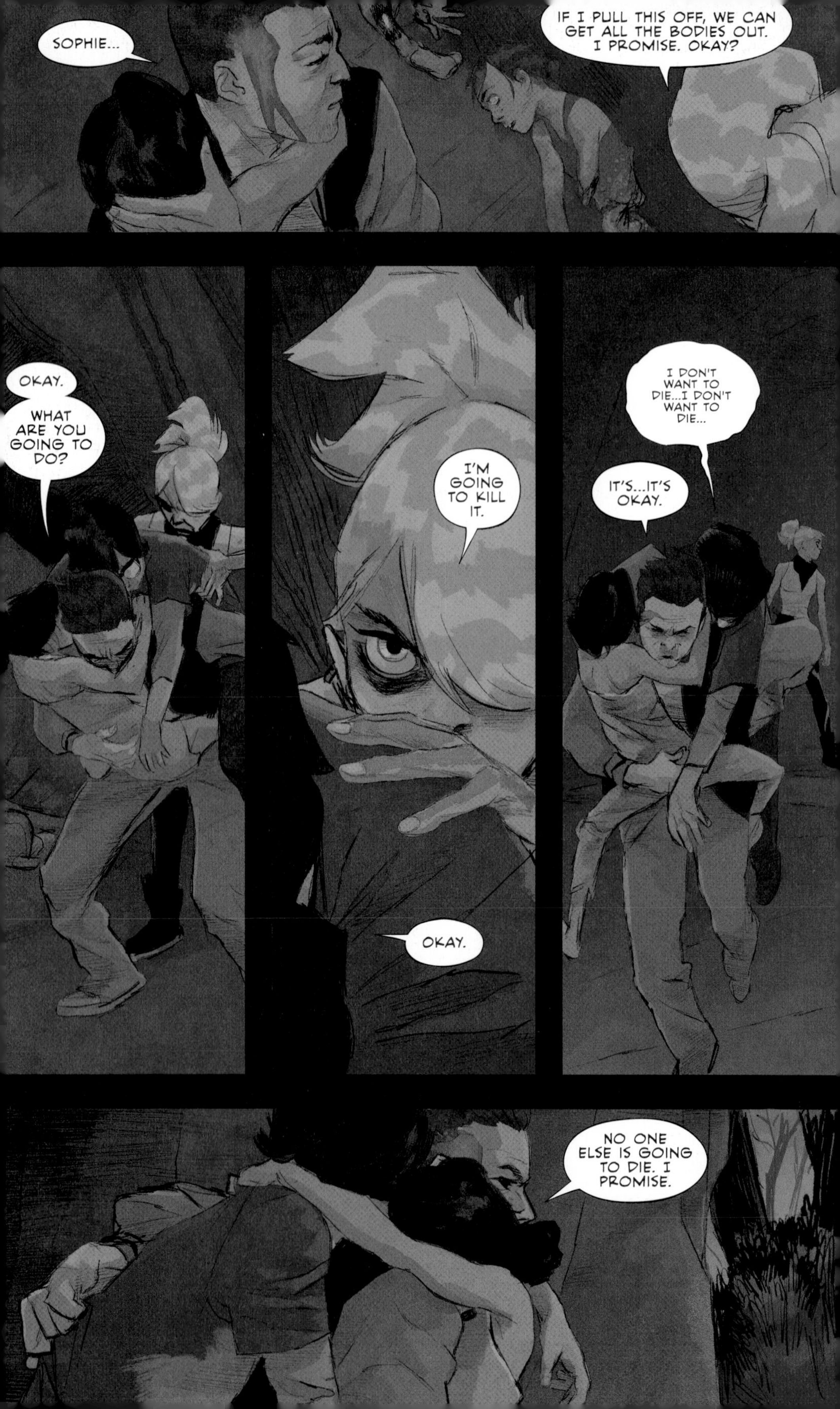
SOPHIE...
IF I PULL THIS OFF, WE CAN GET ALL THE BODIES OUT. I PROMISE. OKAY?
OKAY.
WHAT ARE YOU GOING TO DO?
I'M GOING TO KILL IT.
OKAY.
I DON'T WANT TO DIE...I DON'T WANT TO DIE...
IT'S...IT'S OKAY.
NO ONE ELSE IS GOING TO DIE. I PROMISE.

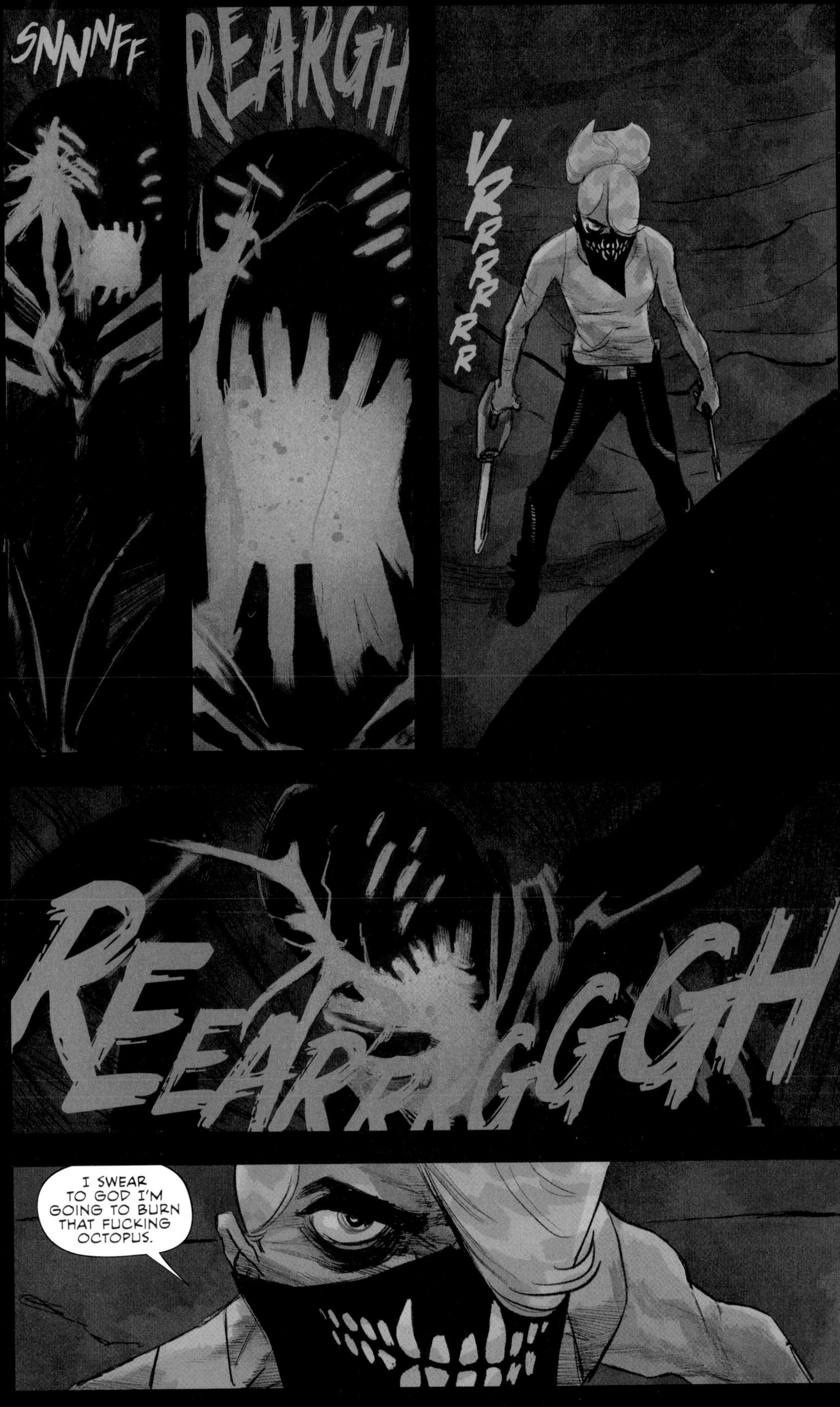
SNNNFF
REARGH
VRRRRRRR
REEARRRGGGH
I SWEAR TO GOD I'M GOING TO BURN THAT FUCKING OCTOPUS.

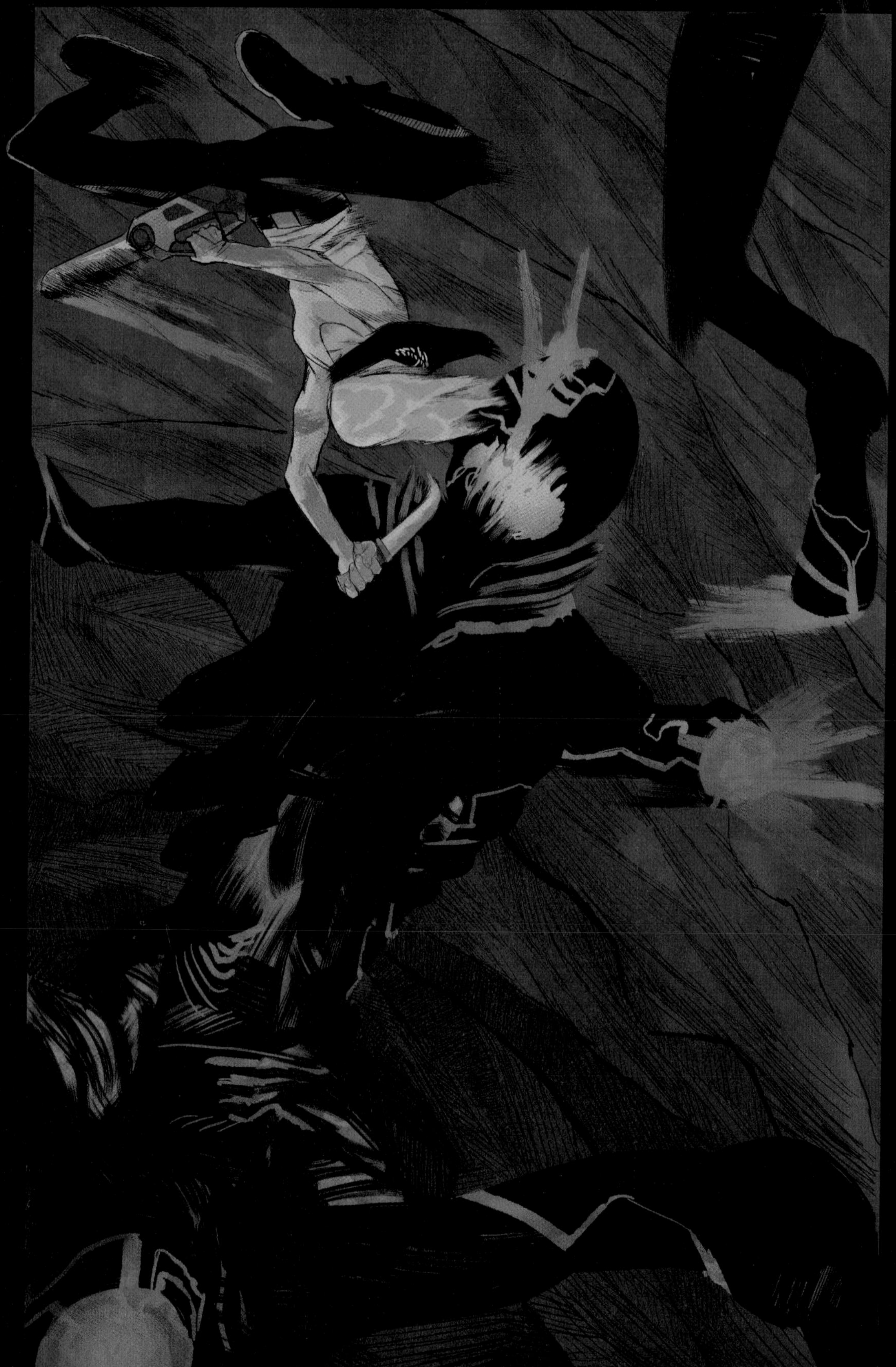

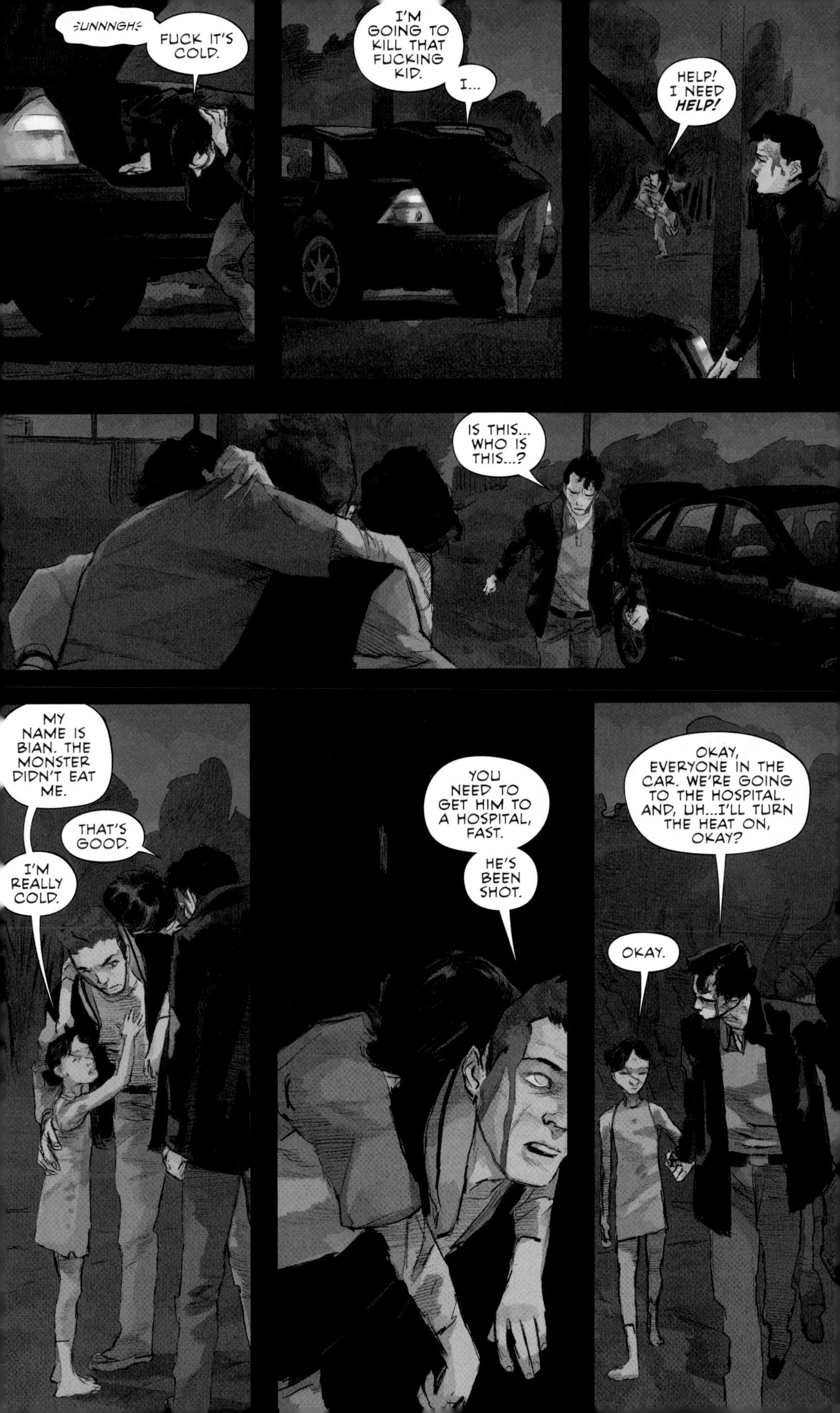

UNNNGH
FUCK IT'S COLD.
I'M GOING TO KILL THAT FUCKING KID.
I...
HELP! I NEED HELP!
IS THIS... WHO IS THIS...?
MY NAME IS BIAN. THE MONSTER DIDN'T EAT ME.
THAT'S GOOD.
I'M REALLY COLD.
YOU NEED TO GET HIM TO A HOSPITAL, FAST.
HE'S BEEN SHOT.
OKAY, EVERYONE IN THE CAR. WE'RE GOING TO THE HOSPITAL. AND, UH...I'LL TURN THE HEAT ON, OKAY?
OKAY.

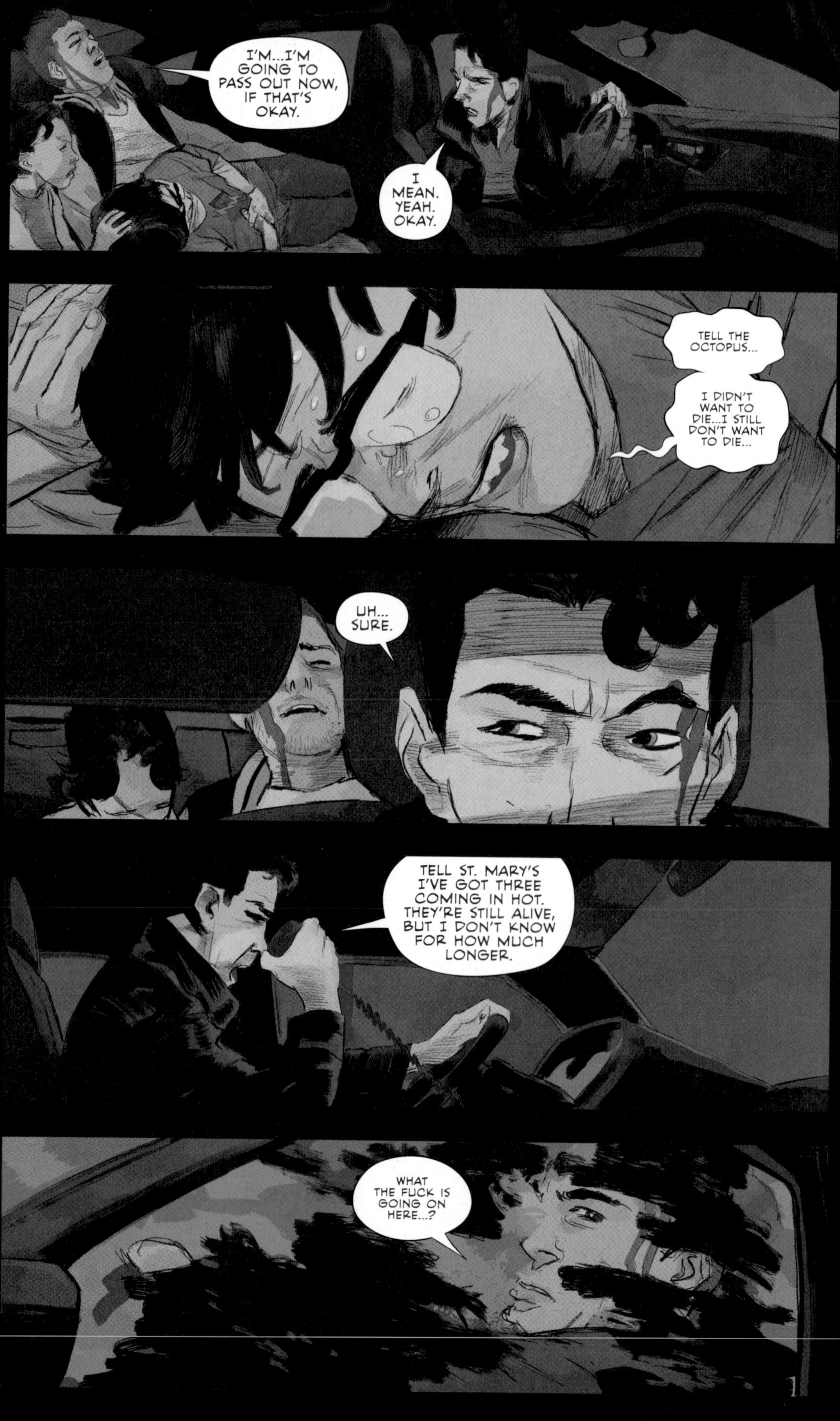
I'M...I'M GOING TO PASS OUT NOW, IF THAT'S OKAY.
I MEAN. YEAH. OKAY.
TELL THE OCTOPUS...
I DIDN'T WANT TO DIE...I STILL DON'T WANT TO DIE...
UH... SURE.
TELL ST. MARY'S I'VE GOT THREE COMING IN HOT. THEY'RE STILL ALIVE, BUT I DON'T KNOW FOR HOW MUCH LONGER.
WHAT THE FUCK IS GOING ON HERE...?

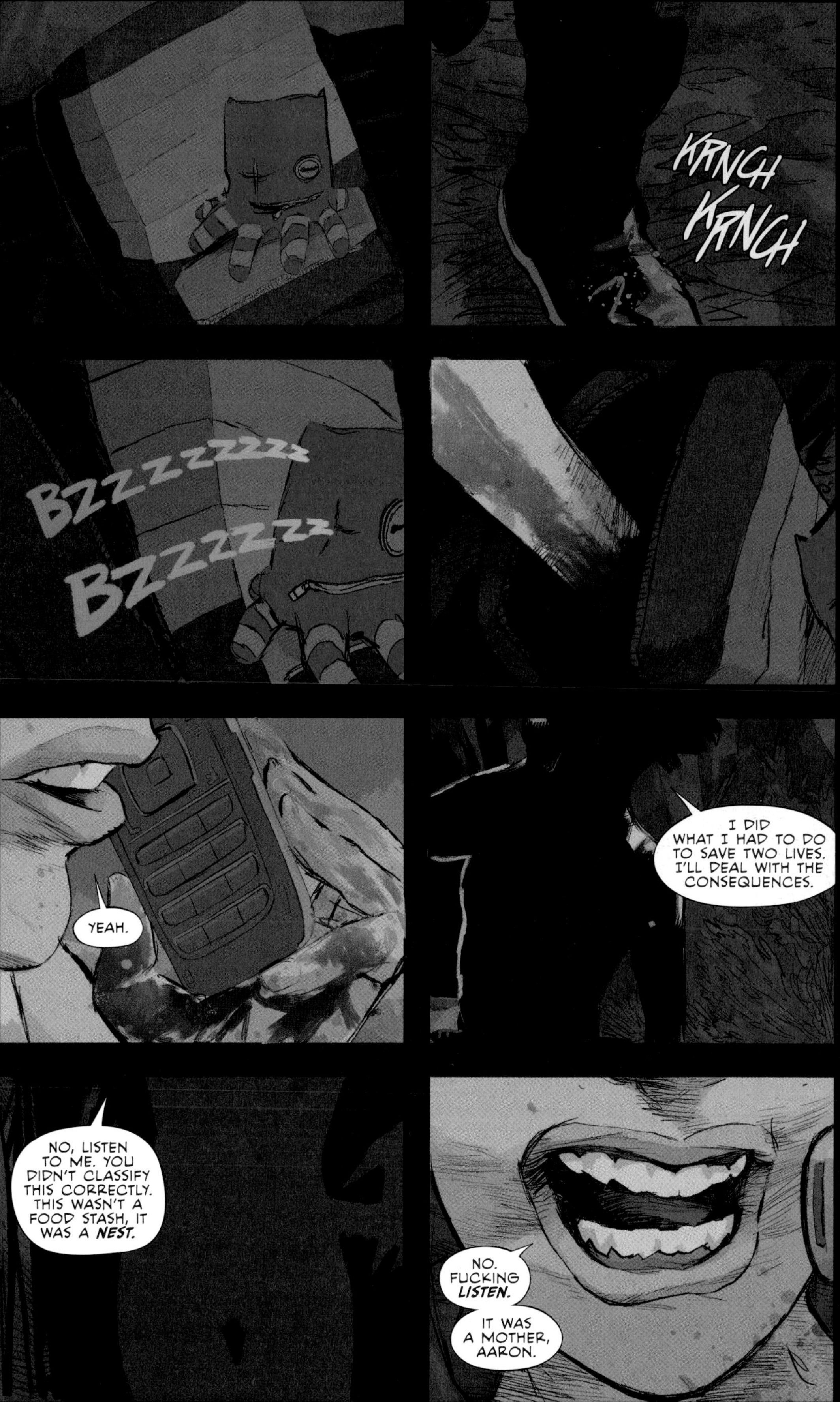
KRNCH
KRNCH
BZZZZZZZZZ
BZZZZZZZ
YEAH.
I DID WHAT I HAD TO DO TO SAVE TWO LIVES. I'LL DEAL WITH THE CONSEQUENCES.
NO, LISTEN TO ME. YOU DIDN'T CLASSIFY THIS CORRECTLY. THIS WASN'T A FOOD STASH, IT WAS A *NEST.*
NO. FUCKING *LISTEN.*
IT WAS A MOTHER, AARON.

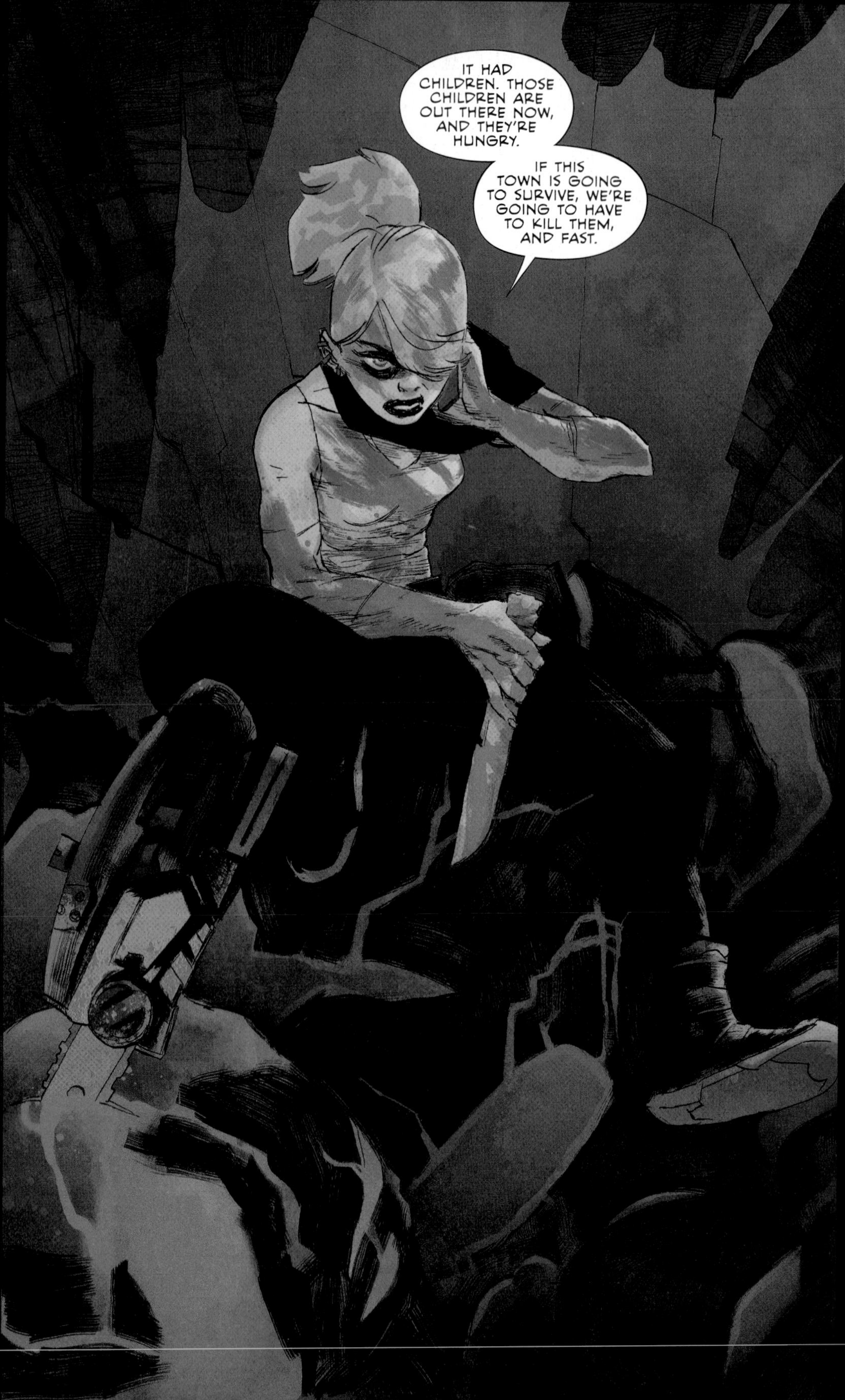
IT HAD CHILDREN. THOSE CHILDREN ARE OUT THERE NOW, AND THEY'RE HUNGRY.
IF THIS TOWN IS GOING TO SURVIVE, WE'RE GOING TO HAVE TO KILL THEM, AND FAST.

TO BE CONTINUED...

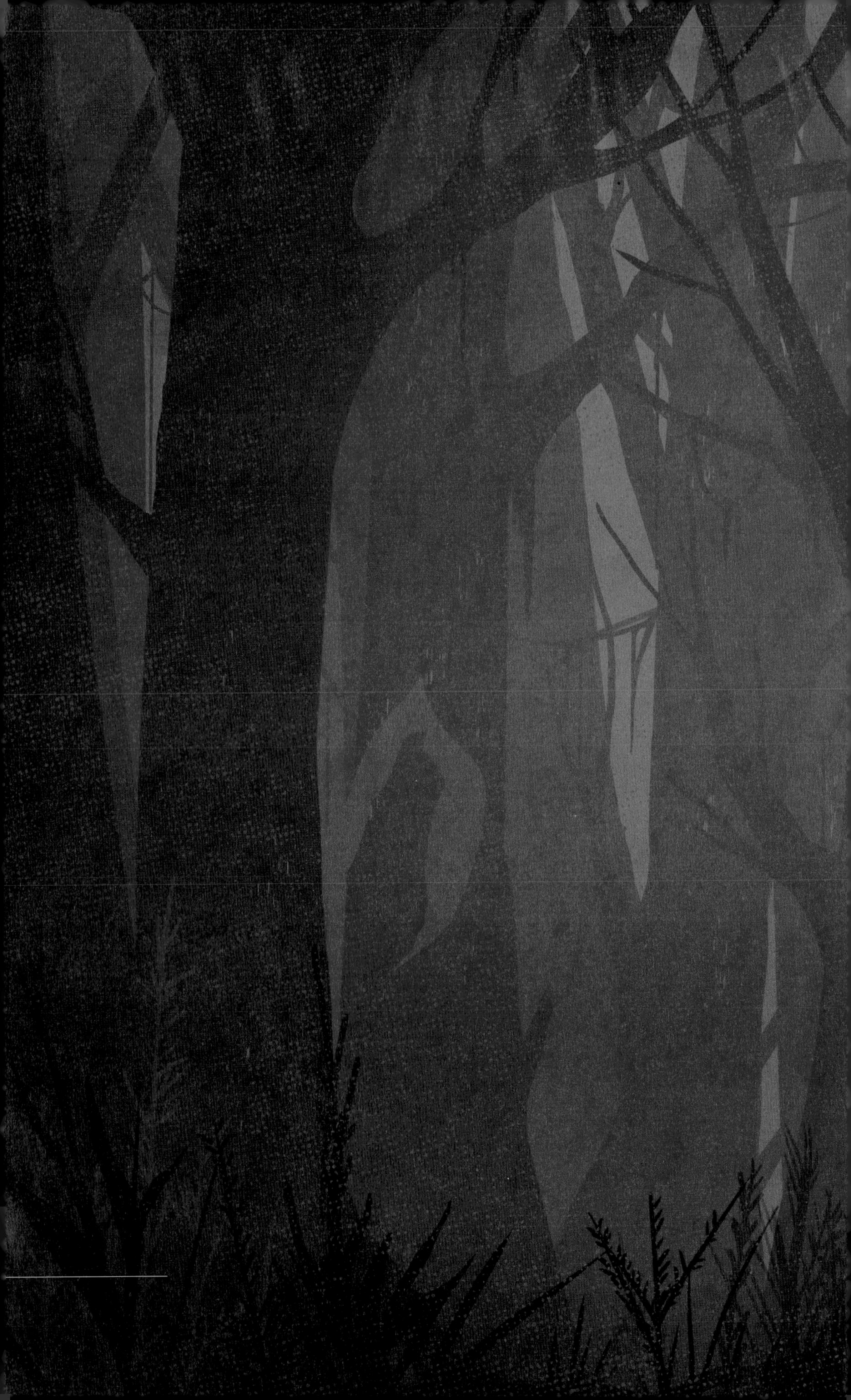

COVER GALLERY

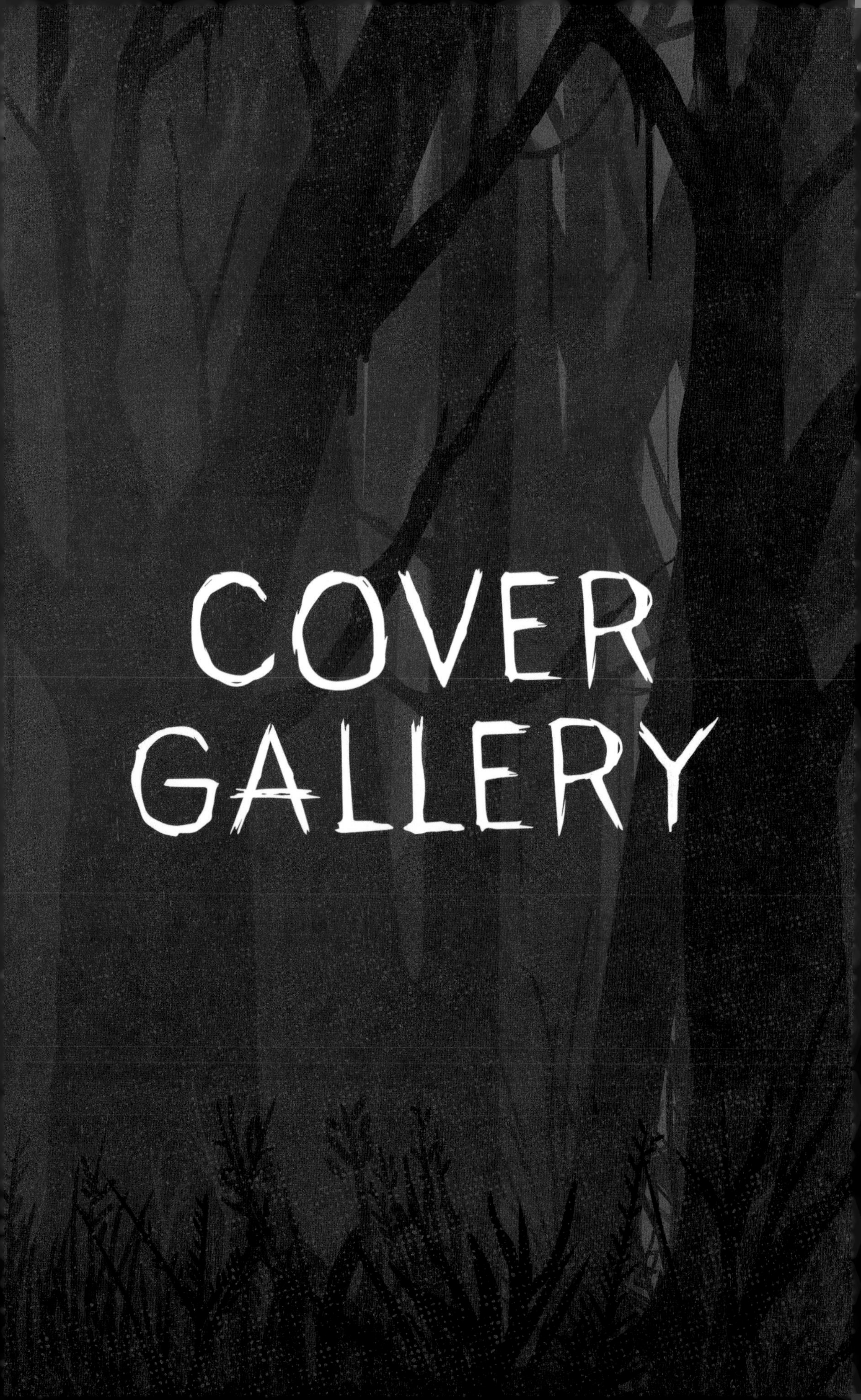

NO. 1 VARIANT COVER BY **JAE LEE** & **JUNE CHUNG**

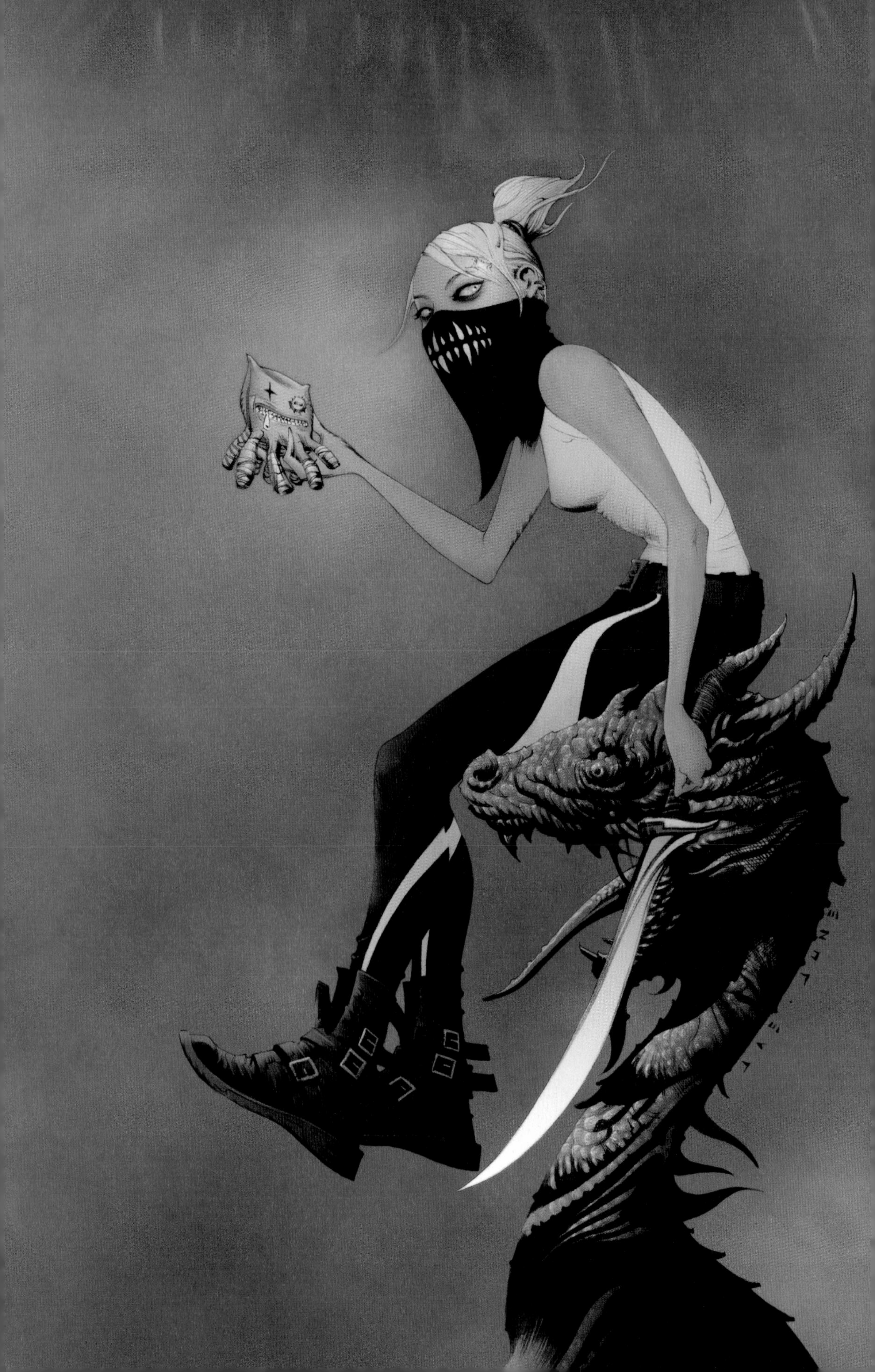

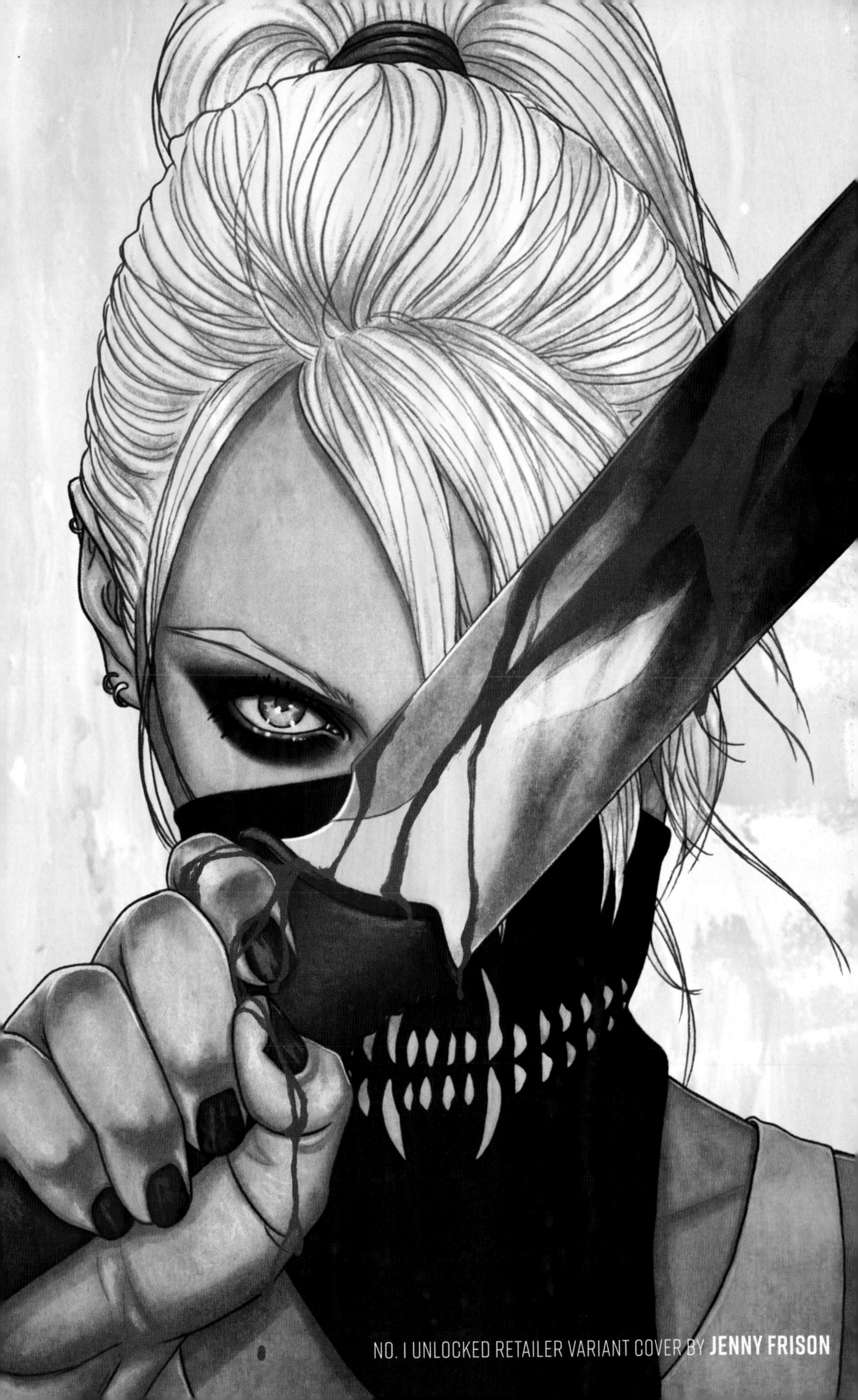

NO. 1 UNLOCKED RETAILER VARIANT COVER BY **JENNY FRISON**

NO. 2 COVER BY **WERTHER DELL'EDERA**
WITH COLORS BY **GIOVANNA NIRO**

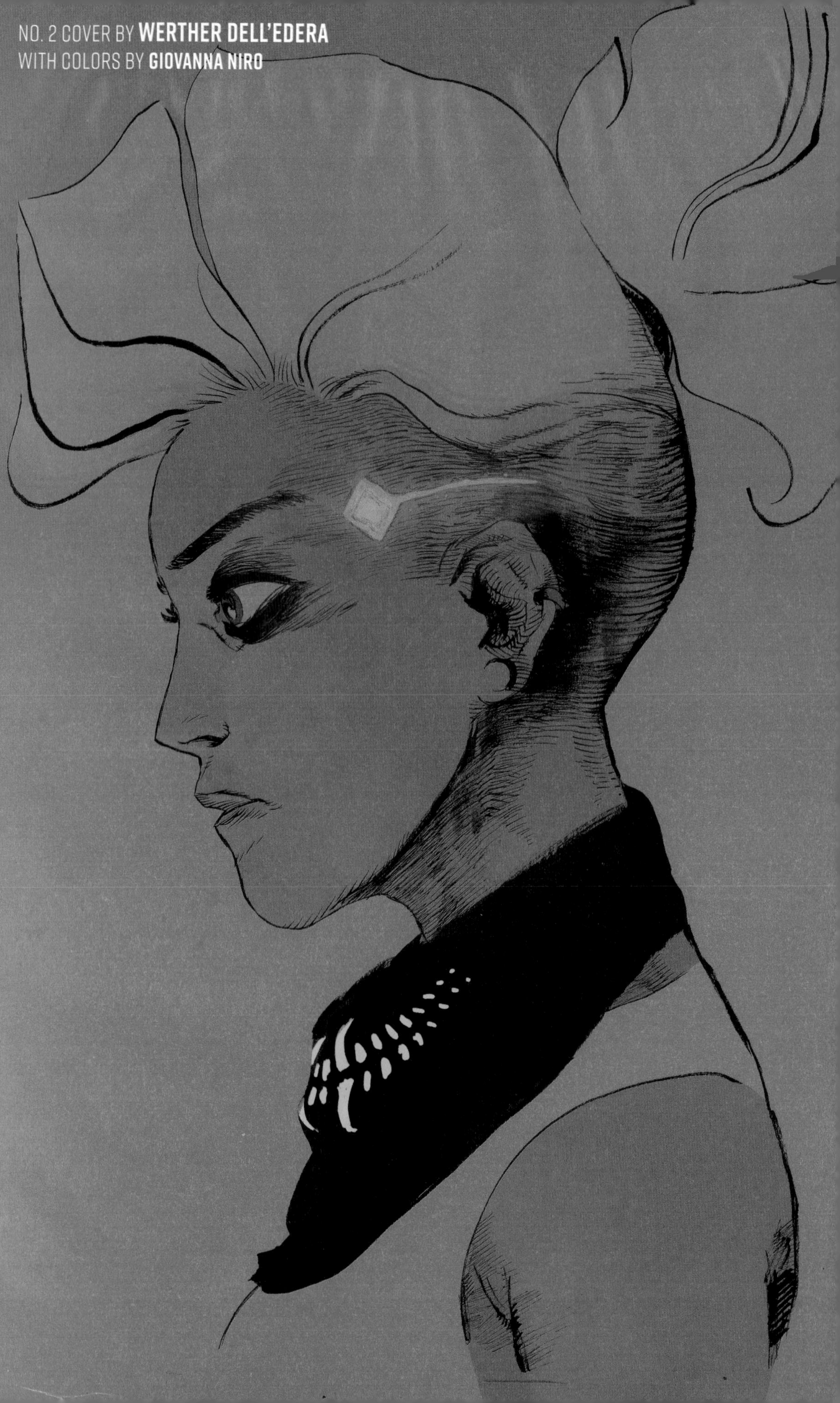

NO. 2 UNLOCKED RETAILER VARIANT COVER BY **IAN BERTRAM**
WITH COLORS BY **MIQUEL MUERTO**

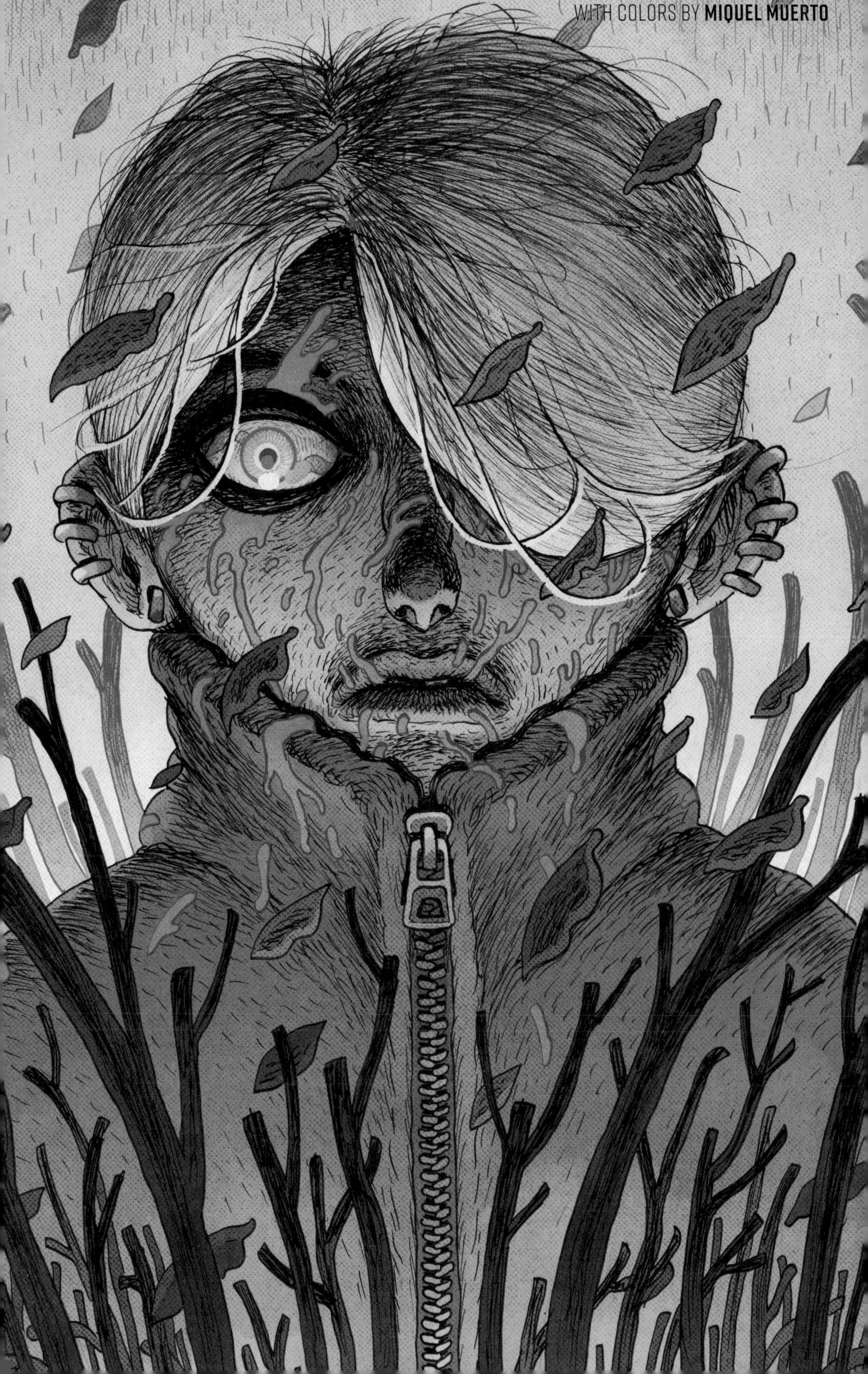

NO. 3 COVER BY **WERTHER DELL'EDERA**
WITH COLORS BY **GIOVANNA NIRO**

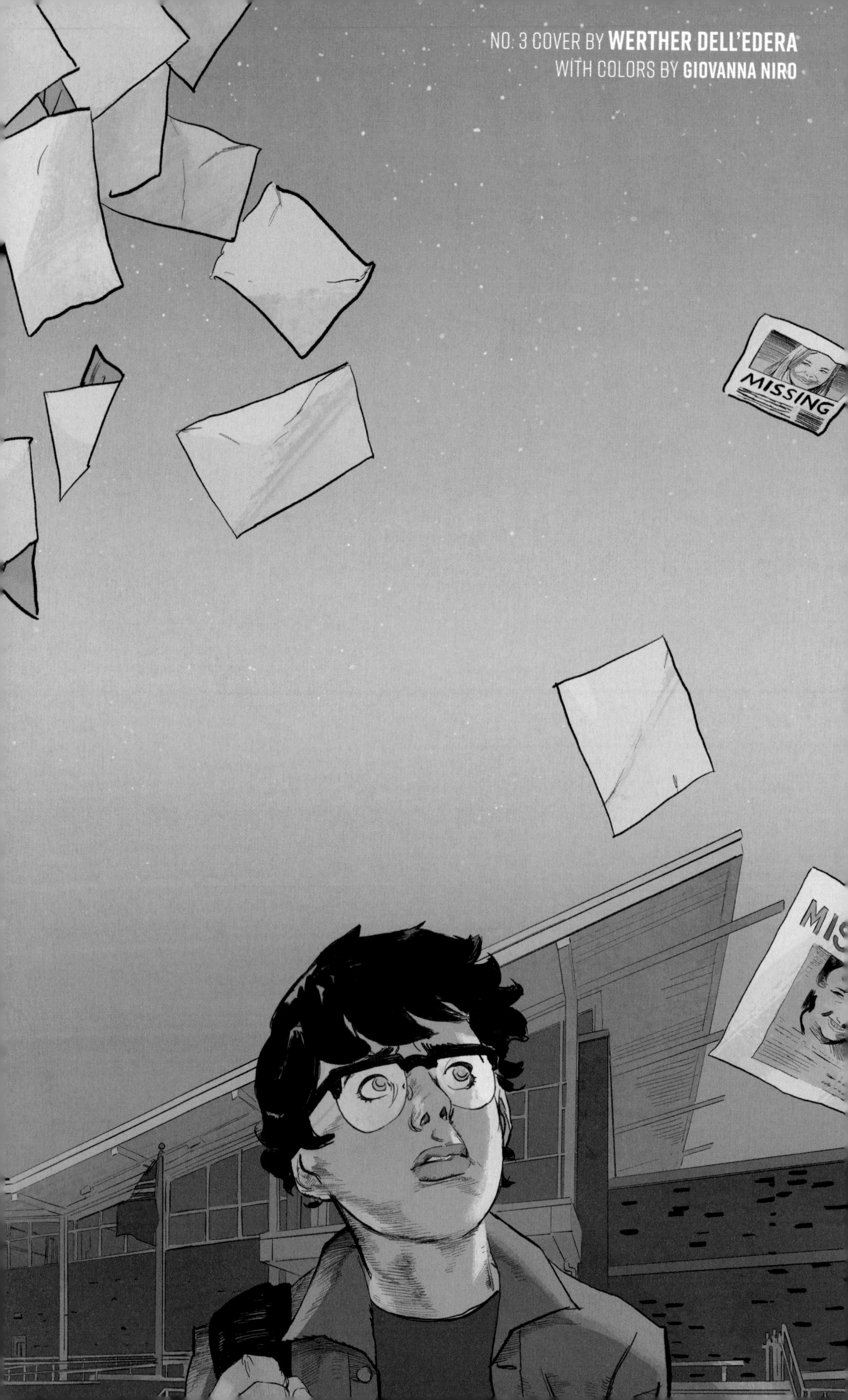
MISSING

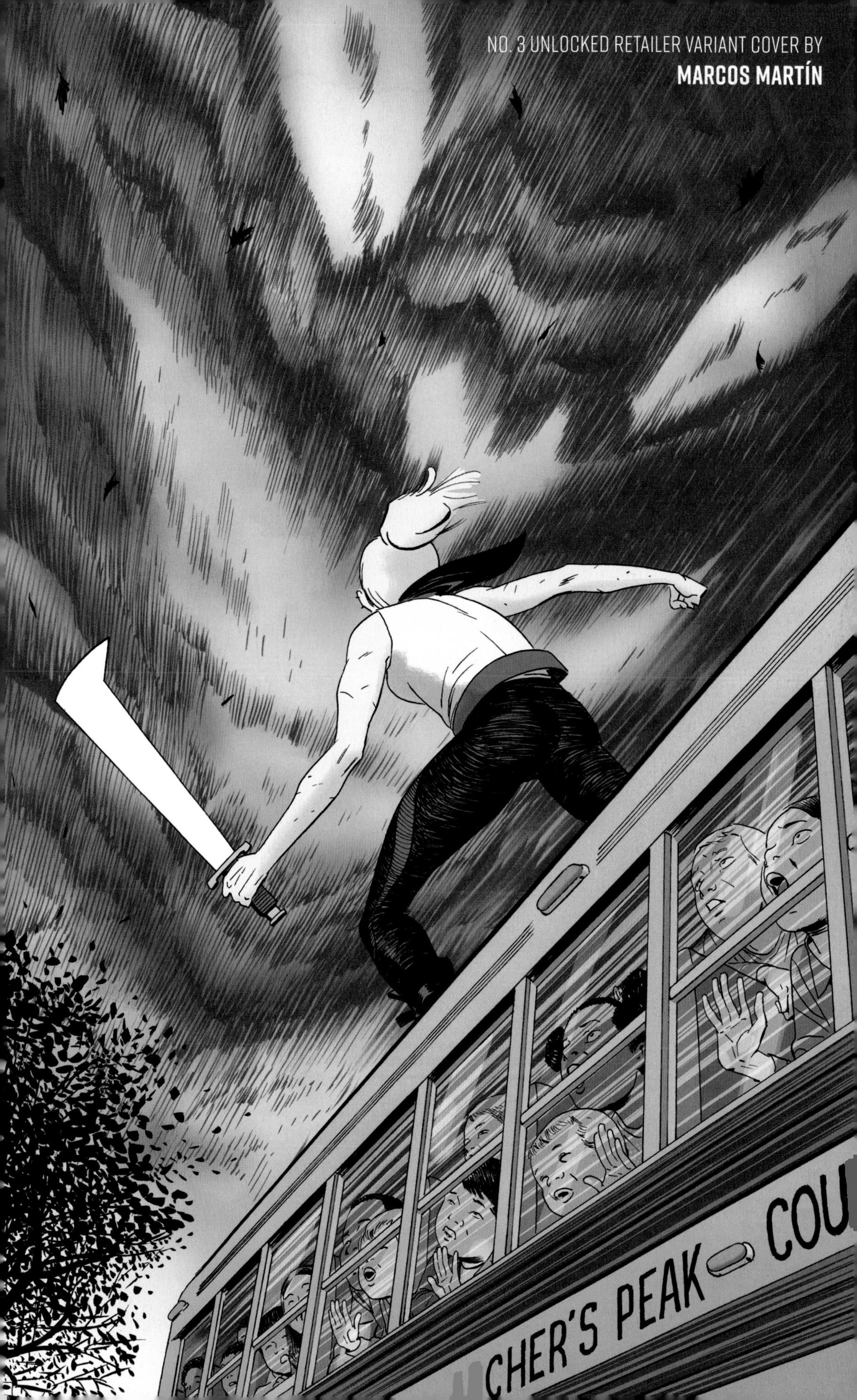
CHER'S PEAK
COU
NO. 3 UNLOCKED RETAILER VARIANT COVER BY
MARCOS MARTÍN

NO. 4 COVER BY **WERTHER DELL'EDERA**
WITH COLORS BY **GIOVANNA NIRO**

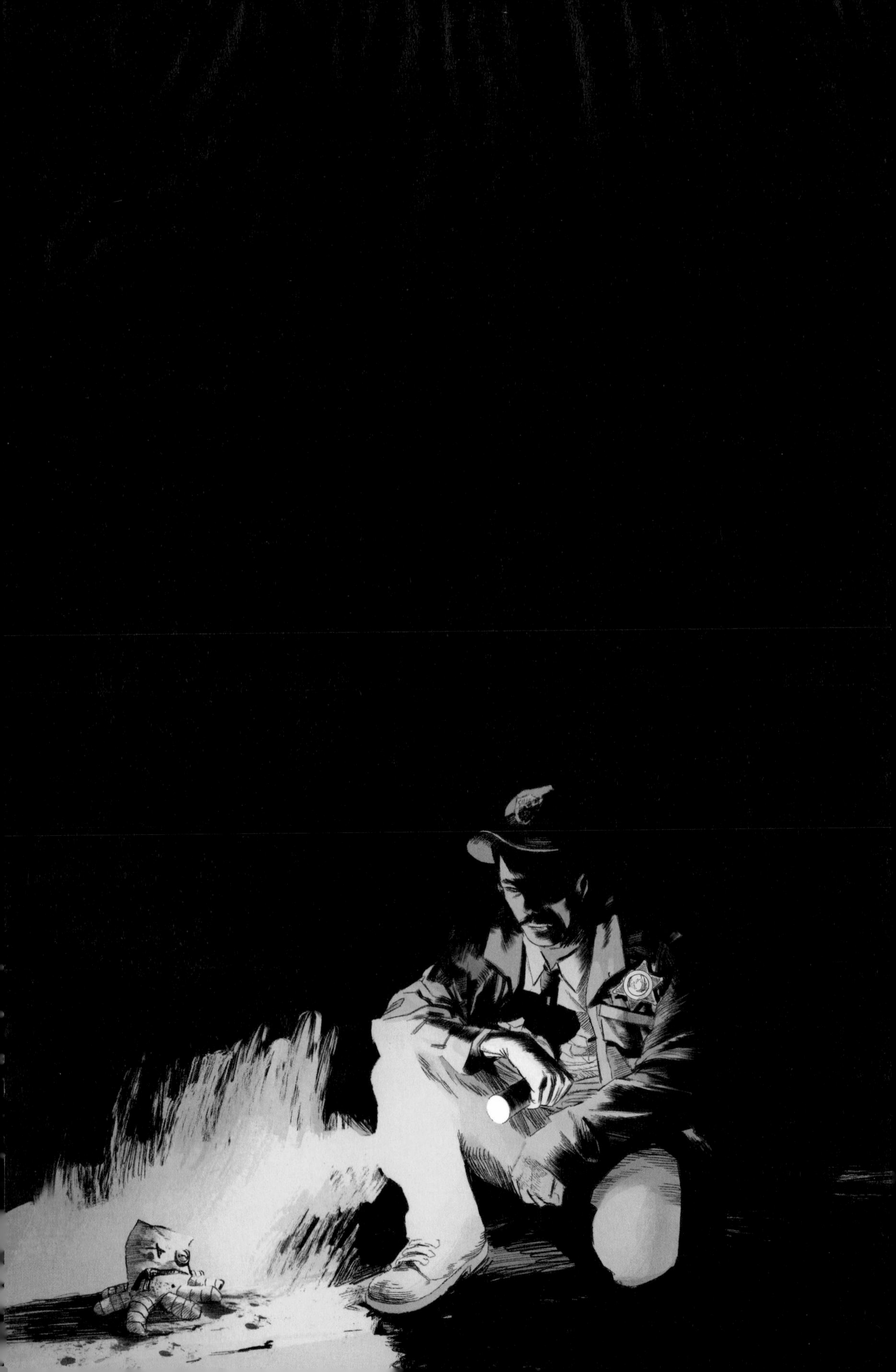

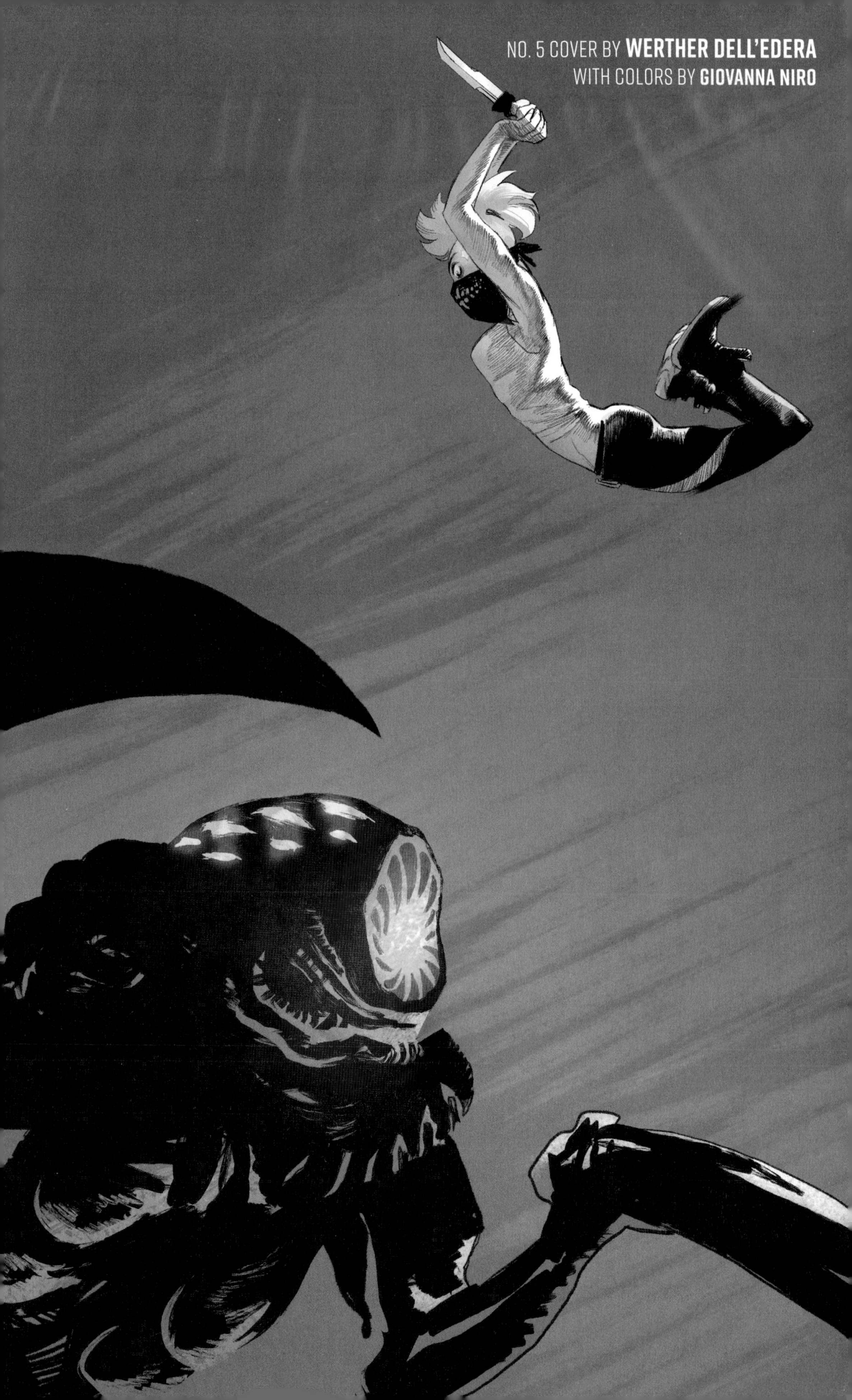

NO. 5 COVER BY **WERTHER DELL'EDERA**
WITH COLORS BY **GIOVANNA NIRO**

2017 GLAAD AWARD WINNER OUTSTANDING COMIC BOOK

JAMES TYNION IV MICHAEL DIALYNAS

THE WOODS™

YEARBOOK EDITIONS

EXCLUSIVE PREVIEW

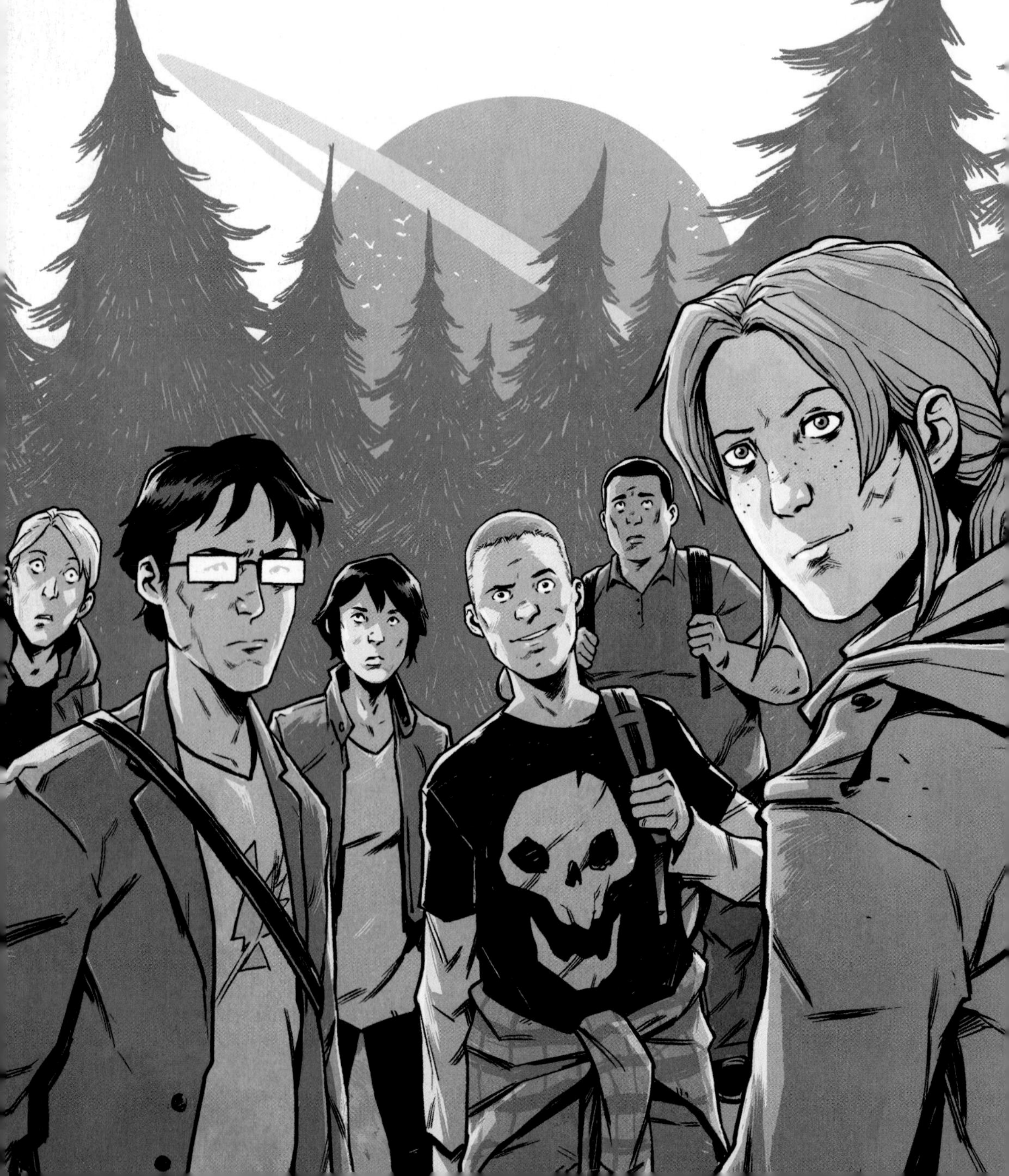

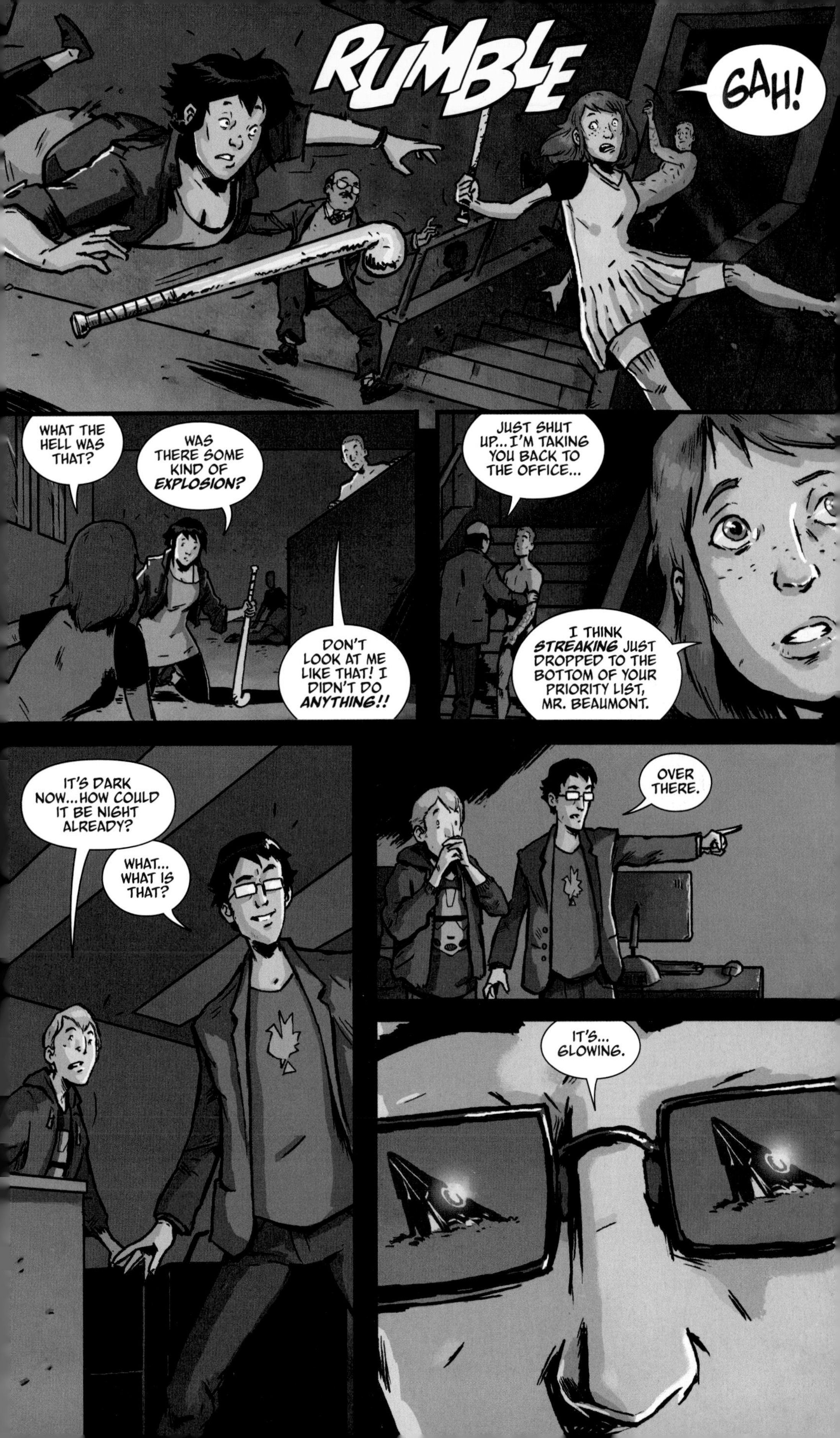
RUMBLE
GAH!
WHAT THE HELL WAS THAT?
WAS THERE SOME KIND OF EXPLOSION?
DON'T LOOK AT ME LIKE THAT! I DIDN'T DO ANYTHING!!
JUST SHUT UP...I'M TAKING YOU BACK TO THE OFFICE...
I THINK STREAKING JUST DROPPED TO THE BOTTOM OF YOUR PRIORITY LIST, MR. BEAUMONT.
IT'S DARK NOW...HOW COULD IT BE NIGHT ALREADY?
WHAT... WHAT IS THAT?
OVER THERE.
IT'S... GLOWING.

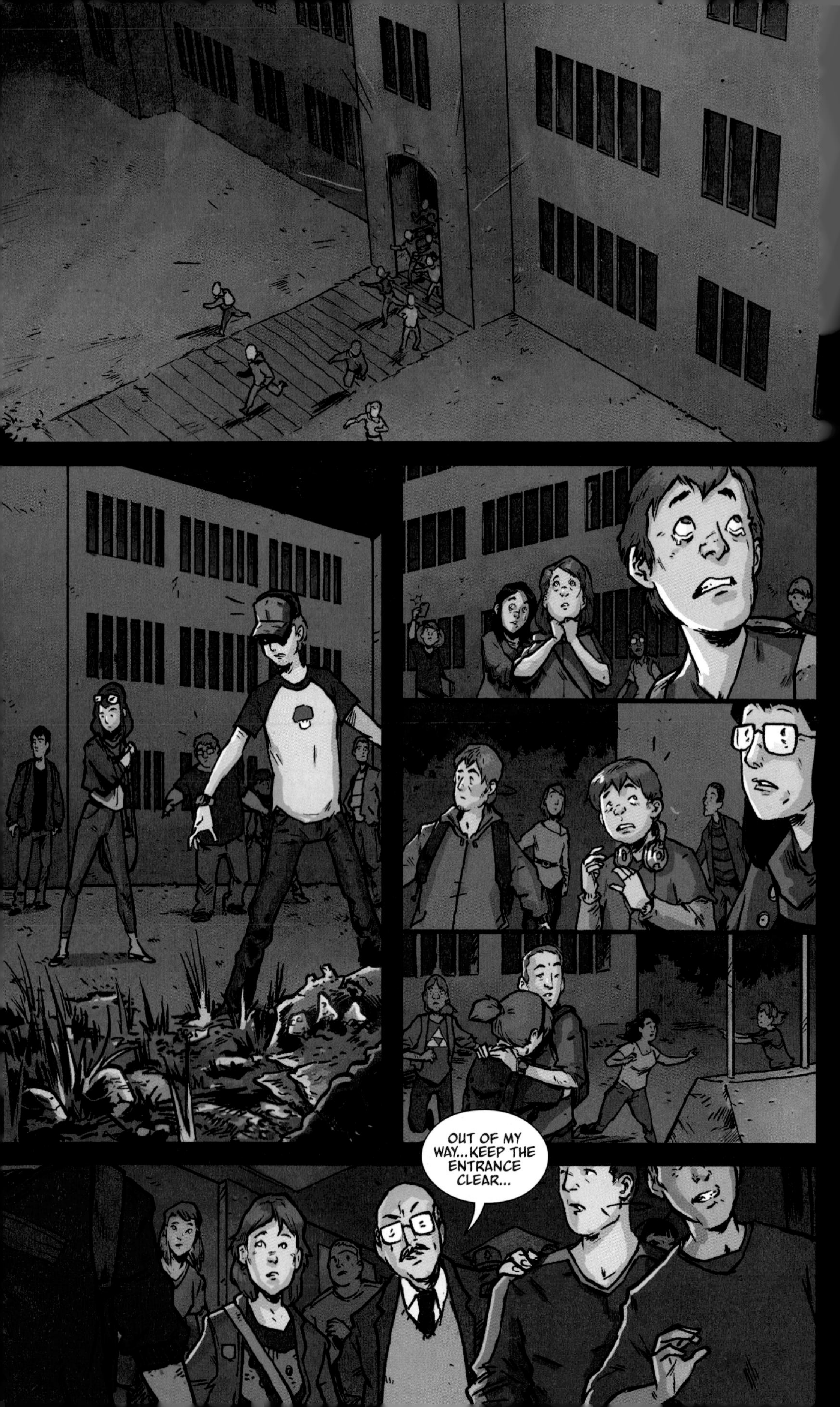
OUT OF MY WAY...KEEP THE ENTRANCE CLEAR...

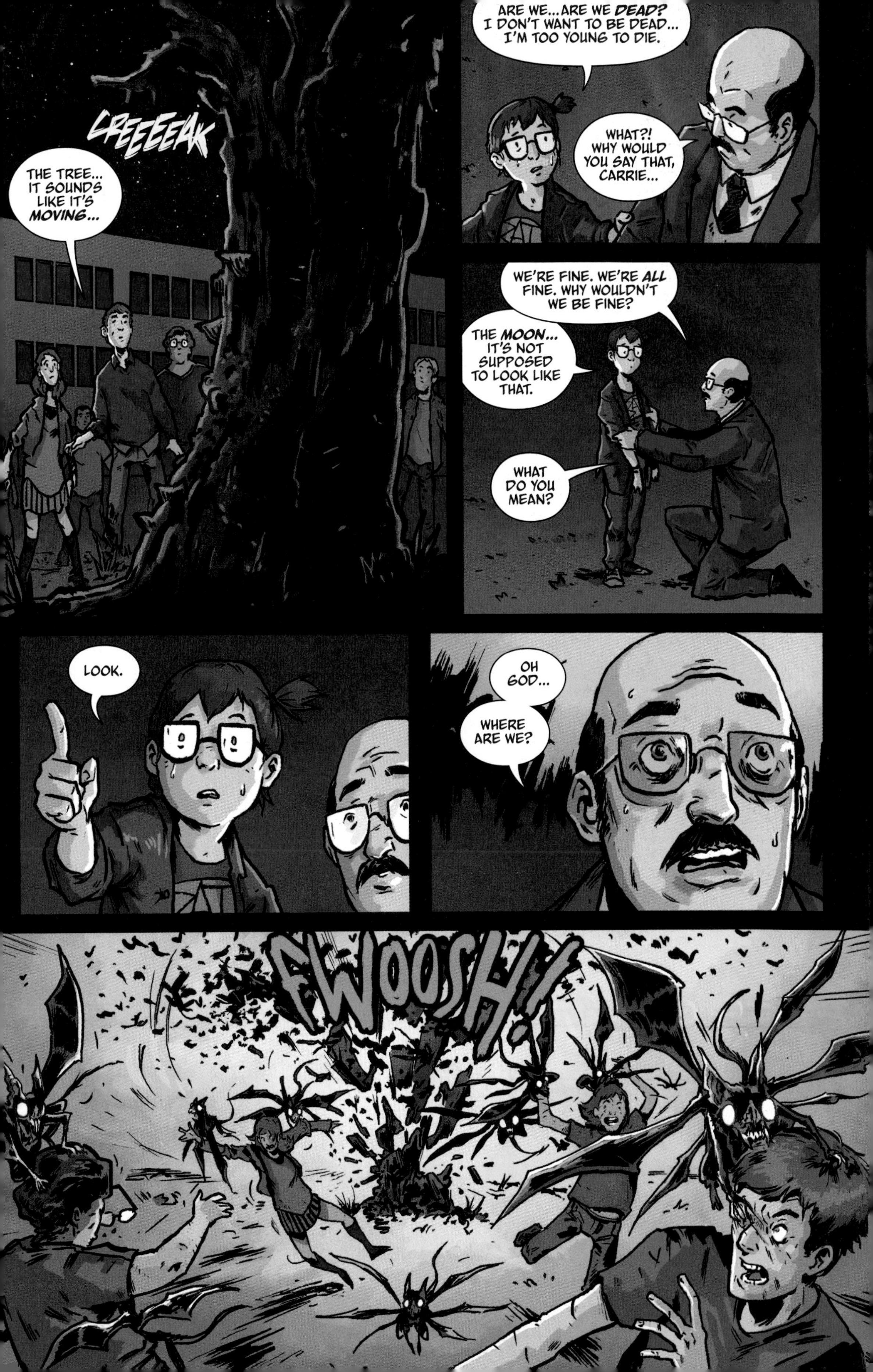
CREEEEAK
THE TREE... IT SOUNDS LIKE IT'S MOVING...
ARE WE...ARE WE DEAD? I DON'T WANT TO BE DEAD... I'M TOO YOUNG TO DIE.
WHAT?! WHY WOULD YOU SAY THAT, CARRIE...
WE'RE FINE. WE'RE ALL FINE. WHY WOULDN'T WE BE FINE?
THE MOON... IT'S NOT SUPPOSED TO LOOK LIKE THAT.
WHAT DO YOU MEAN?
LOOK.
OH GOD...
WHERE ARE WE?
FWOOSH!!

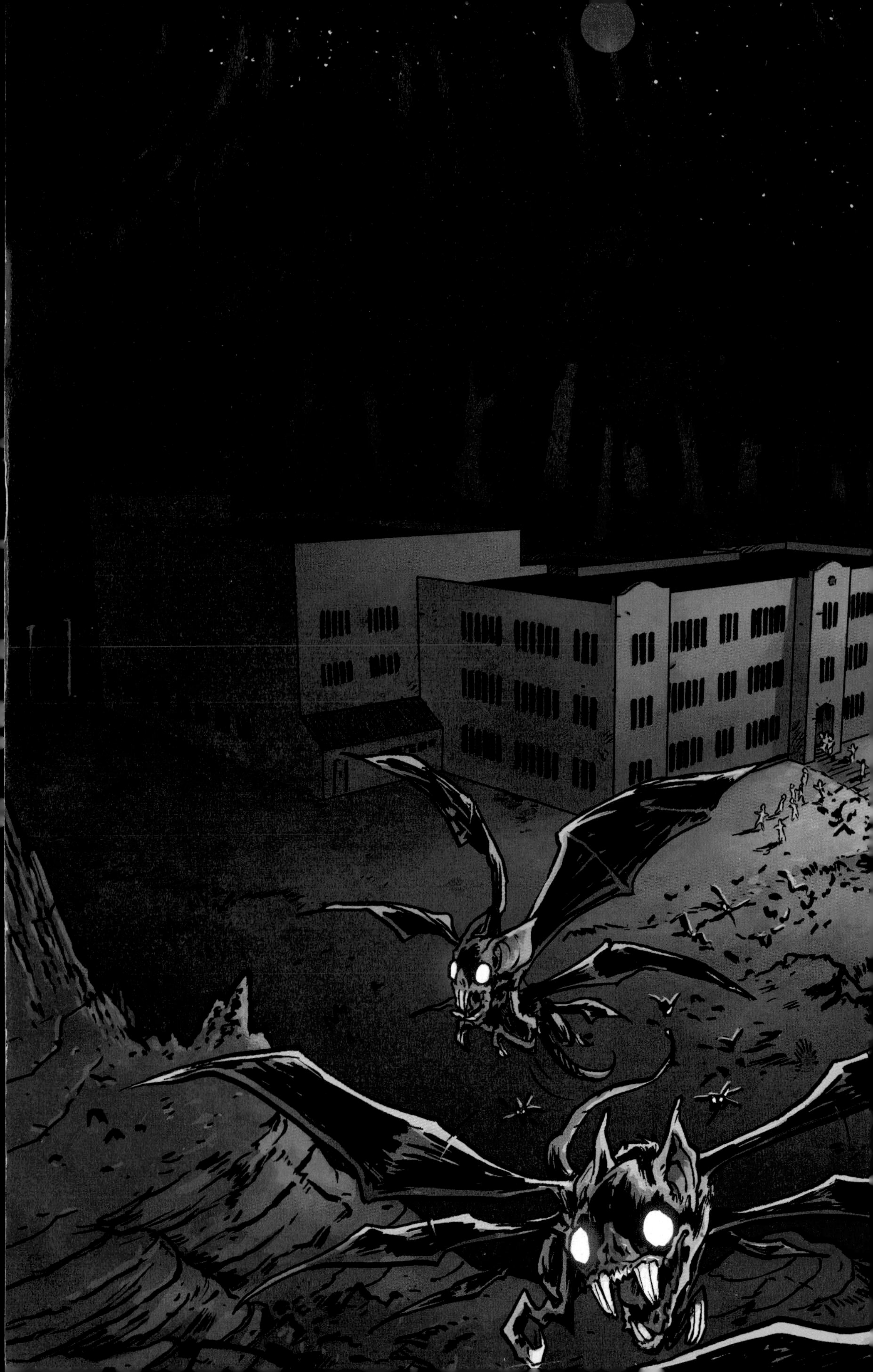

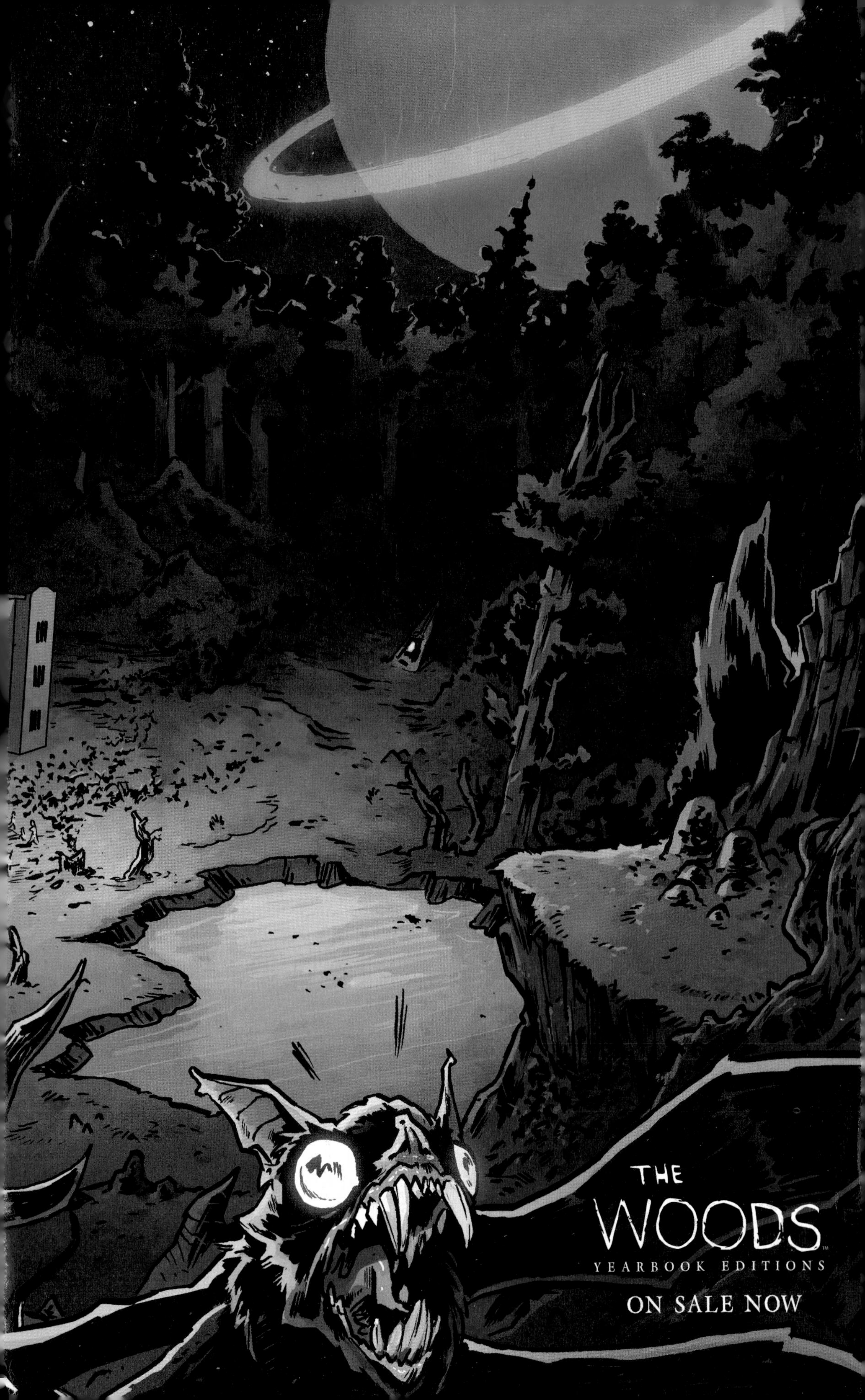
THE
WOODS™
YEARBOOK EDITIONS
ON SALE NOW

ABOUT THE AUTHORS

JAMES TYNION IV is a comic book writer, best known as the writer for DC Comics' flagship series, *Batman*. In addition to the 2017 GLAAD Media Award-winning series *The Woods* with Michael Dialynas, James has also penned the critical successes *Memetic*, *Cognetic*, and *Eugenic* with Eryk Donovan, *The Backstagers* with Rian Sygh, and *Ufology* with Noah J. Yuenkel and Matthew Fox from BOOM! Studios. An alumni of Sarah Lawrence College, Tynion now lives and works in New York, NY.

WERTHER DELL'EDERA is an Italian artist, born in the south of Italy. He has worked for the biggest publishers in both Italy and the U.S., with his works ranging from *Loveness* (DC Vertigo) to the graphic novel *Spider-Man: Family Business* (Marvel). He has also worked for Image, IDW, Dynamite, and Dark Horse. In Italy, he has drawn Sergio Bonelli's *Dylan Dog* and *The Crow: Memento Mori* (a co-production between IDW and Edizioni BD), for which he has won awards for Best Cover Artist, Best Series, and Best Artist.

Not dead, MIQUEL MUERTO has lived in Barcelona since 1992, where he studied illustration, ran a small press, and worked as a graphic designer until feeling entitled to chase his dream: doing comics! *The Druid's Path* (2016) was his comic book debut as a full artist, a traumatic experience he swore would never happen again. Coloring comics was the first good step he has taken in his career and he has been happily following that path ever since.